AF526656

Women, Social Justice and Human Rights

Women, Social Justice and Human Rights

Vijay Kumar Gupta

MD PUBLICATIONS PVT LTD
NEW DELHI
www.mdppl.com

Copyright © 2009 by MD Publications Pvt Ltd.

All rights reserved. No part of this book may be reproduced or utilized in any form or by any means, electronically or mechanically, including photocopying, recording, or by any information storage and retrieval system, without the prior permission in writing from the publisher.

Published by :

MD Publications Pvt Ltd
"MD House", 11, Darya Ganj,
New Delhi-110 002
Phone : +91-11-41563325 (Customer Service)
+91-11-41562846 (Editorial)
E-mail (orders) : order@mdppl.com
Website : www.mdppl.com

ISBN : 978-81-7533-216-4

Published and Printed by Mr. Pranav Gupta on behalf of
MD Publications Pvt Ltd at Printext, New Delhi.

PREFACE

The term women's rights refer to freedoms and entitlements of women and girls of all ages. These rights may or may not be institutionalized, ignored or suppressed by law, local custom, and behavior in a particular society.

Since the beginning of what we call civilization, when men's dominance over women was firmly established until the present day, our history has been marred with oppression of and brutality to women. The system of male domination, known as patriarchy, forced in all its forms, both subtle and overt - from oppression, inequality, and discrimination to domestic violence, rape, trafficking and forced slavery. The change the world is crying for cannot occur unless women's voices are heard. Democracy cannot work without equality for a woman that provides equal participation and representation.

Issues commonly associated with notions of women's rights include, though are not limited to, the right: to bodily integrity and autonomy; to vote (universal suffrage); to hold public office; to work; to fair wages or equal pay; to own property; to education; to serve in the military or be conscripted; to enter into legal contracts; and to have marital, parental and religious rights. Women and their supporters have campaigned and in some places continue to campaign for the same rights as modern men. We believe that equality should be a given, and we must work toward that end.

In traditionally patriarchal societies any improvement in the status of women has far-reaching consequences and produces fundamental political changes. Therefore it is always resisted by the established powers. However, it seems certain that they will ultimately have to relent, because the emancipation of women is both necessary and desirable. It will provide for a greater degree of social justice and thus benefit everyone. Indeed, from the beginning, the great "feminists" or champions of women's rights have always insisted that they worked in the interest of the whole human race. The feminist movement therefore has always been a humanist movement. Much can be learned from their experiences. They often suffered ridicule, persecution, and defeat, but also won admiration, support, and victory. Gradually, they achieved many of their goals. We are committed to increasing participation of women in politics, government and leadership so they can change laws, make decisions, and create policy solutions that affect and will improve women's lives.

The emancipation of women, i.e. their liberation from religious, legal, economic, and sexual oppression, their access to higher education, and their escape from narrow gender roles is not easily achieved. The struggle for sexual equality has a long history and is likely to continue for some time. Even if it should soon be won in the industrial nations, it may well rage on in many "underdeveloped" countries.

I am very grateful to Mr. Pranav Gupta, Director of MD Publications Pvt Ltd, New Delhi, for his kind cooperation and support for this book.

Vijay Kumar Gupta

CONTENTS

1

Social Justice
An Introduction

SOCIAL JUSTICE

Historically, America led the world in establishing a society with democratic values such as equal opportunity and protection from discrimination. Today, however, our country is among the most extreme examples of industrialized nations that have a widening gap between the wealthy and the rest of its citizenry - the working poor, the struggling middle class, and those who increasingly cannot make ends meet. Our public schools, from kindergarten through college, are forced to cut back countless programs and services. Fees for community colleges are up sharply, and many public universities must turn away qualified students. More than 43 million Americans have no medical insurance coverage. The crisis in publicly subsidized housing is intensifying, while publicly funded "corporate welfare" continues unabated. Our tax code favors the wealthy. Our criminal justice system assigns long prison terms to hundreds of thousands of perpetrators of victimless crimes, such as selling marijuana.

Our civil liberties of privacy and free speech are impaired by the excesses of the USA PATRIOT Act and kindred new laws that use a national tragedy (the attacks on September 11, 2001) as an excuse to impose ubiquitous surveillance and control over citizens. In addition, discrimination based on gender, ethnicity, or race continues to sap the potential of our society and to violate personal dignity. Feelings of isolation and helplessness are common in America today. Children are increasingly shaped by an "electronic childhood" with little direct experience of nature and free play. Our families are scattered, our popular culture is crassly manipulated by the profit motives of increasingly concentrated media conglomerates, and our sense of community is a pale shadow of what earlier generations of Americans knew.

The Green Party strongly believes that the quality of life is determined not only by material aspects that can be measured and counted but also by elements that cannot be quantified. We firmly support the separation of church and state, but we also acknowledge the spiritual dimension of life, and we honor the cultivation of various types of spiritual experience in our diverse society. We believe that artistic expression and a thriving structure of art institutions are key to community well-being. We believe that a deep and broad embrace of nonviolence is the only effective way to stop cycles of violence, from the home to the streets to the international level. We advocate a diverse system of education that would introduce children early to the wonders of the *Great School* (Nature), and would cultivate the wisdom of eco-education, eco-economics, eco-politics, and eco-culture.

We seek to protect our children from the corrosive effects of mass culture that trains them to regard themselves first and foremost as consumers. We support the shift in modern medicine to include healing through complementary therapies and engagement with the *Great Hospital* (Nature). We seek, in short, to facilitate the healthy unfolding of the person within the unfolding story of the family, community, bioregion, state, nation, and Earth community.

CIVIL RIGHT AND EQUAL RIGHTS

One of our key values is respect for diversity. We are committed to establishing relationships that honor diversity; that support the self-definition and self-determination of all people; and that consciously confront the barriers of racism, sexism, homophobia, class oppression, ageism, and the many ways our culture separates us from working together. We support affirmative action to remedy discrimination, to protect constitutional rights and to provide equal opportunity under the law.

WOMEN'S RIGHTS

Since the beginning of what we call civilization, when men's dominance over women was firmly established until the present day, our history has been marred with oppression of and brutality to women. The Green Party deplores this system of male domination, known as *patriarchy*, in all its forms, both subtle and overt - from oppression, inequality, and discrimination to domestic violence, rape, trafficking and forced slavery. The change the world is crying for cannot occur unless women's voices are heard. Democracy cannot work without equality for women that provides equal participation and representation. It took an extraordinary and ongoing fight over 72 years for Women to win the right to vote. However, the Equal Rights Amendment has still not been ratified.

We believe that equality should be a given, and that all Greens must work toward that end. We are committed to increasing participation of women in politics, government and leadership so they can change laws, make decisions, and create policy solutions that affect and will improve women's lives, and we are building our party so that Greens can be elected to office to do this. In July 2002 the Women's Caucus of the Green Party of the United States was founded to carry out the Party's commitment to women.

We also support, and call on others to support, the many existing and ongoing efforts for women.

Social Equality

a. We support the equal application of the Constitution to all citizens, and therefore call for passage of the Equal Rights Amendment (ERA). We urge accelerated ratification by three or more of the remaining 15 states that are required to pass ERA into law and into the Constitution. We urge renewed efforts and campaigns to ratify the ERA. We support House Resolution 98, using the precedent of a three-state strategy for ratification.

b. We call for equal representation of women in Congress instead of the current 13%.

c. The Green Party calls for U.S. passage of CEDAW, the Convention on the Elimination of all forms of Discrimination Against Women, which was adopted in 1979 by the U.N. General Assembly and ratified by 173 countries. The U.S. is one of the very few countries, and the only industrialized nation, that have not ratified it.

d. The Equal Employment Opportunities Commission should actively investigate and prosecute sexual harassment complaints. Women who file complaints must not be persecuted and should be protected under federal and state law. We must enshrine in law the basic principle that women have the same rights as men, and promote gender equality and fairness in the work force to ensure that women receive equal pay for jobs of equal worth.

e. We support the inclusion of an equal number of women and men in peace talks and negotiations, not only because these efforts directly affect their lives and those of their husbands, children and families, but also because when women are involved, the negotiations are more successful.

Reproductive Rights

f. Women's rights must be protected and expanded to guarantee each woman's right as a full participant in society, free from sexual harassment, job discrimination or interference in the intensely personal choice about whether to have a child.

g. Women's right to control their bodies is non-negotiable. It is essential that the option of a safe, legal abortion remains available. The "morning-after" pill must be affordable and easily accessible without a prescription, together with a government-sponsored public relations campaign to educate women about this form of contraception. Clinics must be accessible and must offer advice on contraception and the means for contraception; consultation about abortion and the performance of abortions, and; abortion regardless of age or marital status.

h. We endorse women's right to use contraception and, when they choose, to have an abortion. This right cannot be limited to women's age or marital status. Contraception and abortion must be included in all health insurance policies in the U.S., and any state government must be able to legally offer these services free of charge to women at the poverty level. Public health agencies operating abroad should be allowed to offer family planning, contraception, and abortion in all countries that ask for those services. We oppose our government's habit of cutting family planning funds when those funds go to agencies in foreign countries that give out contraceptive devices, offer advice on abortion, and perform abortions.

i. We encourage women and men to prevent unwanted pregnancies. It is the inalienable right and duty of every woman to learn about her body and to be aware of the phases of her menstrual cycle, and it is the duty for every man to be aware of the functions and health of his and his partner's bodies. This information is necessary for self determination, to make informed decisions, and to prevent unintended consequences. Unplanned conception takes control away from individuals and makes them subject to external controls. The "morning-after" pill and option of a safe and legal abortion need to remain available.

Economic Equality

j. Since, nationally, women still earn only 70% of men's wages for equal jobs, the Green Party calls for the introduction and passage of federal and state laws to achieve pay equity, and funding for the enforcement of such laws.

k. Single mothers are the largest and most severely impoverished group in the United States, which explains why 25% of the children in our country live below the poverty line. Welfare reform has forced mothers to abandon their children to travel to minimum wage jobs. With the extreme pay inequity, single mothers cannot afford child care, nurture their children, and move out of poverty.

l. The Green Party supports real reforms to end poverty and return dignity and opportunity to all mothers. We call for implementing innovative programs that work with the particular and special needs of motherhood. We also support other programs such as a universal basic income (known also as a guaranteed income or Citizen Dividend, as described in True Cost Pricing and Tax Fairness) that will provide for those who nurture the next generation - work that is of incalculable importance to our society.

Violence and Oppression

m. Language is often used as a weapon by those with power, and women have traditionally borne the brunt of inflicted injuries. Freedom of speech is vital to democracy. However, we believe that this freedom should not be used to perpetuate oppression and abuse.

n. Rape, domestic violence and other violence to women are increasing nationwide. We must address the root cause of all violence even as we specifically address violence to women. We cannot allow this to continue and call for increased funding for programs to address it.

o. The Green Party has zero tolerance for the illegal international trafficking in humans. Of the millions of humans trafficked worldwide, the large majority are women and children who are bought and sold as slaves and forced to labour against their will primarily in prostitution, but also in agriculture, sweat shops, domestic service and in other forms of servitude. According to Human Rights Watch, in all cases coercive tactics - including deception, fraud, intimidation, isolation, threat and use of physical force, or debt bondage - are used to control women. Figures from 2003 show 50,000 victims, both women and children, were trafficked to the U.S.

p. The Green Party supports all efforts to eradicate this extreme abuse of human rights, including but not limited to enforcement of existing laws and passage of tough new ones, punishing traffickers, aiding victims, increasing public awareness, reforming immigration laws, supporting existing programs and creating new ones.

q. We support the State Department's annual Trafficking in Persons Report as an important document to begin to combat this abuse. We support and urge enforcement of the Victims of Trafficking and Violence Protection Act (HR 3244) signed into law on October 28, 2000. This Act authorizes funding for the prevention of trade in human beings and for protecting victims. It gives the State Department a historic opportunity to create an office with the exclusive responsibility of ending traffic in humans and protecting the victims of this worldwide trade. We urge committed political support to achieve the cooperation of all different levels of government.

RACIAL DISCRIMINATION

The development of the United States has been marked by conflict over questions of race. Our nation was formed only after Native Americans were displaced. The institution of slavery had as its underpinnings the belief in white supremacy, which we as Greens condemn. In slavery's aftermath, people of color have borne the brunt of violence and discrimination. The Green Party unequivocally condemns these evils which continue to be a social problem of paramount significance.

a. We support efforts to overcome the effects of over 200 years of racial discrimination.

b. We call for an end to official support for any remaining

symbols of slavery and specifically call for the removal of the Confederate battle flag from all government buildings.

c. People of color in this country have legitimate claims to reparations in the form of monetary compensation for centuries of discrimination. We also uphold the right of the descendants of African slaves to self-determination, as we do for all indigenous peoples.

d. We condemn the practice of racial profiling by law enforcement agencies, which are guilty of stopping motorists, harassing individuals, or using unwarranted violence against suspects with no other justification than race or ethnic background.

e. We favor strong measures to combat official racism in the forms of police brutality directed against people of color.

f. We support effective enforcement of the Voting Rights Act, including language access to voting.

g. We oppose discriminatory English-only pressure groups. We call for a national language policy that would encourage all citizens to be fluent in at least two languages.

h. We strongly support the vigorous enforcement of civil rights laws, the aggressive prosecution of hate crimes, and the strengthening of legal services for the poor.

INDIGENOUS PEOPLES

We have great respect for Native American cultures, especially their deference for community and the Earth.

a. We recognize both the sovereignty of Native American tribal governments and the Federal Government's trust obligation to Native American people. Native American nations are just that - *nations* - and should be treated in like fashion, with the special circumstance that they are located within the United States.

b. The federal government is obligated to deal in good faith with Native Americans; honor its treaty obligations; adequately fund programs for the betterment of tribal governments and their people; affirm the religious rights of Native Americans in ceremonies (American Indian Religious Freedom Act); provide funds for innovative economic development initiatives, education and public health programs; and respect land, water and mineral rights within the borders of reservations and traditional lands.

c. We support efforts to broadly reform the Bureau of Indian Affairs to make this vast agency more responsible and more responsive to tribal governments.

d. We support the just settlement of the claims of the thousands of Native American uranium miners who have suffered and died from radiation exposure. We condemn the stance of secrecy taken by the Atomic Energy Commission during this era and its subsequent claim of government immunity, taken knowingly and immorally at the expense of Native people. We support the complete clean-up of those mines and tailing piles, which are a profoundly destructive legacy of the Cold War.

e. Native American land and treaty rights often stand as the front line against government and multinational corporate attempts to plunder energy, mineral, timber, fish, and game resources; pollute water, air, and land in the service of the military; expand economically; and consume natural resources. We support legal, political, and grassroots efforts by, and on behalf of, Native Americans to protect their traditions, rights, livelihoods, and sacred spaces.

Since illegal annexation in 1898, the Federal and State governments have cheated and neglected the native Hawaiian people. In 1993, the U.S. Congress passed, and President Clinton signed into law, the "Apology Bill" (U.S. Public Law 103-150). This admission of crime states in part, "the native Hawaiians have never lost their inherent sovereignty nor their national home base."

The Green Party demands justice for *kanaka maoli*. We

support the following:

a. Protecting sacred and culturally significant sites.

b. Efforts to nurture native Hawaiian culture.

c. Kanaka maoli leadership and guardianship in protecting gathering rights, and lobbying the legislature to safeguard these rights without interference.

d. Return of, or fair compensation for, ceded lands.

e. Immediate distribution of Hawaiian Homelands, with government funds allocated for the necessary infrastructure.

f. Prohibition of future sale or diminishments of the Ceded Land Trust.

g. A call for open dialogue among all residents of Hawai'i on the sovereignty option of full independence.

h. Hawaiian sovereignty in a form that is fair to both native Hawaiians and other residents of Hawai'i.

i. We acknowledge and actively endorse the inherent and absolute right of indigenous nations to self-determination, and thereby call upon the U.S. government to reverse its opposition to enactment of the proposed United Nations Declaration on the Rights of Indigenous Peoples in its entirety.

SEXUAL ORIENTATION AND GENDER IDENTITY

In keeping with the Green Key Values of diversity, social justice and feminism, we support full legal and political equality for all persons, regardless of sex, gender, or sexual orientation.

a. The Green Party affirms the rights of all individuals to freely choose intimate partners, regardless of their sex, gender, or sexual orientation.

b. We support the recognition of equal rights of persons

gay, lesbian, bisexual, or transgender to housing, jobs, civil marriage, medical benefits, child custody, and in all areas of life provided to all other citizens.

c. We support the inclusion of language in state and federal anti-discrimination law that ensures the rights of intersex individuals and prohibits discrimination based on gender identity, characteristics, and expression. We are opposed to intersex genital mutilation.

d. We support the right of all persons to self-determination with regard to gender identity and sex. We therefore support the right of intersex and transgender individuals to be free from coercion and involuntary assignment of gender or sex. We support access to medical and surgical treatment for assignment or reassignment of gender or sex, based on informed consent.

e. We support legislation against all forms of hate crimes, including those directed against people who identify as lesbian, gay, bisexual, queer, transgender, and intersex.

RIGHTS OF THE DISABLE

We support the full enforcement of the Americans with Disabilities Act to enable all people with disabilities to achieve independence and function at the highest possible level. Government should work to ensure that children with disabilities are provided with the same educational opportunities as those without disabilities. The physically and mentally challenged are people who are differently-abled from the majority, but who are nevertheless able to live independently. The mentally ill are people with serious mental problems who often need social support networks. Physically and mentally challenged people have the right to live independently in their communities.

The mentally ill also have the right to live independently, circumscribed only by the limitations of their illness. These people are their own best advocates in securing their rights and for living in the social and economic mainstream. Current Medicaid policy forces many challenged people to live in costly state-funded institutions. Excluding these people from society alienates them; excluding them from the work force denies them the chance to use their potentials. The diminishing funds available to provide care for the growing number of the mentally ill often result in their homelessness, vagrancy and dependence on short-term crisis facilities. Lack of funding also increases the necessity of placing them in long-term, locked facilities.

The Green Party urges the government to:

a. Increase rehabilitation funding so that persons with disabilities can pursue education and training to reach their highest potential. The differently-abled should participate fully in the allocation decisions of state rehabilitation departments' funds.

b. Aggressively implement the Americans with Disabilities Act.

c. Fund in-home support services to allow the differently-abled to hire personal care attendants while remaining at home.

d. Allocate adequate funding to support community-based programs that provide outpatient medical services, case management services and counseling programs. We should provide a residential setting within the community for those who do not need institutional care but who are unable to live independently.

e. Make it easier for the chronically mentally ill to apply for and receive Supplemental Security Income.

f. Mainstream the differently-abled. Increase the training of teachers in regards to the needs of differently-abled students.

g. Discourage stereotyping of the mentally and physically challenged by the entertainment industry and the media.

h. Fund programs to increase public sensitivity to the needs of the mentally ill and differently-abled.

RELIGIOUS FREEDOM AND SECULAR EQUALITY

The United States Bill of Rights guarantees freedom of religion. We affirm the right of each individual to the exercise of conscience and religion, while maintaining the constitutionally mandated separation of government and religion. We believe that federal, state, and local governments must remain neutral regarding religion.

We call for:

a. Ending discriminatory federal, state, and local laws against particular religious beliefs, and non-belief. The U.S. Constitution states that there shall be no religious test for public office. This requirement should apply to oaths (or affirmations) for holding public office at any level, employment at all government levels, oaths for witnesses in courts, oaths for jury membership, and the oath for citizenship.

b. Prosecution of hate crimes based on religious affiliation or practice.

c. Elimination of displays of religious symbols, monuments, or statements on government buildings, property, websites, money, or documents.

d. Restoration of the Pledge of Allegiance to its pre-1954 version, eliminating the politically motivated addition of "under God."

e. Ending faith-based initiatives and charitable choice programs, whereby public funds are used to support religious organizations that do not adhere to specified guidelines and standards, including anti-discrimination laws.

f. Ending school vouchers whereby public money pays for students in religious schools.

g. Ending governmental use of the doctrines of specific religions to define the nature of family, marriage, and the type and character of personal relationships between consenting adults.

h. Ending religiously-based curricula in government-funded public schools.

i. Ending the use of religion as a justification to deny children necessary medical care or subject them to physical and emotional abuse.

j. Ending the use of religion by government to define the role and rights of women in our society.

k. Revocation of the Congressional charter of the Boy Scouts of America. Any private organization that practices bigotry against certain religious beliefs and classes of people should not have a Congressional endorsement or access to public property and funds.

YOUNG RIGHTS

All human beings have the right to a life that will let them achieve their full potential. Young people are one of the least protected classes of human beings, yet they represent our future. We must ensure they have an upbringing that allows them to take their place as functioning, productive, and self-actualized members of their community.

a. Youth are not the property of their parents or guardians, but are under their care and guidance.

b. Youth have the right to survive by being provided adequate food, shelter and comprehensive health care, including prenatal care for mothers.

c. Youth have the right to be protected from abuse, harmful drugs, violence, environmental hazards, neglect, and exploitation.

d. Youth have the right to develop in a safe and nurturing early environment provided by affordable child care and preschool preparation.

e. Youth have the right to an education that is stimulating, relevant, engaging, and that fosters their natural desire to learn.

f. Young people's creative potential should be encouraged to the greatest extent possible.

g. Young people should have input into the direction and pace of their own education, including input into the operation of their educational institutions.

h. Young people should be provided with education regarding their own and others' sexuality at the earliest appropriate time.

i. Young people should be provided the opportunity to express themselves in their own media, including television, radio, films and the Internet. Young people should also be given skills in analyzing commercial media.

j. Young people should be kept free from coercive advertising at their educational institutions.

VETERANS' RIGHTS

Support for men and women in the armed forces must go far beyond the rhetoric used to discredit the peace movement in the U.S. today. We believe that the ill-advised and illegal actions of the U.S. administration have unnecessarily put our troops in harm's way. We further believe that the dangerous burden of fighting the unnecessary war in Iraq, and the wars that may follow, due to the administration's overly narrow and militaristic response to terrorism is disproportionately borne by families of lesser means. Those who are required to carry out militaristic policies, often with great hardship to themselves, their families, and even the risk of their lives, deserve our respect and our commitment to adequate compensation and benefits.

We recommend the following actions:

a. Increase the current pay levels, monthly imminent danger pay, and family separation allowances for those risking their lives in combat zones.

b. Ensure that all pre-deployment physicals are completed and carried out within the standard allotted time period and that medical follow-ups are routinely done on all soldiers.

c. Establish a panel of independent medical doctors to examine and oversee the policies of the military regarding forced vaccinations and shots, often with experimental drugs.

d. Honor all laws concerning time limits on deployments.

e. Provide better care for the wounded, sick, and injured soldiers returning home. The Pentagon must take all steps necessary to fully diagnose and treat both physical and mental health conditions resulting from service in all combat zones.

f. Ensure a smooth transition from active military service to civilian life by providing counseling, housing, emergency management, job protection, and other support systems.

g. Restore full funding for veterans' health programs.

h. Request Congress to enact a new GI Bill, similar to the one that began after World War II and ended in 1981, to provide the following benefits:

Tuition grants for four years of college or other educational opportunities.

Low interest loans for housing or business start-ups.

Free medical care for military personnel and their families for ten years following separation from the armed forces - until universal health care becomes a reality.

i. Support and respect Conscientious Objector status during all phases of the process. We fully support the right of individuals in the military service to modify or completely separate from military involvement because of conscientious objection. We call upon all military entities and officers to support a transparent and democratic conscientious objection process free of harassment, imprisonment, or deployment to war zones for those pursuing the conscientious objection process.

j. Recognized, independent veteran organizations must have access to military personnel to ensure they are being informed of their rights. This is especially true for those who are hospitalized due to service related injuries or illnesses.

CONSUMER PROTECTION

Consumers have the right to adequate enforcement of the federal and state consumer protection laws. Health and safety are of paramount importance, so we oppose lax or inappropriate regulatory actions.

a. Consumers should have the right to participate in decisions that affect their lives and protect their interests, beyond simply voting on Election Day.

b. We support the creation of consumer advocacy agencies in order to protect the interests of consumers against corporate lobbyists who have too often successfully argued before regulatory agencies against consumer rights. We would require legal monopolies and regulated industries (including electric, gas, water, and telephone utilities) to set up statewide consumer action groups to act on behalf of and advocate for consumer interests.

c. We call for better information for consumers about the products they buy, and where and how they are made. We endorse *truth in advertising,* including the clear definition of words like "recycled" and "natural."

d. We defend the rights of individuals to participate in class action lawsuits against manufacturers of unsafe products. We call for restrictions on secrecy agreements that may prevent lawsuits by not revealing damaging information.

e. We support laws to protect "whistle blowers."

The so-called *war on terrorism* must not become an assault on the civil liberties that are enshrined in our Constitution. The price of freedom is not the loss of liberty. Constitutionally protected rights - fought for by American patriots - are rights the Green Party patriotically holds in the highest regard. Greens demand that the Justice Department cease and desist its wholesale rollback of constitutional protections and its daily dismantling of legal safeguards. The use of Homeland Defense monies to spy on citizens exercising First Amendment rights is particularly onerous, as are "sneak and peek" provisions of the U.S.A. PATRIOT Act that allows surveillance of libraries, readers, the Internet, and computer users. Basic rights ensuring individual privacy are under attack. The U.S. government's use of high tech tools, including intrusive monitoring, data mining and analysis to identify and disrupt citizen activists, should be seen as an attack on fundamental rights of an engaged, active citizenry. The Green Party calls on Congress and the courts to reign in constitutional and civil liberties abuses that have become prevalent in the Bush administration and the John Ashcroft Justice Department.

ENVIRONMENTAL JUSTICE

Low-income citizens and minorities suffer disproportionately from environmental hazards in the workplace, at home, and in their communities. Inadequate laws, lax enforcement of existing environmental regulations, and weak penalties for infractions undermine environmental protection.

Therefore, the Green Party advocates:

1. Devoting greater efforts to full enforcement and prosecution of environmental crimes.
2. Funding environmental crime units for district attorneys in counties with significant pollution problems.
3. Imposing a moratorium on siting new toxic chemical or waste facilities in those counties with the highest percentage exposure to hazardous substances.
4. Not forcing workers to choose between a hazardous job or no job at all.
5. Preventing communities, especially low-income or minority communities, from being coerced by governmental agencies or corporations into siting hazardous materials, or accepting environmentally hazardous practices in order to create jobs.
6. Preceding the siting of hazardous materials or practices with public hearings, conducted in the language of those community members who will be directly affected.

ECONOMIC JUSTICE / SOCIAL SAFETY NET

We have a special responsibility to the health and well-being of the young. Yet we see the federal safety net being removed and replaced with limited and potentially harsh state welfare programs. How will social services be adequately provided if local resources are already stretched thin? We believe our community priorities must first protect the young and helpless. Yet how will state legislatures and agencies, under pressure from more powerful interests, react? We believe local decision-making is important, but we realize, as we learned during the civil rights era, that strict federal standards must guide state actions in providing basic protections.

As the richest nation in history, we should not condemn millions of children to a life of poverty, while corporate welfare is increased to historic highs. The Green Party opposes the privatization of Social Security. It is critical that the public protections of Social Security are not privatized and subjected to increased risk. The bottom 20% of American senior citizens get roughly 80% of their income from Social Security, and without Social Security, nearly 70% of black elderly and 60% of Latino elderly households would be in poverty.

COMMITMENT TO ENDING POVERTY

It is time for a radical shift in our attitude toward support for families, children, the poor and the disabled. Such support must not be given grudgingly; it is the right of those presently in need and an investment in our future. We must take an uncompromising position that the care and nurture of children, elders and the disabled are essential to a healthy, peaceful, and sustainable society. We should recognize that the work of their caregivers is of social and economic value, and reward it accordingly. Ensuring that children and their caregivers have access to an adequate, secure standard of living should form the cornerstone of our economic priorities. Only then can we hope to build our future on a foundation of healthy, educated children who are raised in an atmosphere of love and security.

1. All people have a right to food, housing, medical care, jobs that pay a living wage, education, and support in times of hardship.
2. Work performed outside the monetary system has inherent social and economic value, and is essential to a healthy, sustainable economy and peaceful communities. Such work includes: child and elder care; homemaking; voluntary community service; continuing education; participating in government; and the arts.
3. We call for restoration of a federally funded entitlement program to support children, families, the unemployed, elderly and disabled, with no time limit on benefits. This program should be funded through the existing welfare budget, reductions in military spending and corporate subsidies, and a fair, progressive income tax.
4. We call for a graduated supplemental income, or negative income tax, that would maintain all individual adult incomes above the poverty level, regardless of employment or marital status.
5. We advocate reinvesting a significant portion of the military budget into family support, living-wage job development, and work training programs. Publicly funded work training and education programs should have a goal of increasing employment options at finding living-wage jobs.
6. We support public funding for the development of living-wage jobs in community and environmental service. For example, environmental clean-up, recycling, sustainable agriculture and food production, sustainable forest management, repair and maintenance of public facilities, neighborhood-based public safety, aides in schools, libraries and childcare centers, and construction and renovation of energy-efficient housing. We oppose enterprise zone give-aways which benefit corporations more than inner-city communities.
7. The accumulation of individual wealth in the U.S. has reached grossly unbalanced proportions. It is clear that

we cannot rely on the rich to regulate their profit-making excesses for the good of society through "trickle-down economics." We must take aggressive steps to restore a fair distribution of income. We support tax incentives for businesses that apply fair employee wage distribution standards, and income tax policies that restrict the accumulation of excessive individual wealth.

8. Forcing welfare recipients to accept jobs that pay wages below a living wage drives wages down and exploits workers for private profit at public expense. We reject workfare as being a form of indentured servitude.
9. Corporations receiving public subsidies must provide jobs that pay a living wage, observe basic workers' rights, and agree to affirmative action policies.

EDUCATION AND THE ARTS

Access to quality education for all Americans is the difference that will lead to a strong and diverse community. Fundamental changes in our priorities are needed at the national and local levels, within the public and private sectors, in the classroom, and at home to make education our first priority.

Education

Greens support educational diversity. We hold no dogma absolute, continually striving for truth in the realm of ideas. We open ourselves, consciously and intuitively, to truth and beauty in the world of nature. We view learning as a lifelong process to which all people have an equal right. Education starts with choice, and within public education we believe in broad choices. Magnet schools, Site-based Management, Schools within Schools, alternative models, and parental involvement are ways in which elementary education can be changed to make a real difference in the lives of our children. Curricula should focus on skills - both basic skills that serve as a solid foundation for higher learning, and exploratory approaches that expand horizons, such as distance learning, interactive education, computer proficiency, perspectives that bring an enriched awareness of nature (biological literacy), intercultural experiences, and languages. Greens view learning as a lifelong and life-affirming process.

In learning, and openness to learning, we create the foundation of our platform:

a. We advocate creative and noncompetitive education at every age level, and the inclusion of cultural diversity in all curricula. We encourage hands-on approaches that promote a multitude of individual learning styles.

b. Parental responsibility should be encouraged by supporting parenting, as more families confront economic conditions that demand more time be spent away from home. Parents should be as involved as possible in their children's education; values do start with parents. Teaching human sexuality is a parental and school responsibility.

c. Student responsibility is a key to developing capabilities. Greens hold strongly to the empowerment of individuals. Students should recognize their own personal responsibilities and strive to achieve their fullest potential as individuals.

d. Federal policy on education should act principally to ensure equal access to a quality education.

e. Educational funding formulas at the state level need to be adjusted as needed to avoid gross inequalities between districts and schools. Educational grants should provide balance to ensure equal educational access for minority, deprived, special needs, and exceptional children. In higher education, federal college scholarship aid should be increased and offered to any qualified student.

f. Our teachers are underpaid, overworked and rarely supplied with the resources necessary to do their work. It is time to stop disinvesting in education, and start placing it at the top of our social and economic agenda.

g. We call for equitable state and national funding for education and the creation of schools controlled by parent-teacher governing bodies.

h. We oppose vouchers, or any scheme that will transfer

money out of the public school system. That course only leads to a separate and unequal educational system. We also oppose charter schools or the administration of public schools by private, for-profit entities.

i. We support after-school programs for "latchkey" children.

j. We advocate state funding for day care that includes school children under the age of ten when after-school programs are not available.

k. Classroom teachers at the elementary and high school levels should be given professional status and salaries comparable to related professions requiring advanced education, training and responsibility.

l. Principals are also essential components in effective educational institutions. We encourage state Departments of Education and school boards to deliver more programmatic support and decision-making to the true grassroots level- the classroom teacher and school principal.

m. Use of computers in the early grades should not supplant the development of basic interpersonal, perceptual, and motor skills as a foundation for learning.

n. Dispute resolution is an important part of resolving classroom or after-school disputes, and a life skill that all children should learn. We call for the teaching of nonviolent conflict resolution at all levels of education.

o. We recognize the viable alternative of home-based education.

p. We support a host of innovative and critical educational efforts, such as bi-lingual education, continuing education, job retraining, monitoring and apprenticeship programs.

q. We are deeply concerned about the intervention in our schools of corporations that promote a culture of consumption and waste. Schools should not be vehicles for commercial advertising. Schools must safeguard students' privacy rights and not make private student information available on corporate (or federal government) request.

r. Within higher education, we oppose military and corporate control over the priorities and topics of academic research.

s. We support tuition-free post secondary (collegiate and vocational) public education.

t. In an economy that demands higher skills and a democracy that depends on an informed, educated electorate, opportunities for universal higher education and life-long learning must be vastly expanded.

u. Until tuition-free schooling is available to all, student loans should be available to all students attending college, and should be repayable as a proportion of future earnings rather than at a fixed rate.

v. Individualized training accounts should be made available to students who choose to pursue vocational and continuing education.

w. The Leave No Child Behind Act must be repealed, especially the section that gives the military access to student records.

THE ARTS

Freedom of artistic expression is a fundamental right and a key element in empowering communities, and in moving us toward sustainability and respect for diversity. Artists can create in ways that foster healthy, non-alienating relationships between people and their daily environments, communities, and the Earth. This can include both artists whose themes advocate compassion, nurturance, or co-operation; and artists whose creations unmask the often-obscure connections between various forms of violence, domination, and oppression, or effectively criticize aspects of the very community that supports their artistic activity. The arts can only perform their social function if they are completely free from outside control.

The Green Party supports:

a. Alternative, community-based systems treating neither the artwork nor the artist as a commodity.

b. Eliminating all laws that seek to restrict or censor artistic expression, including the withholding of government funds for political or moral content.

c. Increased funding for the arts appropriate to their essential social role at local, state and federal levels of government.

d. Community-funded programs employing local artists to enrich their communities through public art programs, including public performances, exhibitions, murals on public buildings, design or re-design of parks and public areas, storytelling and poetry reading, and publication.

e. The establishment of non-profit public forums for local artists to display their talents and creations. Research, public dialogue, and trial experiments to develop alternative systems for the valuation and exchange of artworks and for the financial support of artists. Some examples include community subscriber support groups, artwork rental busts, cooperative support systems among artists, legal or financial incentives to donate to the arts or to donate artworks to public museums.

f. Responsible choices of non-toxic, renewable, or recyclable materials. Funding sources not connected with social injustice or environmental destruction.

g. Education programs in the community that will energize the creativity of every community member from the youngest to the oldest, including neglected groups such as teenagers, senior citizens, prisoners, immigrants, and drug addicts. These programs would provide materials and access to interested, qualified arts educators for every member of the community who demonstrates an interest.

h. Funding and staffing to incorporate arts education into every school curriculum. We encourage local artists and the community to contribute time, experience, and resources to these efforts.

i. Diversity in arts education in the schools including age-specific hands-on activities and appreciative theoretical approaches, exposure to the arts of various cultures and stylistic traditions, and experiences with a variety of media, techniques and contents.

j. The integration of the arts and artistic teaching methods into other areas of the curriculum to promote a holistic perspective.

The United States must respect the measures other nations take to ensure public health, and must not use medication, medical equipment, and other medical necessities, or threats of withholding them, as leverage for political reasons or as extortion for the sake of commercial profit. We oppose any embargo or economic sanction that would cause the suffering or death of civilians.

HEALTH CARE

Medicare, which provides health care for over 40 million Americans, is at risk. We would vigorously pursue savings and cuts from abundant waste and fraud, eliminate unnecessary services that benefit providers more than patients, and rein in pharmaceutical industry price-gouging. 70% to 85% of illness in America is due to unmanaged stress. This means that national measures to reduce work hours, promote cyber-commuting for work, and increased vacation time for workers will significantly improve the public's health. We advocate access for all, irrelevant of income, to stress management training such as meditation techniques, yoga, tai chi, qigong, and biofeedback.

A large percentage of illness is diet-related; therefore, improving the quality of our nation's food supply and our personal eating habits will lessen the strain on our health care system. We advocate subsidies for organic foods, as well as removing sugar/caffeine snacks from schools. This could save our nation as much as $700 to $850 billion of the $1 trillion annual health costs. We support the teaching of holistic health approaches and, as appropriate, the use of complementary and alternative therapies such as herbal medicines, homeopathy, acupuncture, and other healing approaches. We call for wider implementation of hospice care. We oppose the arrest, harassment or prosecution of anyone involved in any aspect of the production, cultivation, transportation, distribution or consumption of medicinal marijuana. We also oppose the harassment, prosecution or revocation of license of any health-care provider who gives a recommendation or prescription for medicinal marijuana.

We support informed consent laws to educate consumers to potential health impact of types of treatment. For truly informed consent, a professional must explain the limitations of his or her professional training, and make the patient aware of what other professionals could offer differently or in addition. Primary care, through a renewed attention to family medicine as opposed to increased medical specialization, is necessary. We unequivocally support a woman's right to reproductive choice, no matter her marital status or age, and that contraception and safe, legal abortion procedures be available on demand and be included in all health insurance coverage in the U.S., as well as free of charge in any state where a woman falls below the poverty level.

Medical research must be increased, and alternative therapies actively sought, to combat diseases and eliminate their causes, especially cancer and HIV/AIDS. We call for competent social and health services for those who have special needs: the mentally ill, the handicapped, and those who are terminally ill. Public policy needs to move in the direction of a voluntary, community-based mental health system that safeguards human dignity, respects individual autonomy, and protects informed consent. A wide variety of humane, effective, and empowering alternative and complementary approaches should be available for anyone who experiences a psychiatric problem or mental disability.

UNIVERSAL HEALTH CARE

The United States is the only industrialized nation in the world without a national health care system. The current system's high costs and widely recognized failures demand that bold steps be taken. The Green Party supports a universal, comprehensive, national single-payer health insurance program as the only solution to the current disastrous for-profit system. Under a universal national single-payer health care system, the administrative waste of private insurance corporations would be redirected to patient care. If the U.S. were to shift to a system of universal coverage and a single payer plan, as in Canada, the savings in administrative costs would be more than enough to offset the cost.

Expenses for businesses currently providing coverage would be reduced. State and local governments would pay less because they would receive reimbursement for services provided to the previously uninsured, and because public programs would cease to be the "dumping ground" for high-risk patients and those rejected by HMOs when they become disabled and unemployed. Most importantly, the people of America will gain the peace of mind in knowing that needed health care will always be available to them. No longer will people have to worry about facing financial disaster if they become seriously ill, are laid off their jobs, or are injured in an accident.

The Green Party supports a universal, comprehensive, national single-payer health plan that will provide the following with no increase in cost:

a. A publicly funded health care insurance program, administered at the state and local levels.
b. Lifetime benefits for everyone. No one will lose coverage for any reason.
c. Freedom to choose the type of health care provider, with a wide range of health care choices.
d. Decision-making in the hands of health providers and their patients.
e. Comprehensive benefits, as good or better than existing plans, including dental, vision, mental health care, hospice, long-term care, substance abuse treatment and medication coverage.
f. Participation of all licensed and/or certified health providers, subject to standards of practice in their field.
g. Portable health plan benefits.

h. Primary and preventive care as priorities, including wellness education about diet, nutrition and exercise.
i. Greatly reduced paperwork for both patients and providers.
j. Fair and full reimbursement to providers for their services.
k. Preservation of all health care services currently available.
l. Cost controls via streamlined administration, national fee schedules, bulk purchases of drugs and medical equipment, and coordination of capital expenditures. Prices of medications must be publicly supervised.
m. Hospitals that can afford safe staffing levels for registered nurses.
n. Establishment of national, state, and local Health Policy Boards consisting of health consumers and providers to oversee and evaluate the performance of the system, expand access to care, and determine research priorities. All meetings of the boards shall be open to the public.
o. Establishment of a National Health Trust Fund that would channel all current Federal payments for health care programs directly into the Fund, in addition to employees' health premium payments.

AID/HIV

We call for comprehensive, humane, and competent care of all people with AIDS/HIV. An all-out campaign must be waged against AIDS and HIV. The AIDS epidemic has not been adequately addressed at the local, state, federal, or international levels. All people in all countries, including those with AIDS/HIV, have a right to medical care, protection from discrimination, and confidentiality. Drug corporations have a strong profit motivation to make this disease a manageable one (like diabetes) with guaranteed sales of very expensive drugs, in the billions of dollars every year. Drug companies have not emphasized research that targets a cure. While new drugs have dramatically saved lives, many have side effects so debilitating that the quality of life is poor, if not intolerable during the extended lifetime of the patient. But even these need to be produced generically to stop the devastation resulting from corporate refusal to provide these drugs to the millions dying throughout the world who cannot afford these basic lifesaving drugs. Drug researchers should have a cure for AIDS as their ultimate goal.

The Green Party calls for:

a. Increased funding for AIDS education and patient care.

b. Increased funding for comprehensive sex education that includes AIDS education.

c. Increased funding for research focusing on a cure, methods of prevention, and on bolstering the immune system.

d. Improved technology, facilities, laboratories, researchers, staff and personnel to cure AIDS/HIV. A "Manhattan Project" for a cure is required.

e. Complete sharing of information between researchers, funding agencies (including corporations), and the public on AIDS/HIV before awarding the next research grant.

f. More research into better methods of prevention of HIV infection. While we support condom use, better condoms are also required. We support more vaccine research.

g. Equal access to AIDS education, treatment and medications for all affected. Accordingly, funding and accountability should be increased.

h. Allowing all prisoners affected with AIDS/HIV in all countries to have the same access as free citizens to education, treatment, preventive measures (including condom use), and medical care.

i. A uniform international definition of AIDS.

j. Protecting the confidentiality of all people diagnosed with AIDS/HIV or tested for HIV.

k. More careful and timely approval of effective AIDS drugs by the FDA.

l. Production of affordable and available versions of patented medicines in all countries.

m. Targeting the young for age-appropriate education about AIDS/HIV and appropriate methods of prevention. We support sex education and the distribution of condoms in schools.

n. Prevention awareness and access to condoms to prevent the spread of AIDS. We condemn HIV-related discrimination.

o. Make drug treatment and other programs available for all addicts who seek help.

p. Expand clinical trials for treatments and vaccines.

q. Speed-up the FDA drug approval process.

r. Providing housing for homeless and poor people with AIDS/HIV.

s. Providing treatment for homeless people with AIDS/HIV.

t. Support for needle exchange programs and for programs to help drug addicts.

u. No mandatory screening for AIDS/HIV; anonymous screening must be available.

v. Lifting the ban prohibiting HIV positive people from entering the U.S. as visitors or as immigrants.

And as union membership falls, so do the wages of all working people, union and non-union alike. We support efforts to overcome these legal handicaps, especially in the South and Southwest where the laws are most hostile. We also must dedicate ourselves to fighting for a complete overhaul of this country's labour laws. We support the irreducible right of the working people in a company, without hindrance, to form a union and to bargain collectively with their employer. This right was guaranteed under The Fair Labour Standards Act of 1936.

Furthermore, we support the right of workers, without penalty, to inform other workers on the premises of a union being formed. This includes advertising and recruiting.

The 1936 Act has been eroded and diluted over the years by incremental infringements and restrictions, especially by the Taft- Hartley Act of 1947 (which includes the union shop) passed over President Truman's veto. We stand for repeal of the Taft-Hartley Act.

It is imperative that employees in a company or business enjoy workplace democracy, which includes the following:

- The right to elect representatives to sit equally with management on the Board of Directors.
- The right to fair and democratic elections of their own union officers.
- No permanent replacement of striking workers.
- No forced overtime.
- Encourage flexible working schedules so employees can arrange our own time to deal with personal and family concerns
- All workers, temporary or permanent, must be paid a living wage.
- All workers must have health care coverage, at least half paid by employer, until the passage of universal health care.
- All workers must have unemployment insurance, workers' compensation, and access to a jobs search program when they are unemployed. This security applies to farm workers as well.
- Require minimum pensions for all workers, fully vested and portable, that do not reduce social security benefits
- Mediation must be the first available solution to labour - management disputes with an agreed-upon time limit.
- New union members must have the right to submit a first contract to binding arbitration at the request of the union.
- Labour has the first right to buy out a company that is for sale or is going bankrupt, or being outsourced to another state or another country.
- We support a law requiring employers who purchase or merge with other companies to honor all existing collective bargaining agreements and contracts.

- Labour has the right to stock ownership and oversight of the investment of its own funds in the company where it works.

We support the enactment of living wage laws that apply to all workers. A major consequence of this law will be the lessening of the ever-widening gap between CEOs' income and workers' pay. Agricultural and other excluded workers must be covered by federal labour laws, except where existing state laws offer more protection. We encourage cooperative ownership and management of enterprises whenever a buy-out is possible. We support day-care service offered at every workplace when feasible, or reasonably nearby when not feasible at the workplace. Management's unhindered right to close its workplace and move to a lower-pay locale must be circumscribed to the degree that it protects the local workforce and their job security. We support the establishment of a reduced-hour work week and at least one month of vacation per year for all workers.

The ever-widening gap between rich and poor is destructive of democracy and creates an uneven playing field for economic opportunity. Public welfare that depends on hand-outs from the corporate rich reduces democracy by that same amount. Every citizen must have the leverage necessary to become a productive member of the economy and the society in which we live. All workers have a right to a safe and humane working environment. A lack of adequate enforcement of Occupational Safety and Health Administration (OSHA) laws and/or insufficient standards put many workers at risk.

We support the following safety policies:

- Protect and enforce OSHA laws. We insist on adequate testing of equipment and funding of enforcement procedures.
- Inform workers of workplace hazards. Employers have a responsibility to protect workers from those hazards.
- Legislate full funding for worker safety programs at both the state and federal levels.

- Insist on agricultural practices that don't endanger farm workers. Put agricultural practices under the jurisdiction of OSHA.

We stand firmly opposed to privatization and contracting-out of public services. A government that works for us would provide critical goods and services that should not be run for profit.

CRIMINAL JUSTICE

The effects of imprisonment are largely negative. Prisoners are increasingly isolated from the communities they came from and are often denied contact with the outside world or the media. Access to educational and legal materials is disappearing. Boredom and hopelessness prevail. The United States has the highest recidivism rate of any industrialized country. Rape is a serious problem in prison. The increasingly widespread privatization of prisons renders some prisoners virtual corporate slaves.

Law enforcement is placing too much emphasis on drug-related and petty street crimes, and not enough on prosecution of corporate, white collar, and environmental crimes. Defrauding someone of their life savings is the same as robbery. Spraying pesticides while workers are in the fields, negligently maintaining dangerous workplaces that result in death or maiming, or dumping toxic substances should be treated the same as other crimes. At the same time, we must develop a firm approach to law enforcement that directly addresses violent crime, including trafficking in hard drugs. Violence that creates a climate of further violence must be stopped.

Police brutality has reached epidemic levels in the United States and we call for effective monitoring of police agencies to eliminate police brutality. We support a citizen's right of access to justice. Our system of justice must be made convenient to rich and poor alike, guarding it against big business' attempts to regulate and, in effect, control our civil justice/civil jury system.

The Green Party proposes the following policies:

Alternatives to Incarceration

Any attempt to combat crime must begin with restoration of community. We encourage positive approaches that build hope, responsibility and a sense of belonging. Prisons should be the sentence of last resort, reserved for violent criminals. Those convicted of nonviolent offenses should be handled by other programs including halfway houses, electronic monitoring, work-furlough, community service and restitution programs. Substance abuse should be addressed as a medical problem requiring treatment, not imprisonment, and a failed drug test should not result in revocation of parole. Incarcerated prisoners of the drug war should be release to the above programs. Prisons are presently serving some of the population formerly held in the mental health system. Ninety-five percent of those who commit suicide in jail or prison have a diagnosed mental disorder. Mentally ill prisoners need separate psychiatric facilities providing psychological and medical care, rehabilitation, and release to appropriate community mental health facilities.

The aging of our prison population will lead to huge needless expenditures in the next decade. Prisoners too old and those too infirm to be a threat to society should be released to less expensive, community-based facilities. Juvenile offenders must not be housed in needlessly restrictive settings. They must never be housed with adults. Their education must continue while in custody. A single judge and a single caseworker should be assigned to oversee each juvenile's placement and progress in the juvenile justice system. Our parole system is a failure. Reduction of recidivism should be a goal of parole. Parole should be treated as a time of reintegration into the community, not as a continuation of a person's sentence.

Parolees need community reentry programs before release. Paroled prisoners should have access to education, drug treatment, psychological treatment, job training, work and housing. Their persons and homes should not be subject to search without reasonable cause. Appropriate services should also be available to the members of a parolee's family, to help them with the changes caused by the paro-lee's return. We call for more funding for rape and domestic violence prevention and education programs, and stiffer sentences for people convicted of domestic violence.

PRISON CONDITIONS

Private prisons should be illegal. Corrections Corporation of America ranks among the top five performing companies on the New York Stock Exchange during the late 1990's, and operates the sixth largest prison system in the country. These prisons treat people as their product, and provide far worse service than government-run prisons. Profits are derived from understaffing, which severely reduces the acceptable care of inmates. Prison conditions must be humane and sanitary and should include heat, light, exercise, clothing, nutrition, libraries, possessions, and personal safety. Prisoners are entitled to psychological, drug, and medical treatment, including access to condoms and uninterrupted access to all prescribed medication. Isolation of prisoners from staff and one another should be minimal and only as needed for safety.

Prison officials must institute and enforce policies that discourage racism, sexism, and homophobia in prison. End racially segregated housing. The First Amendment rights of prisoners must not be revoked. Prisoners have the right to talk to journalists, write letters, publish their own writings, and become legal experts on their own cases. Encourage all prisoners to have the opportunity to obtain a G.E.D. (high school equivalency diploma) and higher education. Inmates who earn a diploma have a recidivism rate of 10%, compared with 60% for other inmates. Prisons should be community-based where possible.

Where they are not, transportation for visits should be made available and subsidized. Unless the reason for imprisonment indicates otherwise, parents should have access to their children if it is in the interest of the child. Incarcerated individuals should retain the right to vote by absentee ballot in the district of their domicile, and should retain the right to vote during parole. We support the reinstatement of voting rights and the right to hold public office to ex-felons who have completed their prison sentence.

Legislation

Establish programs to strengthen self-help and community action through neighborhood centers that provide well-funded legal aid, alternative dispute-resolution practices, mediated restitution, community team policing, and local crisis/assault care shelters. Establish elected or appointed independent civilian review boards with subpoena power to investigate complaints about prison guard and community police behaviour.

Maximize restrictions on police use of weapons and restraining techniques such as pepper spray, stun belts, and choke holds. Abolish the death penalty. Repeal state "Three Strikes" laws. Restore judicial discretion in sentencing, as opposed to mandatory sentencing. Freedom on bail must be the right of all defendants charged with non-violent crimes. Mental health and social services should be incorporated in the bail agreement. Laws giving prosecutors the power to deny defendants the right to remain free on bail must be repealed. Stop forfeiture of the property of unconvicted suspects. It is state piracy and denial of due process. Implement a moratorium on prison construction. The funds saved should be used for alternatives to incarceration.

Compensation for jurors should be increased and child care provided for those serving on a jury. Employers should be encouraged to continue paying an employees' wages while they serve. Thoughtful, carefully considered gun control laws such as the "Brady Bill" and the waiting period for record search before gun dealers may sell a gun should be supported. Enact tough DWI (driving while intoxicated) laws. A consistent policy of protection against violence in schools should be developed and enforced. Victims' rights must be guarded and protected. Victim-impact statements are a method for achieving full justice, and restitution should be considered in many cases. We call for decriminalization of victimless crimes. For example, the possession of small amounts of marijuana. We call for legalization of industrial hemp and all its many uses. We call for an end to the "war on drugs." We support expanded drug counseling and treatment.

Population

Limiting the discussion to population numbers and birthrates diverts attention from over-consumption in the industrial world and historic patterns of exploitation of developing countries. Consumption-oriented lifestyles that have evolved in the industrial world have resulted in a minority of people consuming a majority of resources. This is as significant a threat to the Earth's carrying capacity as the high birth rates in low-consumption countries. Current global demographics demonstrate that economic well-being promotes low birthrates. Any discussion of population must also be a discussion of women throughout the world. There is documented evidence that the economic and social status of women is a primary factor in birthrates - when women have control over their lives, birthrates decrease. Also, a major barrier to the improvement of women's reproductive health is a lack of shared responsibility between men and women in family planning.

Combinations of male attitudes and cultural traditions have resulted in most men being under-educated and uninvolved in the planning of their families. Globally, human population is increasing while food production has leveled off. When population increases faster than the economy grows, the disparity between rich and poor also increases. Higher human consumption rates and populations increase the pressure on the environment in every ecological problem area.

Those living in the industrialized world must end the habits of waste and overconsumption that place as much stress on the environment as does population growth in developing nations. We must remove the political and economic barriers that prevent women around the world from having all the resources necessary to become skilled family planners. Funds must be allocated for expanded scientific research into safer and more effective birth control techniques and devices. We demand better-than-adequate health care for women and children—especially prenatal care. There must be access to free birth control devices, information counseling, and clinics to all who desire them. We call for implementation of family planning education for both genders in all levels of the state school system. We must promote new traditions and images of men becoming fully involved in all aspects of the family planning process.

FREE SPEECH MEDIA REFORM

Free speech and free press are constitutionally and politically guaranteed rights. Democracy requires a wide variety of opinions and information, which is not currently provided by corporate controlled media outlets. The Green Party calls for the establishment of citizen initiated and controlled radio and television stations. These citizen-managed media networks would be financed by requiring corporations to pay for the right to use our publicly owned air waves. Mechanisms must be established to prevent political manipulation and exploitation of this essential and valuable resource, so that all citizens are adequately informed.

The Green Party supports:

1. Returning ownership and control of the electromagnetic spectrum to the public. We urge the public to *reclaim the public airwaves*. The privatization of the broadcast airwaves - one of our most important taxpayer assets - has caused serious deformations of our politics and culture.
2. The problem is that private broadcasters control what the public owns. In return for free licenses to use taxpayer property, broadcasters give us a steady stream of

increasingly coarse, redundant, superficial programming, and exclusively decide who says what on our public airwaves.

3. Market-priced leasing of any for-profit use of the electromagnetic spectrum.
4. Reasonable restriction on media consolidation, using a public interest standard.
5. Restoring of full public funding of the National Public Broadcasting System to provide in-depth coverage of issues and the widest possible range of viewpoints.
6. Community ownership of broadcast outlets and public oversight of licensing.
7. Free and equal airtime for political candidates on radio and television networks.
8. Taxing electronic advertising sales to fund democratic media outlets.
9. The repeal of the Telecommunications Act of 1996.
10. The prohibition of commercial advertising in public places such as schools, parks, and governmental buildings.
11. Developing community radio, particularly those rule-making petitions before the FCC that allow for a new service of small, locally-owned FM stations.
12. Limiting the concentration of power that has characterized the telecommunications industry. We need a wide span of programming and information, genuine citizen access, diversity of views, respect for local community interests, news, public affairs and quality children's programming. The FCC should closely monitor applications for license renewals to the public airwaves to ensure that these public interest criteria are met.
13. Opposing censorship in the arts, media (including the World Wide Web and Internet), and press. We encourage individual and social responsibility by artists, creative media, writers and all citizens.

IMMIGRATION/EMIGRATION

While it would be ideal to erase borders between countries, that would be impractical without reciprocity between nations. We seek that reciprocity as a practical goal. While we recognize that there must be some controls on immigration, if only for the sake of national security, the Green Party would endorse a friendlier (less intimidating) attitude towards immigration in all nations within certain guidelines. The Green Party must consider immigration issues from an international standpoint, taking into account international labour and environmental standards, and human rights.

1. Preferential quotas based on race, class, and ideology should be abandoned for immigration policies that promote fairness, non-discrimination and family reunification.
2. We support policies that reflect our constitutional guarantees of freedoms of speech, association, and travel.
3. Particular attention should be given to those minorities who are political exiles and refugees.
4. Our relationship with our neighbor to the south, Mexico, needs to be given added attention due to the special historical and cultural relation it has with the southwest portion of the United States. Our border relations and reciprocal economic opportunities should be a central concern of a government that is looking to improved economic, environmental, and social conditions for both peoples.
5. The Green Party calls for permanent border passes to all citizens of Mexico and Canada whose identity can be traced and verified. Work permits for citizens of Mexico and Canada must be easily obtainable, thereby decriminalizing the act of gainful employment. This action would help eliminate exploitation of undocumented persons by criminals engaged in human contraband (*coyotes*) and unethical employers. It would also help ensure that taxes will be paid in each corresponding nation per its laws. These measures will also help temporary residents from Mexico and Canada to secure driving privileges and liability insurance.

6. Labour laws must be adjusted to take into account seasonal foreign workers. Employers must provide full rights to wages and health benefits to immigrant workers who make voluntary contributions to pension plans and pay Social Security taxes.
7. We advocate an end to employer sanctions, which have been shown to hurt not only undocumented workers but also U.S.-born workers (especially those of color). A fair and equitable legalization program will provide equal access to working people of all nationalities, not tied to a specific employer or guest worker program. Programs involving temporary worker status must include the option of permanent residency for immigrants already in the U.S. and protection of migrant worker savings.
8. Greens oppose "English-only" legislation. We would advocate legislation to ensure that federal funds marked for communities to provide ESL (english as second language) training, and health and social support services to immigrants actually go to them. When funds are spent in other areas, immigrants are being deprived of benefits that they earn as productive workers in their communities.
9. We oppose the use of racial profiling. We are concerned about reports of illegal raids and traffic stops based on ethnic appearance and not probable cause of a traffic violation. We would further advocate funding or education programs designed to reduce racism and bias against ethnic minorities.
10. We advocate adoption of certification standards for translators.
11. We oppose those who seek to divide us for political gain by raising ethnic and racial hatreds, and by blaming immigrants for social and economic problems.

HOUSING AND HOMELESSNESS

Rents have soared due to real estate speculation. One out of five renters pays more than fifty percent of their income for housing. Fewer than one in ten renters can afford to buy a median-priced house in the area where they live. In an era of deregulation, tenants have had few legal protections, and those that exist have begun to erode. Rent control and eviction protection for tenants does not exist in most jurisdictions, and where it does, it is usually inadequate and under attack. Landlords who, in violation of housing code requirements, fail to keep their property in habitable condition are tolerated, or at most given lenient penalties. Housing discrimination remains rampant against people of color, immigrants, disabled, single people, gays and lesbians, and families with children.

It is conservatively estimated that one million people are homeless. Today, homeless people are hounded, threatened, and often can not obtain badly needed services. Though affordable housing could help alleviate the problem of homelessness, the homeless have needs that go beyond housing. The twenty-year decline in real wages for workers is also a major contribution to the current crisis in housing availability and affordability. Certain laws have also contributed to the problems of housing supply and cost, and are in some cases consciously used to exclude households with lower incomes from higher income communities.

Areas of local law that should be revisited include: ordinances that prohibit a shift toward co-housing; land use plans that provide excessive amounts of land for industrial and commercial use; and inflexible building codes that prevent alternative (often less expensive) construction approaches that still meet health and safety requirements. The Green Party recognizes housing as a human right, and will work toward eliminating economic and other forms of discrimination in the construction and use of housing through the following policies:

Renter's Rights

1. Protect tenants with rent control laws, including vacancy control.
2. Prevent evictions without just cause. Restrict owner

move-in evictions of long-term tenants, the elderly, and disabled persons.

3. Crack down on landlords who refuse to maintain their properties in habitable condition, or who engage in illegal evictions, with hefty fines and, in extreme cases, jail terms.

Increase Affordable Housing Supply

4. Enforce laws against illegal hotel conversions.
5. Use vacant housing - whether at closed military bases, housing kept off the market by speculators, or landlords delinquent in taxes - to shelter homeless persons.
6. Build human-scale, low income housing (as does Habitat for Humanity).
7. Pursue more efficient use of our existing housing supply, such as home-sharing and cooperative conversions of existing dwellings.
8. Subsidies, trade-offs with developers, and the creative use of city and county zoning ordinances should be used to increase affordable housing.

Measures to Help Homeless Persons

9. Expand community-based services for homeless persons and make them more readily available.
10. Repeal all laws that criminalize any facet of homelessness or helping homeless persons.
11. Abolish anti-sleeping laws, especially in areas which don't have adequate open space, shelter and sleeping areas for homeless persons.
12. Strictly enforce all the laws that are designed to provide for the homeless, such as the laws that require opening National Guard armories to homeless persons during inclement weather.
13. Allow homeless people to take part in decisions about long- and short-term solutions to their situation.

14. Strengthen and increase funding of mental health and drug rehabilitation systems.

Strong Fair-Housing Laws

15. Strengthen and enforce fair-housing laws against discrimination based on race, sex, familial status (children), marital status, disability, or sexual orientation.
16. Fully fund the Fair Employment and Housing Commission and provide generous government funding to non-profit organizations engaged in fair housing monitoring and enforcement.
17. Insist that architectural review boards and planning commissions represent the concerns of citizens, rather than the concerns of economic segments of the community.

Reform Zoning and Building Codes

18. Implement low-impact, site-specific designs that encourage human-scale development and environmentally sensitive planning. Promote development that encourages urban density - with green spaces - and that discourages urban sprawl.
19. Remove restrictions on converting large, single family homes to multifamily use. Families of today are smaller and there are more single-parent households.
20. Allow industrial and commercial developers to provide housing instead of parking spaces in new developments, and permit housing development in existing industrial and commercial zones.
21. Reform zoning, occupancy, and building ordinances so that residential needs can exist in balance with commercial and industrial needs, and so that alternative approaches are encouraged rather than restricted.

2

Social Justice and Human Rights

Talk, of course, is relatively inexpensive—as witness the fact that most human rights documents are full of fancy language about social and economic rights. In fact, if you look at the UN's Universal Declaration of Human Rights, or the Bills of Rights of most countries, you will notice all sorts of references to housing, education, work, and minimum decent subsistence. Some documents, such as the UN Declaration, speak of these things in the modern language of rights, others in the more biblical language of obligation. Even countries such as the United States that do not have such concepts in their own constitutions have signed UN documents recognizing the basics of subsistence as universal human rights. The question a Vincentian would ask about all that talk, however, is the same sort of question that Abraham Lincoln raised in his Gettysburg Address about the promise of equality in our Declaration of Independence: when are those parchment promises made so long ago going to be carried into action?

1995 CONFERENCE ON WOMEN IN BEIJING

The implementation of prior commitments to social justice was the precise task of the UN's Fourth Conference on Women in Beijing. The 1995 conference was to have been the culmination of a series of women's conferences—the one that developed a plan for putting into practice the principles established at the three previous conferences. The conference title was "Action for equality, development and peace," and the conference document was called a "program of action." On that basis, one might have assumed that the conference would at least try to boldly go where few had gone before. That is one reason that the Holy See delegation looked forward to the Beijing conference with enthusiasm. For one thing, many of the topics on the conference agenda overlapped with the concerns of over 300,000 education, health care and relief organizations that the Catholic Church maintains in all parts of the world.

For another, our team had much to contribute to an action program: its 22 members, mostly women, included many who had firsthand experience in providing services to women in poor countries. We were the most diverse delegation at the conference, with members from 14 countries on five continents. Most importantly, we were all deeply moved and galvanized by the parting words of the Vatican Undersecretary of State, who asked us to try to serve as a voice for the marginalized and voiceless, for women whose concerns are seldom heard in the corridors of power.

We expected that many other delegations, especially from the developing countries, would share that mission. After all, the strife of the Cairo population conference was behind us, and all indications were that the United States would not lead another charge in favor of abortion rights. So our little band left for Beijing in high spirits. With hindsight, I should have remembered the words of my favorite English philosopher, P. G. Wodehouse. As Wodehouse's Bertie Wooster often says, "It's always just when a person is feeling particularly braced with things in general that Fate sneaks up behind you with the old lead pipe." In this case it was not Fate, but the powerful European Union that, with no advance warning, threw a stick into the spokes of the conference.

The 15-country European Union, negotiating as a bloc, stalled negotiations for the entire first week of the two-week conference with its attempts to reopen the compromise on reproductive rights that had been reached in the preceding year's population conference in Cairo. As a result, most of the work scheduled for the women's conference was crammed into one week where many important subjects were given short shrift. Not that the Beijing document doesn't contain some good language about women's education, employment, and the feminization of poverty. But so did the three previous women's conferences! The whole point of the 1995 conference was to develop a program for putting that language into action! Even if more time had been available, however, that would have required some serious thinking about hard, practical problems to which no one has yet found satisfactory solutions. And even if the conference had yielded creative, constructive ideas, any meaningful action program would have required some commitment to funding.

As to funding, however, if there was anything that united the affluent nations who dominated the proceedings at Beijing, it was their determination to keep their pocketbooks firmly closed. And as for serious problem-solving, large, international conferences are obviously not ideal settings for that kind of work, but in any case the prospects were doomed by the fact that so much time and energy were wasted on Europe's special agenda. Some months after the conference, I received a letter from a young Nigerian law student who said she hadn't been able to afford the trip to China, but she had tried to follow the proceedings closely from afar. She wondered why the conference had paid so little attention to the problems that the majority of the world's women struggle with on a daily basis. She was surprised, for example, that the women's health section was focused almost entirely on women's reproductive systems. She wanted to know why it didn't address the health of the whole woman, particularly the problems of poor nutrition, sanitation, and tropical disease that have a disproportionate impact on the women and girls who compose the bulk of the world's poverty population.

She commented that even the treatment of reproductive health was strange, since it concentrated mainly on abortion and birth control—as though reproductive health did not also include prenatal care and childbirth! Now, you might be wondering why the representatives of developing nations did not take the initiative on issues of such vital concern to women in their own countries. That is a subject I hope an investigative reporter will pursue someday. All I can say is that it was disheartening to see many third world delegations remain silent on poverty and development issues, yet show up with well-prepared position papers in support of the agenda of the European Union.

THE SEARCH FOR THE RIGHT TO ASSISTED SUICIDE

Another recent example, close to home, is the current initiative for a new individual right—the right to assisted suicide—at a time when Americans do not even have the right to basic primary health care, not to mention the right to relief of pain! Many opinion leaders in political, business, and academic circles think that's just how it should be. They believe that social and economic rights are bastard rights that never should have been added to human rights instruments. They reason that such language is at best ineffective, and at worst an obstacle to the rising tide of economic progress that they say will lift all boats.

Now, as someone who wants to defend the presence of social justice language in the canon of human rights, I have to concede that I can produce no proof that these sorts of rights (or obligations, as I would prefer to think of them) have any effect at all—for good or ill. For one thing, none of the places that has recognized such rights has made them enforceable in the same way as traditional civil and political liberties. Rights to education, shelter, and a decent level of subsistence are mainly what legal theorists call "programmatic" rights—which mean they represent a commitment to a set of goals and ideals, in short—to a program whose implementation depends on ordinary politics and available economic resources.

Nevertheless, it seems to me that it counts for something when we make social justice concerns highly visible in constitutions or international declarations—according them pride of place with traditional political and civil liberties. When we do this, even in a programmatic way, we are making a statement about what kind of people we want to be, and what kind of societies we hope to bring into being. Personally, I believe that this language in some countries at least has had some influence on the terms of political deliberations, and thus on legislative action and establishment of national priorities. But this is unprovable—because no one knows what those countries would have done without such language. So let us return to the question I posed at the outset: why has all this high-minded language so regularly been ignored in the debates that swirl around human rights? One explanation is fairly obvious. Just as many Americans tend to view our Bill of Rights as a menu with some items we like more than others, so the nations of the world have taken a cafeteria approach to the human rights that they all recognized as fundamental when they signed the UN's Declaration of Human Rights way back in 1948. That's not terribly hard to understand.

Everyone tends to exalt the virtues that he or she finds easiest to practice. So let me ask you to try to imagine the scene when the United Nations Declaration of Human Rights has its 50th birthday party next year. No doubt the friends of traditional political and civil liberties will sip their Chardonnay in one corner of the room; the partisans of entrepreneurial rights, cell phones in hand, will gather in another; and the advocates of social and economic rights will cluster in another. You will look long and hard before you will find anyone ready to give three rousing cheers for what all nations on paper have accepted—that all these good things are mutually dependent—and that all are rooted in the human dignity of each and every man and woman.

The fact is that, for the past 30 years, the single most consistent champion of human freedom and solidarity in international settings has been the Catholic Church. The idea that social justice can and must be harmonized with political and civil liberties has been the touchstone of the Holy See's advocacy in the UN, and the social encyclicals of John Paul II. In his speech on the 50th anniversary of the United Nations two years ago, John Paul II took the occasion to stress the essential unity of the human rights corpus. He reminded the nations that the promises they made in the wake of the horrors of World War II are mutually reinforcing. He celebrated the freedoms of which the liberal democracies are rightly proud, saying that humanity has been "inspired by the example of all those who have taken the risk of freedom." But then he asked: "Can we not recommit ourselves also to taking the risk of solidarity—and thus the risk of peace?"

THE CHALLENGE OF OUR FUTURE

That, will be the challenge at next year's anniversary of the Universal Declaration of Human Rights. It is nothing less than the challenge of bringing together the two halves of the divided soul of the modern human rights movement: its dedication to human freedom and its acknowledgment of common responsibility for our fellow human beings. Now suppose, by some miracle, that the nations of the world were finally persuaded to take a holistic, rather than a cafeteria approach to human rights. Suppose they decided to take "the risk of solidarity." There would still be an equally formidable obstacle to overcome, one that is of special concern to those of us who are engaged in academic work. I am referring to the appealingly primitive state of our practical and empirical knowledge about what kinds of programs and measures, private or public, do or do not work, and under which circumstances. We know embarrassingly little about what helps and what hurts.

To our shame, we've been bogged down for too long in a sterile debate between the partisans of big government programs on the one hand and their laissez-faire critics on the other—a debate, we might say, between the ham-fisted and the hard-hearted. It is a hopeful sign, however, that policy makers all over the world are beginning to think in a more nuanced way about the appropriate or optimal roles and relationships among government, markets, and the mediating institutions of civil society. They are beginning to ask better questions: What does each institution do best? At what level? How can the harmful tendencies of each be checked without killing the geese that lay nutritious eggs? The Doctrine of Subsidiarity, unknown outside Catholic social thought until a few years ago, has found its way into the most influential circles at all points along the political spectrum.

The bad news is that there's so much work to be done, but the good news is that it seems to be beginning, and that there are so many resources to draw upon—including the wisdom and experience of the world's great religious traditions, not least of which is the rich storehouse of Catholic social teaching. In that connection, I would like to express admiration and gratitude to the Congregation of St. Vincent dePaul for the human and intellectual resources it has contributed to the task of building the civilization of life and love. Vincentian education with its emphasis on social action proves that theory and practice are not opposed, but are in fact two blades of the scissors.

While I'm at it, I must also pay tribute to the broad-mindedness of the Vincentians. They invited me to give this talk—even though I spent 18 years teaching in a Jesuit institution! This passage has helped to keep my spirits up over the years, so I pass it on as a parting gift—in thanks for this lovely evening and in hopes it may mean something to you young women and men who are just embarking on your journey through life. Here is what Father Lonergan says about intellectual work in turbulent times:

"There will always be a solid right determined to cling to a past that can never be recaptured, and a scattered left following now this, now that new idea. But what will count is a perhaps not numerous center" —sufficient numbers of men and women who are knowledgeable enough to be at home in the old as well as the new, imaginative enough to recognize the possibilities in the current situation, and painstaking enough to work out the transitions a step at a time.

THEORY OF SOCIAL JUSTICE

John Rawls is widely regarded as one of the most important political philosophers of the second half of the twentieth century. He is primarily known for his theory of justice as fairness, which develops principles of justice to govern a modern social order. Rawls' theory provides a framework that explains the significance, in a society assumed to consist of free and equal persons, of political and personal liberties, of equal opportunity, and cooperative arrangements that benefit the more and the less advantaged members of society. Darrel Moellendorf writes that Rawls' conception of justice, like any conception of justice whatsoever, is an associational conception. It is about relationships between members of an association. Rawls is chiefly concerned with the political association known as the modern nation-state. Moellendorf and other defenders of "cosmopolitan justice" apply the approach Rawls developed for the nation-state to the global community, which may be understood as an economic association even if there is no effective international political association.

More may be said later about cosmopolitan justice. Here the important point is that Rawls' initial concern with justice is related to relationships between persons within an association. Rawls' theory urges us to conceive of society "as a fair system of cooperation over time, from one generation to the next." (PL 14) He says that "the . . . relationship of citizenship . . . [is] a relation of citizens within the basic structure of society, a structure we enter only by birth and exit only by death" (PL xlv).

TWO MORAL POWERS

John Rawls develops a conception of justice from the perspective that persons are free and equal. Their freedom consists in their possession of the two moral powers, "a capacity for a sense of justice and for a conception of the good." Insofar as they have these to the degree necessary to be "fully cooperating members of society," they are equal. A sense of justice is "the capacity to understand, to apply, and to act from the public conception of justice which characterizes the fair terms of cooperation." This sense expresses "a willingness...to act in relation to others on terms that they also can publicly endorse".

A conception of the good includes "a conception of what is valuable in human life." Normally it consists "of a more or less determinate scheme of final ends, that is, ends [goals] that we want to realize for their own sake, as well as attachments to other persons and loyalties to various groups and associations." Rawls says that we also "connect such a conception with a view of our relation to the world...by reference to which the value and significance of our ends and attachments are understood".

An important concept for Rawls is the concept of a comprehensive doctrine or view. These include moral philosophies like utilitarianism and philosophical systems such as Kantianism, Platonism and Stoicism. They also include religious doctrines such as Augustinianism, Thomism, orthodox Judaism, etc. "Utilitarianism...: the principle of utility . . . is usually said to hold for all kinds of subjects ranging from the conduct of individuals to the organization of society as a whole as well as to the law of peoples."

COMPREHENSIVE DOCTRINES

A moral conception is comprehensive when it includes "conceptions of what is of value in human life, and ideals of personal character, as well as ideals of friendship and of familial and associational relationships, and much else that is to inform our conduct, and in the limit to our life as a whole. A conception is fully comprehensive if it covers all recognized values and virtues within one rather precisely articulated system; whereas a conception is only partially comprehensive when it comprises a number of, but by no means all, nonpolitical values and virtues and is rather loosely articulated." The idea of a comprehensive conception or doctrine is crucial for Rawls, because the idea of a political conception of justice that he develops is contrasted with comprehensive doctrines.

A comprehensive doctrine may include a political conception of justice but a political conception of justice falls far short of addressing questions of interest to the comprehensive doctrine. Thus, a political conception may address whether we are to respect freedom of speech and assembly for other comprehensive doctrines than our own, but it will not address the question of precisely how we should conduct ourselves so as to secure our happiness or eternal salvation. A political conception conceives of persons as having the two moral powers mentioned above, as being responsible for their actions, etc., but does not address whether persons are immortal souls or immaterial substances as, say, Plato and most medieval Christian theologians held. Recall, as mentioned above, that Rawls conceives of "society as a fair system of cooperation over time, from one generation to the next." He says that "the fundamental political relationship of citizenship ... [is] a relation of citizens within the basic structure of society, a structure we enter only by birth and exit only by death [and]...a relation of free and equal citizens who exercise ultimate political power as a collective body".

POLITICAL CONCEPTION OF JUSTICE

A political conception of justice, says Rawls, has three basic features. First, "it is a moral conception worked out for a specific kind of subject, namely, for political, social, and economic institutions." Specifically, it is worked out for what Rawls' calls society's basic structure—society's main social, economic, and political institutions, and "how they fit together" into one "system of social cooperation from one generation to the next." Second, says Rawls, the political conception is "presented as a freestanding view." It is neither presented as a comprehensive doctrine, nor as derived from a comprehensive doctrine, applied to the basic structure of society.

This does not mean that it cannot be justified from within a comprehensive doctrine—indeed, it has no chance of success unless a number of comprehensive doctrines support it. What it means is that there exists a network of concepts in the "public political culture" from which the political conception can be explained and justified. "It is expounded apart from" any wider background made up of comprehensive doctrines. Third, "its content is expressed in terms of certain fundamental ideas seen as implicit in the public political culture of a democratic society. This public culture comprises the political institutions of a constitutional regime and the public traditions of their interpretation".

Rawls now regards his own theory of justice as fairness (involving his idea of the original position, the veil of ignorance, and the derivation of two principles of justice) as a political conception of justice. Such a conception does not commit one who holds it to a doctrine about the metaphysical nature of persons (whether we consist of immortal souls or whether we are creatures of an eternal omniscient deity), although such commitments may well be part of a comprehensive doctrine. But it does commit the holder to certain moral stands in relation to fellow citizens in an existing political society, assuming that society does not deviate too far from the principles of justice outlined in Rawls' theory.

REASONABLE CITIZENS

The political conception of justice points to a notion of reasonable citizens. "Citizens are reasonable when, viewing one another as free and equal in a system of cooperation over generations, they are prepared to offer one another fair terms of social cooperation . . . and they agree to act on those terms, even at the cost of their own interests in particular situations, provided that others also accept those terms. For those terms to be fair terms, citizens offering them must reasonably think that those citizens to whom they are offered might also reasonably accept them. . . . They must be able to do this as free and equal, and not as dominated or manipulated, or under the pressure of an inferior political or social position". Rawls calls this the "criterion of reciprocity."

The second aspect of our being reasonable is "our recognizing and being willing to bear the consequences of the burdens of judgment." (PL 58) We are willing to recognize that reasonable persons can disagree without being prejudiced or biased or excessively self- or group interested or willful. We recognize such sources of disagreement or burdens of judgment as:

- conflicting nature and complexity of evidence
- differences about weighting of considerations
- vagueness of concepts, borderline cases
- disparate experiences of diverse people
- different kinds of normative consideration of different force on both sides of an issue
- tendency of social institutions to force us to select some values for emphasis and deselect others

REASONABLE COMPREHENSIVE DOCTRINES

Reasonable persons (in Rawls' special sense of reasonable) affirm only reasonable comprehensive doctrines. Rawls notes three features of such a doctrine. (1) It "covers the major religious, philosophical, and moral aspects of human life in a more or less consistent and coherent manner." In this sense it is an exercise of theoretical reason. (2) In another sense it is an exercise of practical reason, since it determines what values to regard as highly significant and how to weigh them against each other when they conflict. (3) "It tends to evolve over time in the light of what it sees as good and sufficient reasons."

"The political conception of justice is a module, an essential constituent part that fits into and can be supported by various reasonable comprehensive doctrines that endure in the society regulated by it." Finally, "reasonable persons think it unreasonable to use political power, should they possess it, to repress comprehensive views that are not unreasonable, though different from their own." What this means is that reasonable persons are not inclined to repress or outlaw religions different from their own. They would not do so even if their view was to become the majority and they had no fear of being repressed in turn.

"Reasonable persons see that the burdens of judgment set limits on what can be reasonably justified to others, and so they endorse some form of liberty of conscience and freedom of thought." This means that reasonable persons will grant others the freedom to explore religious and spiritual options even if these options differ from their own. They will permit members of their own faith to investigate others and to abandon that their original faith or form of spirituality if they are so moved. (A reasonable Christian or Muslim will not regard it as a crime if another member of his or her faith investigates Buddhism or decides to become a Buddhist.)

SOCIAL CONTRACT THEORY

One of the most discussed elements of Rawls' view of justice as fairness is his "modeling" device known as the Original Position. The Original Position has often been compared to the "state of nature" or the pre-political condition of humanity, which was important in the philosophies of early modern social contract theorists. According to thinkers such as Thomas Hobbes and John Locke, in order to understand political obligation, we should first

I. conceive what human beings were like (or would have been like) before the creation of organized societies under governments and laws, and then (II) ask:

   A. what reasons would have motivated people to form an organized society and

   B. what principles human beings in this pre-political condition would have chosen to guide their interaction in a society under an established government.

In the social contract tradition there are three items to keep distinct: (1) the pre-political condition, (2) the political order established just as people were coming out of the pre-political condition, and (3) the actual (possibly flawed) order under which we now live. Because of its connection with (1), (2) was thought to reveal what arrangements are just or fair. (2) could then be used as a basis for justifying or critically evaluating (3).

THE ORIGINAL POSITION

Rawls' idea of the Original Position is similar, except that he is under no illusions that the Original Position was ever a reality. It is a model, an abstract mental device to help us understand something else, in this case, the principles of (political or social) justice. The three-way distinction basic to social contract theories reappears in Rawls' thought is as follows (I am simplifying somewhat):

1. The Original Position
2. The Just Social Order whose Basic Structure described by the Two Principles of Justice
3. Actual Society

Representative persons in the Original Position are to choose principles of justice that would govern the basic structure of a (just and fair) social order. Each real person in the just social order has a representative in the Original Position. These representatives represent every human being that belongs to the political association of free and equal persons (Rawls focuses on the political community of the national states, but others extend Rawls' approach to global society conceived as an economic association.).

There are three fundamental features of the representatives in the Original Position that reflect the two moral powers of which we spoke earlier. The first is that the representatives are rational in the sense that they wish to secure for those they represent the kind of goods that would enable them to work out (including to revise if necessary) their own conceptions of the good and then try to realize this good. This feature recognizes that each person has a set of interests which are his or her own. These interests are linked to the person's moral power to form, revise, and pursue a conception of the good; in the case of persons with a comprehensive doctrine, the interests will be linked to the comprehensive doctrine.

The second fundamental feature of the representatives in the Original Position is summed up in the phrase The Veil of Ignorance. The representatives, unlike persons in the ideal society and unlike ourselves in a less than ideal society, stand behind the Veil of Ignorance. That is to say, they do not know the following about the persons they represent: their sex, race, physical handicaps, social class, or conception of the good. They rightly assume that the persons represented have these features but they do not know what it is.

A third feature of the representatives in the Original Position is that they possess a great deal of common sense general knowledge about human psychology and sociology. They know, for instance, that humans remember the past, anticipate the future, and interact with things and people in the present. They know that people have diverse talents and interests. They know that humans undertake projects of varying complexity—from traveling to a mall to raising a family to undertaking missionary work to fighting for social justice to undertaking medical research. They are aware of the general types of situations in which humans can find themselves (that people can be sick or healthy, rich or poor, educated or ignorant, skilled or unskilled, indebted or free from debt, in a healthy natural environment or a degraded one, enslaved or free, etc.

Specifically they are aware of that persons possess the two moral powers. They are aware that persons have a conception of the good. The first and second features of the representatives in the Original Position correspond to the two moral powers. Our capacity to frame and pursue a conception of the good is reflected in the rationality of the representatives who choose for us in order to optimize our ability to investigate and pursue the good. Our capacity for a sense of justice is reflected in the operation of the Veil of Ignorance. The Veil of Ignorance is what makes their imaginary choices on our behalf fair.

EXPOUNDING THE PRINCIPLES OR JUSTICE FROM THE IDEA OF THE ORIGINAL POSITION

As stated above, our representatives in the Original Position are given the task of selecting principles of justice that will govern the basic structure of society. To show briefly how they will reason, let us consider whether they would choose a principle of equal opportunity, say, a principle that would make economic discrimination on the basis of race, gender, or religion unjust. Recall that they do not know specifics about the individual persons they represent but they are committed to optimizing the interests of those persons. The best way to achieve this would be to rule out discrimination on the basis of race, gender, or religion. For if discrimination were permitted, then persons at stage who have (and know they have) a specific race, or gender, or religion would find themselves at a disadvantage. They would be denied economic opportunities, and thus they would be prevented, to some extent at least, from pursuing as effectively as they otherwise might their conception of the good. (We assume that pursuit of the good, however one conceives it, requires resources.)

THE TWO PRINCIPLES OF JUSTICE

Rawls offers his notion of justice as fairness as an illustration of a political conception of justice. In its mature form (PL 291), this notion affirms the following principles:

I. Each person has an equal right to a fully adequate scheme of equal basic liberties which is compatible with a similar scheme of liberties for all,

II. Social and economic inequalities are to satisfy two conditions. First, they must be attached to offices and positions open to all under conditions of fair equality of opportunity; and second, they must be to the greatest benefit of the least advantaged members of society.

The first of these is sometimes referred to as the Equal Liberty Principle. The stem of the second ("Social and economic liberties are to satisfy [the condition that]") together with the first condition is called the Principle of Equal Opportunity. The stem of the second together with the second condition is called the Difference Principle. Rawls lists the following among the equal basic liberties: "freedom of thought and liberty of conscience; the political liberties and freedom of association, as well as the freedoms specified by the liberty and integrity of the person; and finally, the rights and liberties covered by the rule of law."

Rawls explains that in justice as fairness ". . . There is . . . a general presumption against imposing legal and other restrictions on conduct without sufficient reason. But this presumption creates no special priority for any particular liberty." Slightly later he writes: "the priority of liberty means that the first principle of justice assigns the basic liberties . . . a special status. They have an absolute weight with respect to reasons of public good and of perfectionist values. . . The equal political liberties cannot be denied to certain social groups on the grounds that their having these liberties may enable them to block policies needed for economic efficiency and growth . . . The priority of liberty implies . . . that a basic liberty can be limited or denied solely for the sake of one or more other basic liberties." A desire to increase the Gross National Product or make airlines run on an efficient schedule cannot alone justify the limitation of basic liberties.

MORE ON THE EQUAL BASIC LIBERTIES

It is important to explain what the first principle means by the phrase "fully adequate scheme of equal basic liberties." First, what are included among the equal basic liberties? Rawls lists:

1. freedom of thought
2. liberty of conscience

He later explains liberty of conscience as "liberty as applied to religious, philosophical, and moral view of our relation to the world."

3. political liberties

These liberties would require representative democratic institutions, freedom of speech and the press, and freedom of assembly.

4. freedom of association
5. freedoms specified by the liberty and integrity of the person

He later elaborates these as including freedom from slavery and serfdom and freedom of movement and choice regarding occupation.

6. rights and liberties covered by the rule of law

How does Rawls get this list? He says that it can be drawn up by considering "which liberties are essential social conditions for the adequate development and full exercise of the two powers of moral personality over a complete life." One of those powers, we recall, is the formation of a conception of the good (life). "The liberty of conscience, and therefore the freedom to fall into error and make mistakes is among the social conditions for the development and exercise of [the] power [to form a conception of the good]

Thus freedom of thought and freedom of assembly are needed to make liberty of conscience effective. Regarding freedom of assembly, Rawls writes, "unless we are at liberty to associate with other like-minded citizens, the exercise of liberty of conscience is denied." On this list, the equal political liberties are singled out for special treatment. Part of what it means to have a *fully adequate scheme* of equal basic liberties is this special treatment of the political liberties. [What must be done is] including in the first principle of justice the guarantee that the political liberties, and only these liberties, are secured by . . . their "fair value." . . . [T]his guarantee means that the worth of the political liberties must be approximately equal, or at least sufficiently equal, . . . that everyone has a fair opportunity to hold political office and to influence the outcome of political decisions.

When the parties in the original position adopt the priority of liberty, they understand that the equal political liberties are treated in this special way. . . . one guideline for guaranteeing fair value seems to be to keep political parties independent of large concentrations of private economic and social power in a private-property democracy, and of government control and bureaucratic power in a . . . socialist regime. In either case, society must bear at least a large part of the cost of organizing and carrying out the political process and must regulate the conduct of elections. The guarantee of fair value for the political liberties is one way in which justice as fairness [Rawls' theory of justice] tries to meet the objection that the basic liberties are merely formal.

The guarantee of fair value for the political liberties is essential to motivate the passing of just laws and to ensure that the fair political process specified by the constitution [constructed around Rawls' two principles] is "open to everyone on a basis of rough equality." Why, it may be asked, should we not go farther and "guarantee the fair value" of the other basic liberties, such as liberty of conscience as applied to religious choices? Rawls points out that this would require that society distribute resources so that everyone would be equally able to fulfill their religious interests. But doing so would mean that members of certain faiths would receive funds needed to build cathedrals or go on pilgrimages to distant places while others, whose religious was less materially demanding, would receive very little. Society's neutrality with respect to comprehensive conceptions of the good, which is an essential feature of the political conception of justice, would be compromised (for it would seem that the basic structure would be under-writiing the comprehensive conceptions that demanded the most materially). As Rawls observes, this would be very divisive and a recipe for religious controversy if not civil strife.

BASIC LIBERTIES AND PROPERTY

Rawls does include among the basic liberties of the person "the right to hold and to have the exclusive use of personal property." This is because this liberty is the basis for a sense of personal independence and self-respect. Two wider conceptions, he says, are not included in the basic liberties: "certain rights of acquisition and bequest, as well as the right to own means of production and natural resources" and "the right to participate in the control of the means of production and natural resources, which are to be socially owned." In other words, precisely how capitalistic or socialistic the economic model should be is to depend on factors that are not entirely dictated by the basic structure of a just social order.

This issue would depend, among other things, upon the habits and attitudes of members of particular societies. Rawls' view on this topic has been criticized by James Nickel, who thinks that a more vigorous defense of private property rights is possible using Rawls' own approach.

RAWLS' SECOND PRINCIPLE

It means that society may undertake projects that require giving some persons more power, income, status, etc. than others, e.g., paying accountants and upper-level managers more than assembly-line operatives, provided that the following conditions are met:

(a) the project will make life better off for the people who are now worst off, for example, by raising the living standards of everyone in the community and empowering the least advantaged persons to the extent consistent with their well-being, and (b) access to the privileged positions is not blocked by discrimination according to irrelevant criteria.

The second principle contains elements of other familiar ethical theories. The "socialist" idea that responsibilities or burdens should be distributed according to ability and benefits according to need is partly contained within the Difference Principle. We may reasonably assume that the "least advantaged" have the greatest needs and that those who receive special powers (hinted at under "social inequalities") also have special responsibilities or burdens. However, the merit principle that the use of special skills should be rewarded is also included in the Difference Principle. What the Difference Principle does not permit is a change in social and an economic institution that makes life better for those who are already well off but does nothing for those who are already disadvantaged, or makes their life worse.

3

Women's Human Rights

The term "women's human rights" and the set of practices that accompanies its use are the continuously evolving product of an international movement to improve the status of women. In the 1980s and 1990s, women's movements around the world formed networks and coalitions to give greater visibility both to the problems that women face every day and to the centrality of women's experiences in economic, social, political and environmental issues. In the evolution of what is becoming a global women's movement, the term "women's human rights" has served as a locus for praxis, that is, for the development of political strategies shaped by the interaction between analytical insights and concrete political practices. Further, the critical tools, the concerted activism, and the broad-based international networks that have grown up around movements for women's human rights have become a vehicle for women to develop the political skills necessary for the twenty-first century. The concept of women's human rights owes its success and the proliferation of its use to the fact that it is simultaneously prosaic and revolutionary. On the one hand, the idea of women's human rights makes common sense. It declares, quite simply, that as human beings women have human rights.

Anyone would find her or himself hard-pressed to publicly make and defend the contrary argument that women are not human. So in many ways, the claim that women have human rights seems quite ordinary. On the other hand, "women's human rights" is a revolutionary notion. This radical reclamation of humanity and the corollary insistence that women's rights are human rights have profound transformative potential. The incorporation of women's perspectives and lives into human rights standards and practice forces recognition of the dismal failure of countries worldwide to accord women the human dignity and respect that they deserve-simply as human beings. A woman's human rights framework equips women with a way to define, analyze, and articulate their experiences of violence, degradation, and marginality. Finally, and very importantly, the idea of women's human rights provides a common framework for developing a vast array of visions and concrete strategies for change.

HISTORY OF HUMAN RIGHTS

The *Universal Declaration of Human Rights* adopted by the United Nations General Assembly in 1948 outlines what is considered in this century to be the fundamental consensus on the human rights of all people in relation to such matters as security of person, slavery, torture, protection of the law, freedom of movement & speech, religion, and assembly, and rights to social security, work, health, education, culture, & citizenship. It clearly stipulates that these human rights apply to all equally "without distinction of any kind such as race, color, sex, language... or other status" (Art.2). Obviously, then, the human rights delineated by the Universal Declaration are to be understood as applying to women. However, tradition, prejudice, social, economic and political interests have combined to exclude women from prevailing definitions of "general" human rights and to relegate women to secondary and/or "special interest" status within human rights considerations.

This marginalisation of women in the world of human rights has been a reflection of gender inequity in the world at large and has also had a formidable impact on women's lives. It has contributed to the perpetuation, and indeed the condoning, of women's subordinate status. It has limited the scope of what was seen as governmental responsibility, and thus has made the process of seeking redress for human rights violations disproportionately difficult for women and in many cases outright impossible. The division between the so-called "public" has compounded the difficulties posed by women's peripheral status within international human rights mechanisms and organizations and "private" spheres prevalent in so many societies. The pervasive division of life into "public" and "private" spheres has its roots in the desire to limit the jurisdiction of the government. In many countries, this has meant that what individuals do in the "public" sphere is subject to regulation, while activities taking place in the "private" sphere are thought to be exempt from governmental scrutiny. Since this "public" sphere is seen as the focus of interaction between state actors and citizens, abuses of that relationship have been the focus of international human rights advocacy.

Of course, the status of citizen has often been exclusionary, formally or informally entailing gender, racial and socio-economic bias and privileges. Thus, for those citizens-primarily men-who predominate in public and governmental realms and who enjoy gender, racial and economic privilege, the issues of primary concern have tended to be those abuses to which they are most vulnerable-abuses of civil and political aspects of human rights such as the violation of the right to speech, arbitrary detention, torture during imprisonment, and summary execution. While women have been able to invoke international human rights machinery when they have found themselves in such situations, some of their specifically gender experiences of such human rights abuse-for example, rape in detention-have not been visible within the prevailing definitions of abuse. This is because women have traditionally been relegated to the "private" sphere of the home and family; the typical citizen has been portrayed as male, and thus the dominant notions of human rights abuse have implicitly had a man as their archetype.

A major effect of the gender nature of the public/private split is that human rights violations of women that occur between "private" individuals have been made invisible and deemed to be beyond the purview of the state. It is particularly important to note that gender is a significant factor in the decisions of governments to intervene in the so-called private sphere to prosecute human rights violations. For example, many activities that take place in the private sphere, such as murder between siblings or the systematic enslavement African peoples in the Americas, are subject to government censure internationally. However, governments overlook much of what happens to women at the hands of men and male family members, for example domestic violence or confinement, even when there are laws against such abuse. Thus, abuses done to women in the name of family, religion, and culture have been hidden by the sanctity of the so-called private sphere, and perpetrators of such human rights violations have enjoyed immunity from accountability for their actions.

The historical emphasis on human rights abuses in the public sphere and the concomitant neglect of the human rights of women were exacerbated by the politics of the Cold War. The United Nations' human rights treaties and mechanisms developed after the horrors of World War II and consolidated during the Cold War. The purpose of many human rights organizations that developed along with them was to monitor the treatment of citizens by their governments and to ensure respect for citizens' human rights as they worked for democratic governance. As positions polarized during the Cold War, western governments attributed priority to civil and political rights, which they believed were integral to a prosperous free market economy.

Meanwhile, the socio-economic rights to work, shelter, and health, for example, became identified with the socialist bloc and were thus suspect to many in the West. Thus, human rights bodies dominated by western conceptions of human rights priorities, focused on violations within the civil and political realm-the "public" sphere. So, in addition to the obstacles for women posed by the split between so-called public and private spheres, the predominance of civil and political rights within human rights organizations eclipsed the ways in which women often do not enjoy the social and economic conditions that make possible the exercise of civil and political rights and participation in public life.

THE CONCEPT OF WOMEN'S HUMAN RIGHTS

During the United Nations Decade for Women (1976-1985), women from many geographical, racial, religious, cultural, and class backgrounds took up organizing to improve the status of women. The United Nations-sponsored women's conferences, which took place in Mexico City in 1975, Copenhagen in 1980, and Nairobi in 1985, were convened to evaluate the status of women and to formulate strategies for women's advancement. These conferences were critical venues at which women came together, debated their differences and discovered their commonalities, and gradually began learning to bridge differences to create a global movement. In the late eighties and early nineties, women in diverse countries took up the human rights framework and began developing the analytic and political tools that together constitute the ideas and practices of women's human rights. Taking up the human rights framework has involved a double shift in thinking about human rights and talking about women's lives. Put quite simply, it has entailed examining the human rights framework through a gender lens, and describing women's lives through a human rights framework.

In looking at the human rights framework from women's perspectives, women have shown how current human rights definitions and practices fail to account for the ways in which already recognized human rights abuses often affect women differently because of their gender. This approach acknowledges the importance of the existing concepts and activities, but also points out that there are dimensions within these received definitions that are gender-specific and that need to be addressed if the mechanisms, programs, and the human rights framework itself are to include and reflect the experiences of the female half of the world's population. When people utilize the human rights framework to articulate the vast array of human rights abuses that women face, they bring clarifying analyses and powerful tools to bear on women's experiences. This strategy has been pivotal in efforts to draw attention to human rights that are specific to women that heretofore have been seen as women's rights but not recognized as "human" rights. Take, for example, the issue of violence against women. The Universal Declaration states: "No one shall be subject to torture or to cruel, inhuman or degrading treatment or punishment."

This formulation provides a vocabulary for women to define and articulate experiences of violence such as rape, sexual terrorism and domestic violence as violations of the human right not to be subject to torture or to cruel, inhuman or degrading treatment or punishment. The recognition of such issues as human rights abuses raises the level of expectation about what can and should be done about them. This definition of violence against women in terms of human rights establishes unequivocally that states are responsible for such abuse. It also raises questions about how to hold governments accountable for their indifference in such situations and what sorts of mechanisms are needed to expedite the process of redress.

The *Universal Declaration of Human Rights* defines human rights as universal, inalienable, and indivisible. In unison, these defining characteristics are tremendously important for women's human rights. The universality of human rights means that human rights apply to every single person by virtue of their humanity; this also means that human rights apply to everyone equally, for everyone is equal in simply being human. In many ways, this universality theme may seem patently obvious, but its egalitarian premise has a radical edge. By invoking the universality of human rights, women have demanded that their very humanity be acknowledged. That acknowledgment and the concomitant recognition of women as bearers of human rights-mandates the incorporation of women and gender perspectives into all of the ideas and institutions that are already committed to the promotion and protection of human rights. The idea that human rights are universal also challenges the contention that the human rights of women can be limited by culturally specific definitions of what count as human rights and of women's role in society. The idea of human rights as inalienable means that it is impossible for anyone to abdicate her human rights, even if she wanted to, since every person is accorded those rights by virtue of being human. It also means that no person or group of persons can deprive another individual of her or his human rights. Thus, for example, debts incurred by migrant workers or by women caught up in sex trafficking can never justify indentured servitude (slavery), or the deprivation of food, of freedom of movement, or of compensation.

The idea of inalienable rights means that human rights cannot be sold, ransomed, or forfeited for any reason. The idea of inalienability has also been important in negotiations over the priority given to social, religious and cultural practices in relation to human rights. For decades, work to transform practices which are physically or psychologically damaging to women and that have often been "protected" under the rubric of religion, tradition or culture has been particularly difficult, given both the integrity of culture guaranteed by the *Universal Declaration* and the history of Northern domination in much of the world. Thus it was important that both the *Vienna Declaration and Programs of Action* from the World Conference on Human Rights held in Vienna in 1993, and the United Nations *Declaration Against Violence Against Women* passed by the General Assembly the same year, affirmed that in cases of conflict between women's human rights and cultural or religious practices, the human rights of women must prevail.

The indivisibility of human rights means that none of the rights that are considered to be fundamental human rights is more important than any of the others more specifically, that they are interrelated. Human rights encompass civil, political, social, economic and cultural facets of human existence; the indivisibility premise highlights that the ability of people to live their lives in dignity and to exercise their human rights fully depends upon the recognition that these aspects are all interdependent. The fact that human rights are indivisible is important for women, since their civil and political rights historically have been compromised by their economic status, by social and cultural limitations placed on their activities, and by the ever-present threat of violence that often constitutes an insurmountable obstacle to women's participation in public and political life.

The idea of indivisibility has provided women with a common framework through which to emphasize the complexity of the challenges they face, and to highlight the necessity of including women and gender conscious perspectives in the development and implementation of policy. By calling upon the indivisibility of women's human rights, women have rejected a human rights hierarchy, which places either political or civil rights or socio-economic rights as primary. Instead, women have charged that political stability cannot be realized unless women's social and economic rights are also addressed; that sustainable development is impossible without the simultaneous respect for, and incorporation into the policy process of women's cultural and social roles in the daily reproduction of life; and that social equity cannot be generated without economic justice and women's participation in all levels of political decision-making.

THE MOVEMENT FOR WOMEN' S HUMAN RIGHTS

The term "women's human rights" does not refer simply to the theoretical approaches that women have used to transform human rights concepts, programs and agendas. In addition to being instrumental in the formulation of the conceptual challenges and demands levied by women, the idea of women's human rights has had immense impact as a tool for political activism. The concept of women's human rights has opened the way for women around the world to ask hard questions about the official inattention and general indifference to the widespread discrimination and violence that women experience everyday. Whether used in political lobbying, in legal cases, in grassroots mobilization, or in broad-based educational efforts, the idea of women's human rights has been a rallying point for women across many boundaries and has facilitated the creation of collaborative strategies for promoting and protecting the human rights of women.

While women have raised questions for a long time about why their rights are seen as ancillary to human rights, a coordinated effort to change this attitude using a human rights framework gained particular momentum in the early part of the 1990s. The opening of space for new debates afforded by the end of the Cold War facilitated the exchange of ideas and experiences among women around the world that led to strategizing about how to make women's human rights perspectives more visible. As women's activities developed globally during and following the United Nations' Decade for Women, more and more women raised the question of why "women's rights" and women's lives have been deemed secondary to the "human rights" and lives of men. Over the past decade, a movement around women's human rights has emerged to challenge limited notions of human rights, and it has focused particularly on violence against women as a prime example of the bias against women in human rights practice and theory.

The United Nations World Conference on Human Rights held in Vienna in 1993 was the first such meeting since 1968, and it became a natural vehicle to highlight the new visions of human rights thinking and practice being developed by women. Its initial call did not mention women nor did it recognize any gender-specific aspects of human rights in its proposed agenda. Since the conference represented an historic reassessment of the status of human rights, it became the unifying public focus of a worldwide Global Campaign for Women's Human Rights-a broad and loose international collaborative effort to advance women's human rights. The campaign launched a petition calling upon the World Conference "to comprehensively address women's human rights at every level of its proceedings" and to recognize "gender violence, a universal phenomenon which takes many forms across culture, race, and class... as a violation of human rights requiring immediate action." The petition was eventually translated into 23 languages, and was used by over 1,000 sponsoring groups who gathered a half million signatures from 124 countries.

The petition and its demands instigated discussions about why women's rights, and gender-based violence in particular, were left out of human rights considerations, and served to mobilize women around the World Conference. Women acted to inject issues of women's human rights into the entire pre-conference preparatory process: Women from all regions demanded that women's human rights be discussed at the preparatory meetings held in Tunis, San Jose, and Bangkok, as well as at other non-governmental and national preparatory events. The idea of women's human rights was a framework for women to articulate and collaborate around broad and similar concerns about the status of women; it also provided women with a way to elaborate on the most pressing human rights issues specific to particular political, geographic, economic, and cultural contexts. By the time the World Conference convened, the idea that "women's rights are human rights" had become the rallying call of thousands of people all over the world and one of the most discussed "new" human rights debates. The *Vienna Declaration and Program of Action*, which is the product of the conference and is meant to signal the agreement of the international community on the status of human rights, states unequivocally that:

> The human rights of women and of the girl-child are an inalienable, integral and indivisible part of universal human rights.

Women continued to lobby for and gain wider recognition of women's human rights at subsequent United Nations Conferences. So, for example, at the International Conference on Population and Development in Cairo in 1994, women's reproductive rights were explicitly recognized as human rights. A particularly significant development was the way in which the Platform for Action at the IV World Conference on Women in Beijing in 1995 became virtually an agenda about the human rights of women. This signaled the successful mainstreaming of women's rights as human rights. The agreements that are produced by such conferences are not legally binding; however, they do have ethical and political weight and can be used to pursue regional, national, or local objectives. Conference documents can also be used to reinforce and interpret inter-national treaties such as the *Covenant on*

Civil and Political Rights, or the *Covenant of Social, Economic and Cultural Rights*.

These covenants, when signed by a country, do have the status of international law and have been used in courts by lawyers seeking redress for human rights violations. The most important international treaty specifically addressing women's human rights is the *Convention on the Elimination of All Forms of Discrimination Against Women (CEDAW)* which was initiated during the UN Decade for Women and has been ratified by over 130 countries. Further, local women's groups have integrated the women's human rights framework into their legal literacy programs and legal strategies. Although the framework of women's human rights has been tremendously useful in efforts to lobby for legislative and policy changes at local, national and international levels, it has been an equally as important tool for grassroots organizing. Women's human rights not only teach women about the range of rights that their governments must honor; it also functions as a kind of gestalt by which to organize analyses of their experiences and plan action for change.

The human rights framework creates a space in which the possibility for a different account of women's lives can be developed. What is so useful about this framework is that it provides women with principles by which to develop alternative visions of their lives without suggesting the substance of those visions. The fundamental principles of human rights that accord to each and every person the entitlement to human dignity give women a vocabulary for describing both violations and impediments to the exercise of their human rights. The large body of international covenants, agreements and commitments about human rights gives women political leverage and a tenable point of reference. And finally, the idea of women's human rights enables women to define and articulate the specificity of the experiences in their lives at the same time that it provides a vocabulary for women to share the experiences of other women around the world and work collaboratively for change.

4

Reports on Human Rights Practices

India is a multiparty, federal, parliamentary democracy with a bicameral parliament and a population of approximately 1.1 billion. Manmohan Singh became prime minister following his Congress Party-led coalition's victory in the 2004 general elections, which were considered free and fair, despite scattered instances of violence. Serious internal conflicts affected the state of Jammu and Kashmir, as well as several states in the north and east. While the civilian authorities generally maintained effective control of the security forces, there were several instances in which some elements of the security forces acted independently of government authority. The government generally respected the rights of its citizens; however, numerous serious problems remained. Major problems included extrajudicial killings of persons in custody, disappearances, and torture and rape by police and other security forces. A lack of accountability permeated the government and security forces throughout the country, creating an atmosphere of impunity.

The Chhattisgarh state government supported the formation of the "Salwa Judum" village militia to fight the Maoist insurgency. In West Bengal, violence in the Nandigram district led to accusations of state government failure to control ruling Communist party cadres, which were accused by human rights groups of killing more than 30 rural villagers and intimidating them through violence and rape.

Although the country has numerous laws protecting human rights, enforcement was inadequate and convictions rare. Poor prison conditions, lengthy pretrial detention without charge, and prolonged detention while undergoing trial remained significant problems. Government officials used special antiterrorism legislation to justify the excessive use of force while combating terrorism and several regional insurgencies. While security officials who committed human rights abuses generally enjoyed impunity, there were investigations into individual abuse cases as well as legal punishment of some perpetrators. Endemic corruption existed at all levels within the government and police, and attempts to combat the problem were unsuccessful. The government continued to apply restrictions to the travel and activities of visiting experts and scholars.

Significant restrictions on the funding and activities of NGOs also continued. Attacks against religious minorities and the promulgation of antireligious conversion laws were concerns. Social acceptance of caste-based discrimination often validated human rights violations against persons belonging to lower castes. Domestic violence, dowry-related deaths, honor crimes, female infanticide, and feticide were serious problems. Trafficking in persons and exploitation of indentured, bonded, and child labour were ongoing problems. Separatist guerrillas and terrorists in Kashmir, the northeast, and the Naxalite belt committed numerous serious abuses, including killing armed forces personnel, police, government officials, judges, and civilians. Insurgents also engaged in widespread torture, rape, beheadings, kidnapping, and extortion.

ARBITRARY OR UNLAWFUL DEPRIVATION OF LIFE

There were numerous reports that the government and its agents committed arbitrary or unlawful killings, including extrajudicial killings of suspected criminals and insurgents, or staged encounter deaths. According to human rights groups, security forces in Jammu and Kashmir targeted suspected terrorists, insurgents, and their supporters, but there was no widely accepted data on the magnitude of extrajudicial killings, which included encounter killings and custodial deaths. For example, according to the Jammu and Kashmir Coalition of Civil Society, 18 cases of custodial killings and extrajudicial killings took place during the year. Of those, six cases were under investigation by the local government at year's end. In March, Jammu and Kashmir Chief Minister Ghulam Nabi Azad claimed that only five custodial deaths occurred during his eighteen-month tenure and that the overall situation improved considerably with a 95 percent reduction in custodial deaths over the last two years. Between January 1994 and December 2006, according to the Home Ministry's 2006-2007 Report, citizens registered 1,222 complaints of human rights abuses against the Army and Central Police Force. Of those, 1,084 cases were investigated; 1,052 cases were found false; 32 cases were considered "genuine;" 61 persons were penalized; and compensation was awarded in six cases. The Justice Makhan Lal Kaul Commission of Inquiry tasked with the investigation of alleged custodial killings and falsified encounters in Jammu and Kashmir, received only five complaints during the year.

There were developments regarding the December 2006 encounter killing of Abdur Rahman Padder, a Kashmiri carpenter. On February 4, police unearthed five unmarked graves, one of them Padder's, in an ongoing investigation of custodial killings. According to press reports, authorities arrested a number of officers directly implicated in the case. In February a civil court in Srinagar charged seven policemen, including Ganderbal Hans Raj, Senior Superintendent of Police, for the murder of Padder. On October 20, the army arrested Mohammed Tariq, a soldier, for the torture and encounter killing of schoolteacher Abdur Rashid Mir in Jammu. At year's end the case was under investigation.

An update of the 2005 alleged false encounter death in Ahmedabad (Gujarat) of Sohrabuddin Shaikh, a suspected Lashkar-e-Tayyiba (LET) operative, his wife Kausarbi, and key witness Prajapti, indicated that in August, the Gujarat Criminal Investigations Department (CID) filed charges against 13 police officers from Gujarat and Rajasthan. At year's end the case was in trial in the Ahmedabad court. On December 6, the Election Commission sent Gujarat Chief Minister Narendra Modi a notice for allegedly justifying the encounter killing at an election rally in the state's Jamnagar district. Modi denied those allegations. On December 19, the Gujarat High Court transferred the judge hearing the case.

There was a consistently high rate of encounter killings by law enforcement and security forces in the northeast, particularly in the states of Assam and Manipur, as law enforcement attempted to combat insurgent groups, many of whom financed their operations through criminal activities such as extortion, kidnapping, and trafficking in narcotics. On March 14, thousands of local villagers in the Nandigram district of West Bengal attacked police and Communist Party of India—Marxist (CPM) supporters who tried to enter an agricultural area earmarked for conversion to an industrial zone. Acting on orders from the CPM-led state government, police fired on the crowd, killing 14 individuals and injuring 45. The Kolkata High Court ordered an inquiry by the Central Bureau of Investigation (CBI), but the court later revoked the CBI's investigative authority and asked the CBI to preserve evidence.

On July 10, members of the Anti-Naxal Special Police Force killed five persons including an alleged leader of the CPI-Maoist cadre at Ammadlu village in Chikmagalur district. According to Karnataka police, all five were members of the local Naxalite unit, while human rights groups alleged that four of those killed were residents of a house caught in the crossfire. At year's end a magisterial inquiry into the encounter was underway. From November 6 to 11, CPM members, whom human rights groups claim had state government support and direction, conducted a violent campaign of intimidation to regain control over the Nandigram area from the Bhumi Uchhed Protirodh Committee (BUPC). The BUPC included those opposed to the CPM's plan to acquire local land for industry, some former CPM supporters, and opposition party workers and was backed by the Trinamul Congress, part of the West Bengal opposition. News reports and eyewitness accounts noted that CPM cadres fired on BUPC supporters and local villagers, killing at least three and injuring others, burned many houses, and engaged in numerous rapes.

On November 27, journalists reported the discovery of mass graves in the area. Following a government order on December 7, the CID initiated an inquiry into the identity of the bodies. On April 1, according to the Asian Human Rights Commission (AHRC), Border Security Forces (BSF) shot and killed Asif Iqbal and Sahin Sk, age 13 and 15 respectively, on the Indo-Bangladesh border in Murshidabad district. Police allegedly shot the two boys as they tried to take two cows across the border. At year's end the government had not taken action t investigate this case. On May 10, Chhattisgarh police registered a First Information Report against "unknown uniformed people" for the March 31 killing of seven villagers near Santoshpur village in Dantewara district. Media reports alleged that police personnel and "Salwa Judum" militia members apprehended villagers from Santoshpur, took them to a nearby forest, and shot them because they were Naxalite sympathizers.

Media reports further claimed that the police buried the bodies to hide the deaths. Because of media pressure, the police exhumed the bodies and performed autopsies, which confirmed death by gunshot. On December 28, police fired on a crowd and killed at least three individuals in Orissa after a village police station was set afire. The actions were part of a period of communal violence that began four days earlier. In November a key witness in a 1984 anti-Sikh riots case involving senior Congress leader Jagdish Tytler resurfaced two months after the CBI declared that he was unreachable. In December a Delhi court ordered the CBI to reinvestigate the 1984 riots case and file a fresh report. Tytler was accused of orchestrating the riots by encouraging Congress party workers, police, and mobs in Delhi to kill Sikhs and destroy their houses and businesses in retribution for the assassination of Indira Gandhi.

There were no developments regarding the January 2006

case in which security forces allegedly abducted and killed a boy in the Barramulla District, the January 2006 killing of Fayaz Ahmad Bhat, or the March 2006 encounter killing of two suspected LET terrorists in Delhi. There were no developments in the August 2006 staged encounter killing of Abu Osama, an alleged Pakistani national. Several journalists had claimed that the police arranged the encounter and that the person killed was associated with the July 2006 perpetrators of the terror attack on Mumbai trains. At year's end the November 2006 encounter killing case of Ram Narayan Gupta was ongoing in the Mumbai High Court. Navi Mumbai police allegedly had apprehended Ram Narayan Gupta and a friend from a shop, and later police claimed they had killed Gupta in an encounter that night. The friend had disappeared. At year's end the 2005 CBI investigation of four army officers, including Senior Superintendent of Police Farooq Khan, for the killing of five civilians in a staged encounter death in 2000 was still pending. Custodial deaths, often made to appear as encounter deaths, remained a serious problem, and authorities often delayed prosecutions.

During 2005 the Home Ministry reported 139 deaths in police custody. However, the National Human Rights Commission (NHRC) confirmed 1,730 deaths in police and judicial custody during the same time period. During 2006 the National Crimes Record Bureau reported 38 unnatural deaths in police custody. According to the Home Ministry's 2006-2007 Report, the NHRC reported 1,159 total deaths in police custody between April and December 2006. Although Andhra Pradesh police recorded an 11 percent decrease in custodial deaths in 2005 compared with the previous year, they also had the largest number of deaths in judicial and police custody with a total of 145. Andhra Pradesh police recorded five custodial deaths throughout the year. In 2004, according to media reports, Maharashtra police transferred officers linked to encounter killings from the Mumbai crime branch; as a result, staged encounter killings in Maharashtra reportedly decreased from 94 in 2001 to 13 in 2004. Figures for encounter killings in Maharashtra for 2005 and 2006 were not available. In June, according to a media report, the Government of Maharashtra retracted its May 21 order requiring a CID probe into each encounter death. The government conducted only internal police department inquiries. The change reportedly was implemented to avoid "demoralizing the police force."

The Kerala State Human Rights Commission (KSHRC) registered 25 cases of custodial deaths from January to June, compared with 39 cases in 2005. According to KSHRC, 46 persons died in state custody throughout the year. The commission-led investigation of these deaths was ongoing at year's end. During the year in Manipur, there were several killings by police. For example, on January 31, Assam Rifles (AR) personnel entered a church campus in Khoken village and opened fire without warning on suspicion that the villagers were insurgents. AR officers shot and killed Henpu Singsit and injured several others. On February 8, police commandos shot and killed Ashangbam Shyamchand while he was shopping at Lamlai Bazaar.

On February 9, according to AHRC, authorities from the Pathor Pratima Police arrested Krishnapada Das, a resident of Purba Dwarikapur village in West Bengal. The next day, Das's body was found hanged at the police station. By year's end authorities had not taken action to resolve the case. On March 17, according to AHRC, authorities from the Beldanga police station arrested Hayat Seikh at his residence, allegedly because his relative had been involved in a murder the previous week. Authorities took Seikh to Beldanga police station where they detained him until March 23. Although he was released, Seikh died March 25 allegedly from beatings while incarcerated. At year's end the government had not taken action to investigate the case.

There were developments concerning the 2005 death in custody of Udayakumar, a citizen from Kerala. According to the Confederation of Human Rights Organizations, police had arrested Udayakumar for "suspicious movements" in a nearby park, questioned, beat, and killed him. After preliminary investigations, authorities arrested three police constables and charged two with murder. In July a key prosecution witness turned hostile in court, denying his previous statement that he had witnessed his co-prisoner being beaten by policemen. Udayakumar's mother petitioned the Kerala High Court for a reinvestigation by the CBI. On September 20, a Division Bench of the Kerala High Court directed the CBI to conduct an investigation into the case. Human rights activists argued that the police response to custodial deaths varied according to the socioeconomic status of the victims. Media reported that Mumbai police routinely conducted internal inquiries into all custodial deaths, but authorities did not convict any officer of a crime in connection with the 15 cases reported since 2001.

Police did not launch any inquiries into the 2005-6 custodial deaths of Shivkumar Jaiswala and Prem Yadav in Mumbai. There were no developments in the January 2006 death in custody of Gurmail Singh, the April 2006 investigation of police officials for the 2004 custodial death of Uday Bhandge, or the June 2006 death in custody of Madan Lal. At year's end the April 2006 custodial death of Premnath Janardan Rao remained under investigation. Developments in the cases of the 14 Mumbai police and constables held for the 2003 custodial killing of Khwaja Yunus included that, in July, the Maharashtra CID sought permission from the Government of Maharashtra (GOM) to prosecute 10 of the 14 and the GOM determined that there was enough evidence to prosecute four out of the 14 officers. By the year's end hearings had not commenced. One of the accused resigned from the police service, while the other three remained suspended.

At year's end the trial of two railway police constables for the May 2005 custodial killing of porter Vijay Singh was still pending. There were no developments in the April 2006 death of Captain Sumit Kohli in Kupwara, Jammu and Kashmir. Kohli's family alleged that he was killed because he was scheduled to testify as a witness against another officer in a 2004 case of an encounter killing. The army stated that suicide was the cause of death. From May to August 2006, newspapers and opposition parties in Kerala reported seven deaths in police custody of persons arrested for misdemeanor offenses. During the same period, another seven individuals drowned in separate incidents, allegedly while being pursued by the Kerala police. In August 2006 following a media outcry, the government of Kerala announced a judicial inquiry into the deaths.

In July the judicial inquiry commission led by Justice Rajendra Babu presented its report to the Kerala state government regarding the investigation of 15 custodial deaths that took place in 2006. The commission refrained from directly accusing any police officer but recommended reinvestigation of four deaths (Prasannan, Mavelikkara; Rajan, Kozhikode; Anandaraj, Thiruvananthapuram; and Milton, Kodungallur). A prominent Kerala human rights organization charged that the judicial inquiry failed to expose effectively the law-breaking officers. The Kerala Home Minister declared that the state government would pay monetary compensation to the families of nine persons who died in custody. On July 11, the Imphal bench of the Guwahati High Court ordered the AR to pay approximately $8,900 (350,000 rupees) to Athokpam Bandana of Imphal, whose husband, Athokpam Purnima Singh, died in AR custody in 2001. The AR claimed he was shot in an encounter.

During the year the killing of civilians continued in the course of counter insurgency and counter terrorism operations, including those that took place in Jammu and Kashmir. Human rights activists stated that accurate numbers were not available due to limited access to the region, but the Asian Centre for Human Rights (ACHR) alleged that 355 civilians were killed and 373 injured in police shootings in 2005. The security forces often claimed that those killed were insurgents or civilians who died in crossfire. According to the NHRC, state governments had not investigated at least 3,575 previous deaths in custody cases. Government agencies funded, exchanged intelligence with, and directed the operations of counter insurgents, former separatist guerillas who surrendered to the Jammu and Kashmir government and participated in the counter-insurgency effort with their own weapons as part of police auxiliary units.

During 2006 killings and abductions of suspected pro-government counter insurgents continued to be a significant problem in Jammu and Kashmir, although the number of such instances declined substantially from the 1990s. Countrywide, there were allegations that military and paramilitary forces engaged in abduction, torture, rape, arbitrary detention, and the extrajudicial killing of insurgents and noncombatant civilians, particularly in areas of insurgency. According to human rights activists and journalists, during the year a few Naxalites (Maoist guerillas) in eastern and central parts of the country who surrendered were allowed to retain their weapons and worked for the police as "anti-People's War Group (PWG) officers." Human rights groups alleged that police used former Naxalites to kill current Naxalites and human rights activists with Maoist links. Police denied the charges, attributing such killings to internal feuds within the PWG.

Unlawful killings due to societal violence, including vigilante action, continued. For example, in September, villagers in Bihar beat to death a group of 10 suspected robbers. There were no further developments concerning the March 2006 public beheading, by 200 villagers in Sonitpur district of Assam, of five members of a family for allegedly practicing witchcraft, or the July 2006 killing of eight civilians during protests of the custodial death of Ajit Mahanta. In 2005 the National Crime Record Bureau (NCRB) reported that there were 26,127 cases of crimes against persons belonging to the Scheduled Castes (SCs) and 5,713 cases of crimes against those belonging to the Scheduled Tribes (STs). The average conviction rate for the crimes against SCs was 29.8 percent and, for crimes against STs, 24.5 percent. In 2006 the NCRB reported that there were 27,070 cases of crimes against SCs and 5,791 cases of crimes against STs, with the average conviction rate for SCs of 27.6 percent and for STs 28 percent. Approximately 55 percent of the population displaced by development projects was tribals, although they constituted only 8.2 percent of the total population of the country according to the 2001 census.

DISAPPEARANCE

Although government complicity was not always confirmed and numbers of those disappeared varied widely, numerous persons disappeared in insurgency-torn areas during the year. Additionally, insurgents in Jammu and Kashmir and the northeastern states continued to use kidnappings to terrorize the population, obtain the release of detained comrades, and extort funds. There were credible reports that police throughout the country often failed to file legally required arrest reports, resulting in hundreds of unresolved disappearances in which relatives claimed that an individual was taken into police custody and never heard from again. Police usually denied these claims, pointing to the lack of an arrest record.

The government maintained that screening committees administered by the state governments provided information about the unacknowledged detainees to their families. Other sources indicated that families could only confirm the detention of their relatives by bribing prison guards. During 2006 the screening committees released 140 persons detained under the (Jammu and Kashmir) Public Safety Act (PSA). During the year, the government did not release any additional detainees. Chief Minister Ghulam Nabi Azad announced that no custodial disappearances occurred in Kashmir during the year. The government made little progress, however, in holding hundreds of police and security officials accountable for many disappearances committed during the Punjab counter insurgency and the Delhi anti-Sikh riots of 1984-94, despite the presence of a special investigatory commission.

The NHRC also continued to investigate 2,097 cases of murder and cremation that occurred between 1984 and the early 1990s. In May 2006 it ordered monetary compensation to the next of kin of 45 persons whom the Punjab governments admitted were in police custody immediately before they were killed and illegally cremated. The NGO Ensaaf estimated that security forces killed and caused to disappear more than 10,000 Punjabi Sikhs and cremated 6,017 Sikhs in Amritsar in counter insurgency operations during the militancy. There were no developments in the 2006 case filed by Paramjit Kaur Khalra, the widow of human rights activist Jaswant Singh Khalra, seeking prosecution of former police chief K.P.S. Gill in the abduction, illegal detention, torture, and murder of her husband.

At year's end Khalra's case had not been tried in court. According to Ensaaf and other human rights organizations, in 1995 members of the Punjab police operating under Gill's command abducted and killed Khalra for investigating and exposing the disappearances and secret cremations of thousands of Sikhs in Punjab by security forces. There were no developments in the May 2006 case of Ghulam Nabi Mir, who disappeared in Pulwama (Jammu and Kashmir) after Rashtriya Rifle (RR) officers allegedly raided his home.

TORTURE AND OTHER CRUEL OR DEGRADING TREATMENT

The law prohibits torture and generally did not allow for confessions extracted by force to be admissible in court; however, authorities often used torture during interrogations to extort money and as summary punishment. There were allegations of confessions derived under torture. In some instances, these confessions subsequently were used as evidentiary support for an execution sentence. The Code of Criminal Procedure (Amendment) Act of 2005 mandated a judicial inquiry into any death or rape of a woman in police custody; however, human rights groups asserted that the new law had not decreased the prevalence of custodial abuse or killings. The ACHR alleged that custodial deaths were a severe problem and that police regularly used torture. Because many alleged torture victims died in custody, and other victims were afraid to speak out, there were few firsthand accounts. Marks of torture, however, were often found on the bodies of deceased detainees.

The prevalence of torture in detention facilities by police throughout the country was reflected in the number of deaths in police custody. Police and jailers typically assaulted new prisoners or threatened violence in exchange for money, favors, and personal articles. In addition, police commonly tortured detainees during custodial interrogation. Although police were subject to prosecution for such offenses, the government often failed to hold them accountable. According to Amnesty International (AI), torture is "endemic" to the justice system and often used against individuals "on the basis of their caste, religion, socioeconomic, and sexual identity." NGOs asserted that custodial torture was common in Tamil Nadu, and one human rights lawyer claimed that all police stations in Punjab, Andhra Pradesh, Haryana, and Chandigarh have torture cells to "soften up" the accused prior to court appearance. However, increased reporting of custodial torture may be the result of greater awareness.

The AHRC claimed that local police in Kerala continued to use torture and assault as a means of criminal investigation. According to the AHRC, though not verified by other sources, Gujarat interrogation centers function in public view. The suspects allegedly are brought in, kept in illegal detention and tortured as part of questioning. Between February 12 and 16, according to AHRC, officers at the Bally police station in the Howrah district of West Bengal tortured Ajay Yadav Kumar, whom they arrested after finding a skeleton in a well near his home. Authorities suspected the skeleton to be that of Kumar's wife, who been missing since December 2006. At year's end, Ajay Yadav remained in jail, and the government had not investigated the case.

On August 2, according to AHRC, Julfikaqr Ali Mollah, the Inspector in Charge of the Deganga Police (West Bengal), allegedly burned with acid Giasuddin Mando, an iron scrap dealer. On August 13, the local magistrate ordered Mando released and sent to the hospital. By year's end the government had not investigated the case.

On December 11, Chennai police arrested 50-year-old Syed Ali, a tea shop worker in Vadapalani, Chennai, for the alleged unlawful sale of lottery tickets. Syed died in custody. The Tamil Nadu government ordered an inquiry into the incident after Chennai shopkeepers alleged that the death was due to police torture. At year's end, the investigation was ongoing. According to media reports, the police in Rajkot, Gujarat, employed public humiliation as a tool to shame and punish certain accused persons. For instance, in September police forced 12 youths accused of vandalism to perform situps in public. In October the police forced a 61-year-old accused of raping his daughter-in-law to crawl on hands and knees through a crowded market place. Media reports indicate that the police, although aware that such treatment was a breach of the rights of the accused, viewed public humiliation as an effective crime deterrent.

There were no developments in the September 2006 torture case of Saju, a private bus driver. According to the AHRC, police demanded a bribe from Saju of $68 (3,000 rupees) and abused him when he refused. Saju later died while in police custody. An official inquiry was ordered into the incident, and authorities suspended three police officers. The investigation was ongoing at year's end. In Jammu and Kashmir, torture victims or their relatives reportedly had difficulty filing complaints, as local police allegedly were instructed not to open a case without permission from higher authorities. In addition, under the (Jammu and Kashmir) Armed Forces Special Powers Act (AFSPA) of 1990, no "prosecution, suit, or other legal proceeding shall be instituted against any person in respect of anything done or purported to be done in exercise of the powers of the act," without the approval of the central government.

The act gives security forces the authority to shoot suspected lawbreakers and those disturbing the peace and to destroy structures suspected of harboring violent separatists or containing weapons. Human rights organizations alleged that this provision allowed security forces to act with virtual impunity. The rape of persons in custody was part of a broader pattern of custodial abuse. NGOs asserted that rape by police, including custodial rape, was more common than NHRC figures indicated. A higher incidence of abuse appeared credible, given other evidence of abusive behaviour by police, and the likelihood that many rapes went unreported due to the victims' shame and fear of retribution.

However, legal limits placed on the arrest, search, and police custody of women appeared to reduce the frequency of rape in custody. There were no recent NHRC data on the extent of custodial rape. There was a pattern of rape by paramilitary personnel in Jammu and Kashmir and the northeast as a means of instilling fear among noncombatants in insurgency-affected areas, but these incidents were not included in NHRC statistics, as the NHRC does not have direct investigative authority over the military.

PRISON AND DETENTION CENTER CONDITIONS

Prison conditions were life threatening and did not meet international standards. Prisons were severely over-crowded and food and medical care inadequate. In March 2006 an NHRC report indicated that the country's prisons were overcrowded on average by 38.5 percent. According to the NHRC report, the country's prisons had a population of 324,852 persons, with an authorized capacity of 234,462. The NHRC reported that it requested the Chief Justices of High Courts to determine how to resolve the problem of overcrowded prisons.

In 2006 the government introduced a plea bargain option for prisoners to reduce the pending time of cases in trial courts and overcrowded prisons. For disposal of long pending sessions and other cases, the government set up 1,562 Fast Track Courts during the year. According to the 2006 NHRC report, a large proportion of the deaths in judicial custody were from natural causes, in some cases aggravated by poor prison conditions. Tuberculosis caused many deaths, as did HIV/AIDS. The NHRC assigned its special rapporteur and chief coordinator of custodial justice to ensure that state prison authorities performed medical checkups on all inmates. By the end of 2006, only a few examinations had been performed.

While local authorities often attempted to hide custodial killings, the NHRC and the courts investigated cases brought to their attention and prosecuted some perpetrators. In most cases, the courts awarded monetary compensation of $400-$2,200 (17,600-97,000 rupees) to the next of kin. NGO sources stated that relatives often had to pay bribes to receive the compensation awarded, and in many cases never received it at all. There were no developments in the Maharashtra State Human Rights Commission investigation into the June 2006 allegations, made by a former inmate of Arthur Road Jail in Mumbai that the prison's medical doctor ignored a prisoner who died after suffering from chest pains.

By law, juveniles must be detained in rehabilitative facilities, although at times they were detained in prison, especially in rural areas. Pretrial detainees were not separated from convicted prisoners. The government allowed selected NGOs to work in prisons, within specific guidelines, but NGO findings remained largely confidential as a result of agreements made with the government. Increased press reporting and parliamentary questioning provided evidence of growing public awareness of custodial abuse. The NHRC identified torture and deaths in detention as one of its priority concerns. According to the Home Ministry, the International Committee of the Red Cross (ICRC) conducted visits to 21 detention centers and 1,174 detainees during the year, including all 25 acknowledged detention centers in Jammu and Kashmir, and all facilities where Kashmiris were held elsewhere in the country.

The ICRC visited and individually monitored 10 females, 26 minors, and 462 newly registered detainees during 41 visits to detention facilities throughout the country. The ICRC was not authorized to visit interrogation or transit centers, nor did it have access to regular detention centers in the northeastern states. August 2006 amendments to the 1993 Protection of Human Rights Act (PHRA) eliminated the requirement that the NHRC had to notify state governments before visiting prisons, thus enabling surprise visits.

ARBITRARY ARREST OR DETENTION

The law prohibits arbitrary arrest and detention, but both occurred during the year. On May 22, authorities arrested Manipur human rights activist Irom Sharmila on charges that she had attempted suicide. Sharmila had returned to Manipur on March 6 following her six-year hunger strike at a government hospital in Imphal, Manipur, against the AFSPA. AFSPA gives security forces the right to "shoot to kill" suspects. At year's end Irom Sharmila remained in government custody, and the AFSPA had not been repealed.

On August 2, authorities acquitted Abdul Nasser Madhani, Chairman of Kerala-based People's Democratic Party, after he had spent nine years in detention while awaiting trial for the 1998 terrorist bombings in Coimbatore. Madhani had been denied bail during his stay in prison despite appeals by the Kerala Legislative Assembly and several human rights organizations who had pointed out his poor health. Madhani's wife filed a habeas corpus case, which authorities rejected. Madhani's eventual acquittal and release focused popular attention on the condition of prisoners who are awaiting completion of long-drawn out trials.

There were no updates concerning the February 2006 report that authorities had incarcerated Shanka Dayal without trial in the Unnao District Jail for 44 years for "wrongfully restraining a person and causing hurt"—an offense that warrants a one year sentence. The NHRC requested Assamese authorities to submit reports on five other pretrial prisoners detained at the LGB Regional Institute of Mental Health in Tezpur, Assam.

THE POLICE AND SECURITY APPARATUS

Although the governments of 28 states and seven union territories have primary responsibility for maintaining law and order, the central government provides guidance and support. The Ministry for Home Affairs controls most paramilitary forces, the internal intelligence bureaus, and the nationwide police service, and provides training for senior police officers of the state-organized police forces. Corruption in the police force was pervasive and acknowledged by many government officials. Officers at all levels acted with considerable impunity and were rarely held accountable for illegal actions. Should authorities find an officer guilty of a crime, transfer to a different post or position was the common response. Human rights activists and NGOs reported that bribery was often necessary to receive police services.

According the Ministry of Home Affairs, the NHRC recorded 6,923 cases against the police; 35 against armed forces, and 39 against the paramilitary forces for violation of human rights during 2006. In 2005 the government worked with a foreign government and the UN Office on Drugs and Crime (UNODC) on a two-year program to train and sensitize law enforcement officials and prosecutors in the country about victims of human trafficking and to bring abusers to justice. Training material developed through this project was used to conduct courses for law enforcement officials in target states and worked on developing standard operating procedures and protocols to be used nationally and in police training academies.

ARREST AND DETENTION

The law requires that detainees be informed of the grounds for their arrest, be represented by legal counsel, and, unless held under a preventive detention law, assigned within 24 hours of arrest, at which time the accused must either be remanded for further investigation or released. However, thousands of criminal suspects remained in detention without charge during the year, adding to already overcrowded prisons. The law provides arrested persons the right to be released on bail and prompt access to a lawyer; however, those arrested under special security legislation received neither in most cases. Court approval of a bail application is mandatory if police do not file charges within 60 to 90 days of arrest. In most cases, bail was set between $11 (485 rupees) and $4,500 (198,000 rupees). By law, detainees should be provided an attorney and allowed access to family members. However, this was rarely implemented.

In 2004 the government repealed the Prevention of Terrorism Act (POTA) and replaced it with the Unlawful Activities Prevention Act (UAPA). Human rights groups reported that the revised UAPA contained important improvements over the POTA. For example, it does not allow coerced confessions to be admitted as evidence in court. The South Asia Human Rights Documentation Centre (SAHRDC) reported that more than 1,000 persons remained in detention awaiting prosecution under lapsed special terrorism legislation, and that cases opened under POTA continued through the judicial system. In June 2005 the POTA review committee reported that there were 11,384 persons wrongfully charged under POTA who should have been charged under regular law. According to the Ministry of Home Affairs, following the repeal of POTA in 2004, three review committees reviewed 263 cases involving 1,529 accused persons and determined that there was no prima-facie evidence under POTA against 1,006 of them.

The Terrorist And Disrupted Activities (TADA) courts curtailed many legal protections provided by other courts. For example, defense counsel was not permitted to see prosecution witnesses, who were kept behind screens while testifying in court, and confessions extracted under duress were admissible as evidence. Despite the fact that the TADA Act was terminated in 1995, cases initiated under the original act are still considered legally valid. UAPA is used to hold people without bail in jail for extended periods prior to the filing of formal charges. For instance, on May 9, Mumbai police arrested and held under UAPA alleged urban sympathizers of Naxalites Arun Ferreira and Vernon Gonsalves, alias Vikram. On August 22, police arrested Sridhar Srinivasan alias Vishnu. At year's end no charges had been filed in either of these cases.

The National Security Act (NSA) permits police to detain persons considered security risks anywhere in the country, except Jammu and Kashmir, without charge or trial for as long as one year on loosely defined security charges. State governments must confirm the detention order, which is then reviewed by an advisory board of three high court judges within seven weeks of the arrest. NSA detainees were permitted visits by family members and lawyers, and must be informed of the grounds of their detention within five days (10 to 15 days in exceptional circumstances). Human rights groups expressed concerns that the NSA would allow authorities to order preventive detention at their own behest after only a cursory review by an advisory board and that no court would overturn such a decision. In January 2006 Lucknow authorities arrested a doctor from the King George Medical University in Uttar Pradesh and charged him with arson and violence. After the state's chief minister, Mulayam Singh Yadav, warned that "trouble-makers" at the university would be punished, authorities charged the doctor on January 19 under the NSA.

The PSA, which applies only in Jammu and Kashmir, permits state authorities to detain persons without charge and judicial review for up to two years. During this time detainees do not have access to family members or legal counsel. According to the Office of Director General of Jammu and Kashmir Police, authorities arrested 473 persons in 2005 and 420 in 2006 under PSA. According to the ACHR, there were 140 foreign nationals in prisons in Jammu and Kashmir under the PSA. Police continued to ignore the 2005 guidelines announced by the NHRC regarding arrest, which included establishing reasonable belief of guilt; avoiding detention if bail is an option; protecting the dignity of those arrested; refusing public display or parading, and allowing access to a lawyer during interrogation.

Police routinely employed arbitrary and incommuni-cado detention, denied detainees access to lawyers and medical attention, and used torture or ill treatment to extract confessions. Human rights experts claimed that discrimination and custodial torture of those too poor to afford legal assistance was common. During 2006 the media reported that lower-caste individuals were more likely to be illegally detained than others. Human rights activists maintained that the government increasingly avoided prosecuting security officers involved in illegal conduct by providing financial compensation to victims' families in lieu of punishment. In some instances victims or their families who distrusted the military judicial system petitioned to have their cases transferred to a civil court. The NHRC has no jurisdiction over any courts, including military courts. On June 25, a Gujarat court convicted 12 persons under POTA for the 2003 killing of former Gujarat Home Minister Haren Pandya. The judge sentenced nine people to life and gave lesser terms to three other persons.

At year's end, according to the Islamic Relief Committee of Gujarat, 130 persons remained in custody in Gujarat under POTA awaiting trial. Since 2003 the Supreme Court has stayed trials in nine high-profile cases, including the Godhra train arson case. The Supreme Court had not determined how these cases would proceed. In March 2006 the Chhattisgarh State Government enacted the Special Public Protection Act, which Human Rights Watch (HRW) deemed "a vague and overly broad law that allows detention of up to three years for unlawful activities." HRW asserted that the law loosely defined what "unlawful activities" entails and threatens the fundamental freedoms and protections set forth in the constitution. The Public Union for Civil Liberties in India filed suit, alleging that the ordinance is "amenable to gross abuse and misuse, arbitrariness and partiality" and "can result in harsh and drastic punishment to innocent persons without hearing or remedy."

HRW noted particular concern that the law also criminalizes any support given to Naxalites, regardless of evidence of duress. On May 14, Chhattisgarh police arrested Dr. Binayak Sen under the provisions of this act, alleging that Dr. Sen provided material support to Naxalites. At year's end Dr. Sen remained in judicial custody and had been denied bail. The AFSPA remained in effect in Nagaland, Manipur, Assam, and parts of Tripura, and a version of the law was in effect in Jammu and Kashmir. Under AFSPA the government can declare any state or union territory a "disturbed area." This allows the security forces to fire on any person in order to "maintain law and order" and to arrest any person "against whom reasonable suspicion exists" without informing the detainee of the grounds for arrest. Security forces are also granted immunity from prosecution for acts committed under AFSPA. In 2005 a Home Ministry committee, chaired by Justice B.P. Jeevan Reddy, reviewed AFSPA and submitted its report and recommendations.

In October 2006 the ministry released the report, which recommended the repeal of the act and gave the central government power to send forces where required to enforce the repeal. In April a working group on Jammu and Kashmir appointed by the prime minister also recommended that the act be revoked. The government had not acted on these recommendations by year's end. The Manipur government extended AFSPA for another six months from June 1 after declaring the state a "disturbed area," as defined under the AFSPA. The AFSPA does not apply to seven assembly constituencies in the Imphal Municipal area that had not been declared a disturbed area. The law provides a person in detention the right to a prompt trial; however, due to a severe backlog, this was not the case in practice. Human rights organizations reported that 60 to 75 percent of all detainees were in jail awaiting trial, drastically contributing to overcrowding. Human rights organizations asserted that approximately 65 percent of those detained were found innocent. Due to persistent inefficiencies in the judicial system, there were numerous instances in which detainees spent more time in jail under pretrial detention than they would have if found guilty and sentenced to the longest possible term.

DENIAL OF FAIR PUBLIC TRIAL

The law provides for an independent judiciary, and the government generally respected this provision in practice; however, serious problems remained. In Jammu and Kashmir, members of the judiciary were subject to threats and intimidation by insurgents and terrorists. The judicial system is headed by a Supreme Court, which has juris-diction over constitutional issues, and includes state high courts, state lower courts, and special tribunals. Lower courts hear criminal and civil cases and send appeals to state high courts. The president appoints judges, who may serve until the age of 62 on state high courts and 65 on the Supreme Court.

TRIAL PROCEDURES

The Criminal Procedure Code provides that trials be conducted publicly, except in proceedings involving official secrets, trials in which statements prejudicial to the safety of the state might be made, or under provisions of special security legislation. Defendants enjoy a presumption of innocence and have the right to choose their counsel. Sentences must be announced publicly, and there are effective channels for appeal at most levels of the judicial system. The state provides free legal counsel to indigent defendants. The law allows defendants access to relevant government-held evidence in most civil and criminal cases; however, the government had the right to withhold information and did so in cases it considered sensitive.

There was continued concern about the failure of the Gujarat government to arrest and convict those responsible for the 2002 violence following the train burning in Godhra in which 59 men, women, and children died. For example, Muslims continued to voice anger over police unwillingness to register or properly investigate complaints against perpetrators of the violence. In June, after agreeing to reexamine the closure of 1,600 complaints per instruction of the Supreme Court, Gujarat police concluded that a majority of cases could not be reinvestigated due to lack of witnesses. Convictions of Hindu perpetrators of the violence were minimal, while acquittals were common. According to an October 2006 report submitted by the federal government to a UN agency, six cases resulted in convictions, whereas 182 cases were acquittals.

According to Government of Gujarat figures, 223 persons remained "missing" after the 2002 violence, a majority of whom were Muslims. Family members and NGOs maintained that many of these persons were killed and their bones interred in mass graves. In December 2005 and August 2006, two such mass graves came to light in Kidiad town and in the Panam river bed near Lunawada town. The victims' kin and an NGO filed a case in the Gujarat High Court that the remains should be identified and returned to the kin. During 2006, on the directives of the Gujarat High Court, the Government of Gujarat sent the remains for DNA analysis. Although the report was submitted to the Gujarat High Court in May 2006, the victims' kin were not able to access it. At year's end the Gujarat High Court had not ruled whether the remains should be returned.

The other high-profile trial from the 2002 Gujarat violence, the Bilkis Bano gang rape case, was ongoing in a Mumbai court at year's end. The Gujarat Government claimed that police initially arrested 5,384 persons in the city of Ahmedabad and 24,683 persons in the state as a whole. However, a 2006 analysis by the Islamic Relief Committee of Gujarat revealed that a very few number of these investigations actually led to convictions. The Gujarat Government's legal department advised against appealing most of the acquittals in the remaining cases. As a result, only a handful of cases were appealed to higher courts. From April 2002 through year's end, the Justice Nanavati-Shah Commission had also conducted public hearings in the Godhra train arson and subsequent Gujarat violence incidents. At year's end the commission's inquiry was ongoing.

HRW reported in 2006 that Hindu extremists threatened and intimidated victims, witnesses, and human rights activists attempting to investigate those who committed crimes during the 2002 Gujarat riots. HRW asserted that instead of pursuing the perpetrators of violence, the Gujarat Government nurtured a climate of fear by launching selective tax probes against some Islamic organizations to pressure Muslim witnesses to withdraw murder and arson charges against Hindu nationalists. According to AI's 2007 annual human rights report, "justice continued to evade" victims and survivors of the riots." Muslims faced difficulty obtaining housing and access to public resources, and few successful prosecutions took place. However, 41 police were being tried for their alleged roles in the violence.

Fast Track Courts concentrated on a specific type of case, allowing judges to develop expertise in a given area of law. These courts gave preference to cases pending for extended periods and often focused on civil issues. Court fees were generally lower for these courts, since trials were shorter. As in previous years, courts were regularly in session and the judicial system began to normalize in Jammu and Kashmir. Nevertheless, the judicial system was hindered because of judicial tolerance of abuses committed as part of the government's anti-insurgent campaign and because of the frequent refusal by security forces to obey court orders. Due in part to intimidation by insurgents and terrorists, courts in Jammu and Kashmir often were reluctant to hear cases involving insurgent and terrorist crimes and failed to act expeditiously, if at all, on habeas corpus cases. According to the Ministry of Home Affairs, in addition to Kashmiris, there were currently 377 persons of unidentified ethnicity and 136 foreigners in jails in 2006.

POLITICAL PRISONERS AND DETAINEES

While the government maintained that there were no political prisoners, the All Parties Hurriyat Conference (APHC) claimed there were approximately 500 political prisoners in Jammu and Kashmir, and human rights activists based in the state placed the number at 150, although among these were persons whom the government claimed had engaged in violent acts. The government permitted international humanitarian organizations, such as the ICRC, access to such persons on a regular basis. In March the trial of 34 Burmese nationals, suspected members of the National United Party of Arakan and Karen National Union who had spent nine years in detention, began in West Bengal. Authorities arrested the Burmese nationals in February 1998.

Due in large part to a campaign by local human rights organizations, the West Bengal Government withdrew a decision to hold the trial in secret in prison. The trial began in the Kolkata High Court but was closed to the public and media; the Central Bureau of Investigation (CBI) prosecuted the men on charges of illegal possession of weapons. In December the government transferred the judge presiding over the case, and the proceedings were placed on hold. There were no reports of political detainees during the year, although the government temporarily detained hundreds of suspected terrorists, insurgents, and separatists.

CIVIL JUDICIAL PROCEDURES AND REMEDIES

There are different personal status laws for the various minority religious communities, and the legal system accommodates religion-specific laws in matters of marriage, divorce, adoption, and inheritance. Muslim personal status law governs many noncriminal matters, including family law and inheritance. The Government of Karnataka formally established the Karnataka Human Rights Commission on July 25 with the appointment of a former Chief Justice of the Chhattisgarh High Court to head the body, along with two other members. It took four months for the Karnataka government to allot the necessary infrastructure for the commission to start operations. According to human rights groups, the commission held approximately ten hearings during the year.

ARBITRARY INTERFERENCE WITH PRIVACY

The law prohibits such actions, and the government generally respected these prohibitions in practice; however, at times the authorities infringed upon them. Police must obtain warrants to conduct searches and seizures, except in cases where such actions would cause undue delay. Police must justify such warrantless searches in writing to the nearest magistrate with jurisdiction over the offense. The authorities in Jammu and Kashmir, Punjab, and Manipur have special powers to search and arrest without a warrant. The Information Technology Act grants police power under certain circumstances to search premises and arrest individuals without a warrant. The act specifies a one-year sentence for persons who fail to provide information to the government on request and a five-year sentence for transmitting "lascivious" material.

The Indian Telegraph Act authorizes the surveillance of communications, including monitoring telephone conversations and intercepting personal mail in cases of public emergency or "in the interest of the public safety or tranquility." The central government and state governments used these surveillance techniques during the year. Although the Telegraph Act gives police the power to tap phones to aid an investigation, they were not allowed to use such evidence in court. The UAPA allows such evidence to be used in terrorist cases, and some human rights activists noted that UAPA confers additional powers on police to use intercepted communications as evidence in terrorism cases. While there were elabourate legal safeguards to prevent police from encroaching on personal privacy, there were no such protections in terrorist cases.

Laws limiting families to two children remained in place in seven states. The laws, lightly enforced, provide government jobs and subsidies to those who have no more than two children and sanctions against those who do. National health officials in New Delhi noted that the central government was unable to regulate state decisions on population issues.

Use of Excessive Force and Other Abuses in Internal Conflicts

Terrorist and insurgent groups killed members of rival factions, government security forces, government officials, and civilians in Jammu and Kashmir, several northeastern states, and in the Naxalite belt in the eastern part of the country.

KILLINGS

Security forces often staged encounter killings to cover up the deaths of captured non-Kashmiri insurgents and terrorists from Pakistan or other countries. Human rights groups noted that police officials often refused to turn over bodies in cases of suspected staged encounters. The bodies were often cremated before their families could view them. Most police stations failed to comply with a 2002 Supreme Court order requiring the central government and local authorities to conduct regular checks on police stations to monitor custodial violence. According to the Jammu and Kashmir Human Rights Commission, insurgent groups killed 678 persons from April 2005 through March. Human rights groups maintained that, in Jammu and Kashmir and in the northeastern states, numerous persons continued to be held by military and paramilitary forces. Human rights activists feared that many of these unacknowledged prisoners were subjected to torture and that some may have been killed.

The AFSPA and the Disturbed Areas Act (DAA) remained in effect in the Jammu and Kashmir districts of Kathua, Udhampur, Poonch, Rajouri, Doda, Srinagar, Bud-gam, Anantnag, Pulwama, Baramulla, and Kupwara, where active and violent secessionist movements existed. The DAA gives police extraordinary powers of arrest and detention, and the AFSPA provides search and arrest powers without warrant. Human rights groups alleged that security forces operated with virtual impunity in areas under the act. The government did not repeal the act despite the January 2006 Supreme Court recommendation that the UAPA provides sufficient authority to combat the insurgency. Accountability by the Jammu and Kashmir government remained a serious problem. Human rights groups estimated that 30,000 to 35,000 persons died during two decades of conflict in Jammu and Kashmir. The Jammu and Kashmir governor, Lt. General S.K. Sinha, reported 39,000 deaths during the conflict. Security forces committed thousands of serious human rights violations over the course of the insurgency, including extrajudicial killings, disappearances, and torture.

Killings of security force members by insurgents and terrorists in Jammu and Kashmir declined to 330 during 2005, according to home ministry statistics. As of August 2005, the Jammu and Kashmir police claimed fighting in Kashmir had resulted in the deaths of 167 security forces, 359 civilians, and 622 insurgents. According to the Jammu and Kashmir police, militants killed 385 civilians, security forces killed 554 terrorists, and insurgents killed 177 members of the security forces. According to South Asia Terrorism Portal (SATP), at year's end, 164 civilians, 121 security force personnel, and 492 terrorists had been killed as a result of terrorist violence. There were continuing reports of civilians killed in crossfire in Jammu and Kashmir during the year. Terrorists and insurgents operating in Rajouri, Poonch, Udhampur, and Doda areas of Jammu and Kashmir repeatedly targeted the minority Pandit (Hindu Brahmin) community, killing entire families in several incidents throughout the year.

There were no further developments regarding the RR killing in 2006 of a 62-year-old village headman, Sanaullah Magray. The army had said the killing was a case of mistaken identity and that the villager had entered an ambushed area and ignored warnings to stop. While the government conducted an investigation and the army ordered a separate inquiry into the incident, authorities did not take corrective action to resolve this case during the year. As in previous years, tension along the Line of Control (LOC) in Kashmir was minimal. The Home Ministry reported no cases of artillery shelling, mortar, or small arms fire across the LOC or on the Siachen glacier. The government did not take action to resolve the February 2006 army killing of four youths in Kupwara district. While the NHRC had asked the Jammu and Kashmir government to provide a detailed report of the killing, the government had not done so by year's end.

In the northeast, human rights groups observed that violence persisted despite ongoing talks between separatist groups and state government officials and a 1997 government cease-fire. In August the government and the National Socialist Council of Nagaland Isak-Muivah (NSCN-IM) extended the cease-fire indefinitely. Factional violence between the NSCN-IM and the National Socialist Council of Nagaland Khaplang (NSCN-K) continued, resulting in numerous deaths. The Institute for Conflict Management's provisional data for 2007 indicates that of the 108 people killed by insurgency violence, 88 were killed due to intra-factional insurgent fighting. On December 17, the NSCN-K, NSCN-IM, and the Naga National council agreed to a six-month cease-fire agreement. On February 2, Border Security Force members operating near Mayai Leikai, Heirok Part II, in Manipur, beat and arrested Wairokpam Ibosana after blaming him for sheltering members of the People's Liberation Army.

On April 6, police commandos stopped three persons riding a moped through Imphal West. According to Human Rights Alert, the persons attempted to flee but police caught them and shot them. Witnesses reported that police then fired blanks at the crowd seeking to aid the victims. Police stated that they acted in self-defense after the young men threw hand grenades at the officers. On August 11, according to Human Rights Alert, members of the AR killed Md. Ramesh and Md. Isir. AR claimed they killed three members of the People's United Liberation Front, but the victims' families denied that the victims had any connection with armed groups. The families filed formal complaints at Heingang police station.

According to the Home Affairs Annual Report, 76 districts in the nine states of Andhra Pradesh, Bihar, Chhattisgarh, Jharkhand, Orissa, Maharashtra, Madhya Pradesh, Uttar Pradesh and West Bengal were affected by Naxalite violence. Chhattisgarh was a center of Naxalite activity, with over 350 insurgent-related casualties from January to December. In Chhattisgarh, the government touted the Salwa Judum Movement, a village level self-defense militia created in June 2005, as a successful counterweight to the Naxalite threat. Naxalite retaliations against the movement resulted in violent civil conflict in Dantewara district and a large number of civilian deaths.

Throughout the year, according to data compiled from news reports by SATP, 619 deaths related to Naxalite violence occurred throughout the country. These deaths occurred during Naxalite attacks on Internally Displaced Persons (IDP) camps, government installations, police patrols, and remote villages, and in police-Naxalite skirmishes. Of the 336 individuals killed in Chhattisgarh, 93 were civilians, 170 police personnel (regular forces, as well as Special Police Officers) and 73 were alleged Naxalites. According to Andhra Pradesh police, Maoists killed 44 civilians throughout the year. The police were responsible for 47 encounter killings of Maoists during the year, compared with 110 in 2006.

During the year SATP reported 426 deaths related to insurgency in Assam, where the United Liberation Front of Assam (ULFA) continued its violent campaign against Hindi-speakers from mainland India. From January through December, ULFA militants killed more than 110 persons in bomb attacks in the Dibrugarh, Tinsukia and Sivsagar districts of Assam. From January through December 18, SATP reported the following deaths as a result of insurgency-related violence in the seven northeast states: 445 civilians, 65 security forces, and 470 militants.

ABDUCTIONS

Human rights groups maintained that, in Jammu and Kashmir and in the northeastern states, numerous persons continued to be held by military and paramilitary forces. Human rights activists feared that many of these unacknowledged prisoners were subjected to torture and that some may have been killed. There were no reliable figures for disappearances in Jammu and Kashmir during the year. According to Association of Parents of Disappeared Persons (APDP) and other NGOs such as ACHR and SAHRDC, the number of newly reported disappearances decreased compared with the early years of the conflict. Reports varied widely on the number of disappearances that occurred in that area. For example, the Jammu and Kashmir Government stated in 2003 that 3,931 persons had disappeared in the state since the insurgency began in 1990, compared with an APDP estimate of approximately 8,000 to 10,000.

ACHR reported in September 2005 that more than 6,000 cases of disappearances remain unresolved in the state. There was virtually no information about the fate of individuals who disappeared since the beginning of the Jammu and Kashmir insurgency. On December 31, the United Liberation Front of Barak Valley insurgents along the Assam-Mizoram border kidnapped three persons, including the son of a Congress party leader and demanded a ransom of approximately $25,000 (1,000,000 rupees).

Section 2 Respect for Civil Liberties, Including:

a. Freedom of Speech and Press

The constitution provides for freedom of speech and expression; however, freedom of the press is not explicitly mentioned. The government generally respected these rights in practice. An independent press, a somewhat effective judiciary, and a functioning democratic political system combined to ensure freedom of speech and of the press. Under the 1923 Official Secrets Act, the government may prosecute any person who publishes or communicates information that could be harmful to the state. However, no cases were reported during the year.

Designed to be a self-regulating mechanism for the press, the Press Council is a statutory body of journalists, publishers, academics, and politicians, with a government-appointed chairman, that investigates complaints of irresponsible journalism and sets a code of conduct for publishers nationwide. This code includes a commitment not to publish stories that might incite caste or communal violence. The council publicly criticized newspapers or journalists it believed had broken the code of conduct, especially regarding communal violence or vandalism.

Independent newspapers and magazines regularly published and television channels regularly broadcast investigative reports, including allegations of government wrong doing, and the press generally promoted human rights and criticized perceived government lapses. Most print media and 80 percent of television channels were privately owned. However, by law only government-controlled radio stations were allowed to report news over the radio. With the exception of radio, foreign media generally was allowed to operate freely, and private satellite television was distributed widely by cable or satellite dish, providing competition for Doordarshan, the government-owned television network. While the public frequently accused the government network of manipulating the news in the government's favor, some privately owned satellite channels often promoted the platforms of political parties their owners supported.

The government often held foreign satellite broadcasters, rather than domestic cable operators, liable under civil law for what it deemed objectionable content on satellite channels—notably, tobacco and alcohol advertisements and adult content. AM radio broadcasting remained a government monopoly. Private FM radio station ownership was legal, but licenses only authorized entertainment and educational content. Local editions of foreign press were prohibited; however, the government allowed country-specific editions published by a local company, with no more than a 26 percent foreign partnership.

The authorities generally allowed foreign journalists to travel freely, including in Jammu and Kashmir, where they regularly met with separatist leaders and filed reports on a range of issues, including government abuses. The Newspapers Incitements to Offenses Act remained in effect in Jammu and Kashmir, which allows a district magistrate to prohibit publication of material likely to incite violence; however, newspapers in Srinagar reported in detail on alleged human rights abuses by the government and regularly published separatist Kashmiri groups' press releases.

There were some attacks on the media that were apparently intended to harass or inhibit the free expression of opinions. On May 9, a faction of Tamil Nadu's ruling DMK party set fire to the *Dinakaran* newspaper offices in Madurai, killing two employees of the newspaper and a security guard. According to the newspaper's staff, the police were present but did nothing to prevent the mob from entering the compound. The mob reportedly was enraged by a published survey in the newspaper that showed their leader, a son of the Tamil Nadu Chief Minister, trailing in the race to succeed the Chief Minister. In August members of the Shiv Sena party damaged the office of *Outlook*, a weekly in Mumbai, to protest the weekly's description of Shiv Sena founder Bal Thackeray as one of the "villains" of India. No one was injured.

In August the Manipur government imposed restrictions on the publication of insurgent group statements they deemed subversive or threatening to the state, following an August 1 incident in which insurgent groups planted a bomb at the office of the daily newspaper *Sangai Express*. In August suspected Communist Party of India (Marxist) (CPI(M)) workers assaulted three journalists of the Malayala Manorama Group during a demonstration at Kannur. The attackers also shouted slogans against the alleged political bias of the newspaper and its television channel.

Violent intimidation of the press by terrorist groups in Jammu and Kashmir caused significant self-censorship, according to journalists based in the state. During the year the threat of losing government revenue contributed to self-censorship by smaller media outlets that relied heavily on state government advertising for their survival. Despite the fact that local police filed a case, there were no developments in the June 2006 death of Arun Narayan Dekate, a rural correspondent with the Marathi daily *Tarun Bharat*, killed by unknown assailants. According to press reports, Dekate had exposed and informed police about an illegal gambling racket headed by alleged gambling boss Dhampal Bhagat. In June the Indian Federation of Working Journalists protested police and government inaction over Dekate's murder. By year's end no suspects had been identified and the police investigation was still pending.

The government maintained a list of banned books that may not be imported or sold in the country. Censors claimed that some books, such as Salman Rushdie's *Satanic Verses*, aggravated communal tensions. On August 9, three legislators of the All India Majlis-e-Ittehadul Muslimeen in Hyderabad attacked Taslima Nasreen for alleged anti-Muslim remarks. The Bangladesh-born writer was there for the release of the Telugu version of her book *Sokhe*. In November Nasreen self-censored her autobiography, *Dwik-handita*, after a series of protests in West Bengal led the state government to ask the author to leave the state. The national government granted

Nasreen asylum in New Delhi but noted that those living in asylum should behave a "certain way: and not disturb public harmony." At year's end charges had not been filed.

In Uttar Pradesh the AHRC reported that the executive magistrate in the Varanasi district assaulted several journalists who attempted to lodge a complaint against treatment of journalists in the area. In March and April 2006 the government of Rajasthan banned *Haqeeqat* (Reality), a Hindi translation of a controversial anti-Hindu book by Kerala-based evangelist M.G. Mathew, claiming it would incite communal violence, and held Samuel Thomas, president of Emmanuel Ministries International (EMI), a Christian charitable institution, in judicial custody from March 17 to May 2 for distributing the publication. The book *Wo Sharm Se Hindu Kahate Hain Kyon?* (Why Do They Say With Shame They Are Hindus) was banned at the same time as Haqeeqat. A government censorship board reviewed films before licensing them for distribution, censoring material it deemed offensive to public morals or communal sentiment.

Internet Freedom

The Informational Technology Act provides for censoring the Internet on public morality grounds, and defines "unauthorized access to certain types of electronic information" as a crime. According to Reporters without Borders, the law theoretically allows police to search the homes or offices of Internet users at any time without a warrant, but that claim had not been tested in court. The government retained the right to limit access to the Internet, specifically information deemed detrimental to national security. The act requires Internet cafes to monitor Internet use and inform the authorities of offenses.

Academic Freedom and Cultural Events

The government continued to apply restrictions to the travel and activities of visiting experts and scholars. In 2003 the Ministry of Human Resources Development (HRD) passed academic guidelines requiring all central universities to obtain HRD permission before organizing "all forms of foreign collaborations and other international academic exchange activities," including seminars, conferences, workshops, guest lectures, and research. While the restrictions remained in force, in most cases, the HRD ultimately permitted the international academic exchanges to take place after bureaucratic delays. During 2006 the Ministry of Home Affairs denied visa to 21 scholars. During the year the Ministry of Home Affairs denied visa to three scholars.

In February cinema owners and distributors in Gujarat refused to screen the film *Parzania*, arguing that its depiction of a Parsi family suffering during the 2002 violence would rekindle communal tension. Hindutva groups threatened to attack theaters that showed the film. The Indian Censor Board had approved the film for countrywide distribution, and the film was shown elsewhere in India. In April the Supreme Court directed the government of Maharashtra to drop criminal proceedings against a foreign scholar. The Government of Maharashtra had banned his book on the 17th century Maratha warrior Shivaji and had charged him with defaming the king and disrupting communal harmony. At year's end, despite the Supreme Court judgment, the Government of Maharashtra had not lifted the ban on the book.

In May Vishwa Hindu Parishad (VHP)-Bajrang Dal activists vandalized the work of art student Chandramohan Srimantula at M.S. University, Vadodara. Initially, the Gujarat police arrested the student for "hurting religious sentiments." Police released him after five days, with assurances that he would not leave the country, after one of his teachers posted bail for him. University Vice Chancellor Manoj Soni suspended Arts Faculty Dean Shivaji Pannikar, allegedly for his support of his student's right to exhibit the works. In December Shiv Sena activists attacked an art exhibition by self-exiled artist M.F. Hussain at Delhi's India International Center because they found his portraits of Hindu goddesses to be obscene.

b. Freedom of Peaceful Assembly and Association

The law provides for freedom of assembly and association,

and the government generally respected this right in practice.

Freedom of Assembly

The authorities normally required permits and notification prior to holding parades or demonstrations, and local governments ordinarily respected the right to protest peacefully, except in Jammu and Kashmir, where the local government sometimes denied permits to separatist parties for public gatherings and detained separatists engaged in peaceful protest. During periods of civil tension, the authorities may ban public assemblies or impose a curfew under the Criminal Procedure Code.

There were some instances of demonstrations where security forces either claimed harsh tactics were warranted or failed to protect demonstrators from violence. On May 18, in Hyderabad, police fired on a crowd protesting a bombing earlier that day at the city's historic Mecca Masjid mosque, killing five persons. After an inquiry, the government awarded each victim's family $12,500 (491,000 rupees) and one government job. On July 28, Andhra Pradesh police shot and killed six villagers in Mudigonda in the Khammam district after a two month political protest demanding free land for the poor. The government announced compensation of $12,500 (491,000 rupees) and a government job for one family member of each person killed, as well as two acres of agricultural land and education for victims' children.

Freedom of Association

The law provides for the freedom of association, and the government generally respected this right in practice. NGOs must secure approval from the Ministry of Home Affairs before organizing international conferences. Human rights groups contended that this provided the government with substantial political control over the work of NGOs and restricted their freedom of assembly and association. NGOs alleged that some members from abroad were denied visas arbitrarily.

c. Freedom of Religion

The law provides for secular government and the protection of religious freedom, and the central government generally respected these provisions in practice; however, occasionally the government did not act effectively to counter societal attacks against religious minorities and attempts by state and local governments to limit religious freedom. This failure resulted in part from legal constraints inherent in the country's federal structure and in part from shortcomings in the law enforcement and judicial systems. There is no state religion, although the fact that the majority of citizens are Hindus adversely affected on occasion the religious freedom of others. Some Hindu hard-liners interpreted ineffective investigation and prosecution of their attacks on religious minorities as evidence that they could commit such violence with impunity.

Legally mandated benefits were assigned to certain groups, including some defined by their religion. For example, the government allowed educational institutions administered by minority religions to reserve seats for their coreligionists even when they received government funding. Benefits accorded Dalits (formerly known as "untouchables") were revoked once they converted to Christianity or Islam, but not to Buddhism or Sikhism, ostensibly because once a Dalit converted to Christianity or Islam, he or she would no longer technically be a Dalit.

The Religious Institutions (Prevention of Misuse) Act of 1988 criminalizes the use of any religious site for political purposes or the use of temples to harbor persons accused or convicted of crimes. While specifically designed to deal with Sikh places of worship in Punjab, the law applies to all religious sites. The Religious Buildings and Places Act requires a state government-endorsed permit before construction of any religious building. The act's supporters claimed that its aim is to curb the use of Muslim institutions by Islamic extremist groups, but the measure became a controversial political issue among Muslims.

The states of Arunachal Pradesh, Chhattisgarh, Madhya Pradesh, and Orissa have laws against forcible conversions. On May 25, the Gujarat High Court ordered police to drop a case filed under Gujarat's anticonversion law on the grounds the law was not fully operational, as the Governor of Gujarat had refused to sign it. The Court instructed the Director General of Police to notify all state police about the decision. In March 2006 the Rajasthan government introduced and the state assembly passed legislation banning conversions by "force, allurement, or fraudulent means." The Governor of Rajasthan refused to sign her state's anticonversion law, effectively nullifying it. In May 2006 the Tamil Nadu Assembly repealed the Tamil Nadu Prohibition of Forcible Conversion of Religion Act, 2002.

In May the Andhra Pradesh Government enacted the "propagation of other religion in places of worship or prayer (Prohibition)" Law. The Andhra Pradesh Government passed an ordinance forbidding the distribution of literature or other propagation of one religion within the vicinity of designated places of worship of a different religion. The Andhra Pradesh assembly passed an act modeled on this ordinance on July 23. At year's end only Hindu sites had been notified, and authorities had not prosecuted anyone under this act.

While there were some reported arrests throughout the country, there were no convictions under anticonversion laws during the year. Reports from faith-based NGOs and the media indicated that there were four arrests under the anticonversion laws in Andhra Pradesh, 14 in Chhattisgarh, 28 in Madhya Pradesh, two in Orissa, and one in Uttar Pradesh between July 2005 and June 2006. In most cases police released on bail those arrested, often after a night in jail. Faith-based NGOs alleged that this was a systematic strategy to discourage Christian prayer meetings. There is no national law barring a citizen or foreigner from professing or propagating his or her religious beliefs; however, the law prohibits visitors in the country on tourist visas from engaging in religious proselytizing without prior permission from the Ministry of Home Affairs. During the year, state officials continued to refuse permits to foreign missionaries to enter some northeastern states on the grounds of political instability in the region.

Missionaries and religious organizations must comply with the Foreign Contribution (Regulation) Act (FCRA) of 1976, which restricts funding from abroad. The government can ban a religious organization that violates the FCRA, provokes intercommunity friction, or has been involved in terrorism or sedition. The legal system accommodates minority religions' personal status laws, and there were different personal laws for different religious communities. Religion-specific laws are paramount in matters of marriage, divorce, adoption, and inheritance. The personal status laws of the religious communities sometimes discriminated against women.

The law limits inheritance, alimony payments, and property ownership of persons from interfaith marriages and prohibits the use of churches to celebrate marriage ceremonies in which one party is a non-Christian. Clergymen who contravene its provisions could face up to 10 years' imprisonment. However, the act does not bar interfaith marriages in other places of worship.

In response to EMI headquarters' distribution of *Haqeeqat,* deemed disrespectful of Hindu beliefs, a prominent Hindu leader offered a bounty of $26,000 (1.15 million rupees) for the mission archbishop's "head on a plate." According to the media, Hindu activists attacked a school run by EMI and burned an effigy of its founder. In February 2006 the Government of Rajasthan suspended the registration of EMI property and froze its assets. By the end of 2006, EMI's bank account had been reopened and its registration had been restored. In May a bomb explosion killed nine persons and injured more than 50 others in the Mecca Masjid in Hyderabad. At year's end, Harkat-ul-Jehad-i-Islami activist Mohammed Abdul Sahed alias Bilal remained the key suspect in the attack.

On July 28, according to the All India Christian Council, authorities in Mayurbhanj, Orissa, arrested two Catholic nuns reportedly on false charges of forcible conversion and torturing students in their school; on February 22, Hindu extremists reportedly demolished a church building under construction at Chandrasekharpur, Bhubaneswar, and on February 28, Hindu radicals entered the campus of Believers Church Bible College at Brajarajnagar, Jharsuguda, Orissa. There were no updates concerning the April 2006 communal clashes between Hindu and Muslim residents in Aligarh, the March 2006 Hindu attack on Muslim shops in Goa, or the May 2006 police killing of two Muslim protesters in Gujarat. The government did not take action on the investigation of the September 2006 attacks against Muslim worshipers in Maharashtra.

SOCIETAL ABUSES AND DISCRIMINATION

Several human rights and religious freedom NGOs, including the All-India Christian Council and the All-India Catholic Union (AICU), expressed concern over continued anti-Christian violence in several states governed by the Bharatiya Janata Party (BJP) and claimed that some of the attackers had affiliations with the Hindu extremist group Rashtriya Swayamsevak Sangh (RSS). The AICU reported there were approximately 190 cases of persecution against Christians throughout the country and noted that the intensity of attacks on Christians increased. Unlike previous years, NGO contacts reported that attacks against Christians occurred in more urban areas. On September 10, a group of approximately 35 people from the Hindu extremist group RSS beat the principal of a Bible college in Geddalhalli village on Hennur Road in Bangalore. On December 5, a group destroyed machinery at a Church construction site in north Delhi.

On December 24, a Hindu group led allegedly by a leader of the RSS shot at two Christian children in the Kand-hamal district of Orissa. A VHP leader leading an anticonservation drive in the area was also injured. The events started a series of communal clashes in the tribal-dominated Kandhamal and Phulbani districts of eastern Orissa, provoking the Prime Minister to call for calm and a return to peace, and ask the state government to ensure security for Christians. A group of NGOs submitted a memorandum to the chairperson of the NHRC alleging that 5,000 persons had been affected by these attacks and about 600 houses had been damaged. They also alleged that the police had sided with the perpetrators of violence and dissuaded the victims from lodging complaints.

The Bangalore-based Global Council for Indian Christians (GCIC) reported a series of attacks against Christian groups in Karnataka following the founding of the short-lived BJP coalition with the Janata Dal. According to GCIC, on September 30, a group of alleged Bajrang Dal activists attacked a church at Kodlipet in Kodagu district, injuring several people. Similarly, on October 7 in Mayasandra village of Tumkur district, Hindu extremists attacked and seriously injured a Christian missionary while he was conducting a service. Muslims in some Hindu-dominated areas continued to experience intimidation and reported a lack of government protection, resulting in their inability to work, reside, or send their children to school. In some areas, primarily in Gujarat, Hindutva groups displayed signs stating "Hindus only" and "Muslim-free area." Hindutva is the ideology that espouses politicized inculcation of Hindu religious and cultural norms above other religious norms.

There were also allegations of prohibitions on the Muslim call to prayer. Hindu organizations frequently alleged that Christian missionaries forced or lured Hindus, particularly those of lower castes, to convert to Christianity. In Christian majority areas, there were occasional reports that Christians harassed members of other communities. On September 21, the body of Rizwanur Rehman, a Muslim who had married the daughter of a Hindu businessman, was found by the railway tracks in Kolkata. Rehman reportedly had been intimidated and threatened by the police, whom the businessman had approached for help in breaking up the interreligious relationship. Amid public protests, the police commissioner stepped down after being held responsible for undue interference in personal issues. The high court ordered a CBI inquiry into Rehman's death. A CBI report indicated "suicide prompted by circumstances" was the cause of Rehman's death.

Most of the Jews from India emigrated to Israel in 1948. There are believed to be only 13 Indian-born Jews from seven families still living in Kochi and approximately 40 Jews living in Delhi. Small but active communities remain in Mumbai. Most of the Jews from Mumbai are known as Baghdadi Jews who come from Iraq, Iran, Syria and Afghanistan and are thought to have arrived 250 years ago. In Northeastern India, an estimated 9,000 Indians started practicing Judaism in the 1970s, saying they were a lost tribe and descendants of the tribe of Manasseh. In recent years, over 1,400 members of the community emigrated to Israel.

d. Freedom of Movement, Internally Displaced Persons, Protection of Refugees, and Stateless Persons

The law provides for freedom of movement, and the government generally respected this in practice; however, in certain border areas the government required special permits. Security forces often searched and questioned occupants at vehicle checkpoints, mostly in troubled areas in the Kashmir Valley or after major terrorist attacks. The government also completed construction (except in areas of difficult terrain) of a 330-mile security fence along the LOC in Jammu and Kashmir, causing occasional difficulties for local residents, as it cut through some villages and agricultural lands. The government erected the security fence to stop arms smuggling and infiltration by Pakistani-based terrorists or insurgents. The government attributed a decline in insurgent crossings during the year in part to the fence.

Under the Passports Act of 1967, the government may deny a passport to any applicant who "may or is likely to engage outside India in activities prejudicial to the sovereignty and integrity of India." In the past, the government used this provision to prohibit foreign travel by some government critics, especially those advocating Sikh independence, and members of the separatist movement in Jammu and Kashmir.

Unlike in previous years, there were no reports of the government using the issuance of passports or travel documents to restrict travel of separatist leaders in Jammu and Kashmir. However, citizens from Jammu and Kashmir continued to face extended delays, often up to two years, before the Ministry of External Affairs would issue or renew their passports. Government officials also regularly demanded bribes before issuing passports from Jammu and Kashmir that required special clearances. Applicants born in Jammu and Kashmir--even the children of serving military officers born during their parents' deployment in the state--were subjected to additional scrutiny, requests for bribes, and police clearances prior to passport issuance. There was no law banning forced exile and no reports of its use during the year.

Internally Displaced Persons (IDPs)

According to the Norwegian Refugee Council, regional conflicts in Jammu and Kashmir, Gujarat, and the northeast displaced at least 650,000 persons. Approximately 300,000 Kashmiri Pandits forced to flee the Kashmir Valley in the early 1990s after the outbreak of separatist violence remained in IDP camps in Jammu and New Delhi. They were unable to return to their homes in Jammu and Kashmir because of safety concerns, including the ongoing killings of Hindus in the state. According to the Ministry of Home Affairs' Annual Report for 2006-2007, there were 55,950 Kashmiri Pandit migrant families, of which 34,562 resided in Jammu, 19,338 in Delhi, and 2,050 in other states. There were 230 migrant families living in 14 camps in Delhi and 5,778 families in 16 camps in Jammu.

In October 2006 according to the National Commission for Minorities (NCM), 5,307 Muslim families still lived in "precarious conditions" in 46 makeshift camps across Gujarat following the violence in 2002. On August 11, Gujarat Chief Secretary Sudhir Mankad reportedly conceded in a meeting with the NCM that 3,600 families in 46 makeshift camps had not been able to return to their original residences. Mankad also acknowledged that many of the poorest families in the camps had not received "Antyodaya" cards, which allow them access to subsidized food grains. More than 87,000 persons lived under poor conditions in IDP camps in Assam as a result of ongoing violence in the northeast. According to press reports, nearly 2,000 families who were riot victims from the Kokrajhar, Bongaigaon, and Dhubri districts in Assam awaited rehabilitation grants sanctioned by the state government following the 1993-99 riots in these areas.

An NGO reported that the Assam state government released part of the grants during the year. The government also provided assistance to IDPs and allowed them access to NGO and human rights organizations during the year. As in previous years, there were no reports that the government attacked or forcibly resettled IDPs. There were no reports of government programs specifically designed to facilitate resettlement. During 2006 the Chhattisgarh government opened IDP camps in Dantewara district for tribals caught in fighting between Naxalites and activists of a counterinsurgent movement called "Salwa Judum."

An estimated 60,000 tribal villagers were encamped in 27 locations. By most accounts the camps lacked adequate shelter, food, and security. There were allegations of trafficking in persons in the camps. Civil society and media alleged there was trafficking in child soldiers by Naxalites and "Salwa Judum" activists. NGOs in Chhattisgarh also criticized the practice of hiring teenage children of police personnel slain in Naxalite attacks as "Bal-police (child police.)" The children were not given actual policing duty but ran errands in police stations. Several such "Bal-police" continued to be employed in police stations in Madhya Pradesh and Chhattisgarh.

Protection of Refugees

The law does not provide for the granting of asylum in accordance with the 1951 UN Convention relating to the Status of Refugees and its 1967 protocol, and the government has not established a system for providing protection to refugees or asylum seekers. In practice, the government provided some protection against refoulement, the return of persons to a country where there is reason to believe they feared persecution, to Tibetans and Sri Lankans. The government provided temporary protection to certain individuals who may not qualify as refugees under the 1951 Convention and the 1967 protocol. According to the Office of the UN High Commissioner for Refugees (UNHCR), by December 31, there were 11,406 refugees under UNHCR mandate in the country. Since 1960, the government has hosted approximately 110,000 de facto refugees from Tibet. During the year Tibetan leaders in India stated that the government treated them extremely well.

The government generally denied NGOs, international humanitarian organizations, and the office of the UNHCR direct access to refugee and IDP camps, particularly in Mizoram. However, UNHCR was given limited access and maintained a local office in Tamil Nadu. The UNHCR had no formal status, but the government permitted its staff access to refugees living in urban centers. The government did not formally recognize UNHCR grants of refugee status, although it provided "residential permits" to many Afghans and Burmese. The government considered Tibetans and Sri Lankans in settlements and refugee camps to be refugees, and provided assistance to them, but since it regarded most other groups, especially Bangladeshis, as economic migrants, it did not provide them with aid. However, in recent years, a number of court rulings extended protection to refugees whom the government had formerly considered economic migrants.

The government permitted recognized refugees to work, and the state and central governments paid for the education of refugee children and provided limited welfare benefits. According to NGOs, conditions in the Sri Lankan refugee camps were generally acceptable, although much of the housing, as well as water and sanitation facilities, were of poor quality. The UNHCR continued to meet outside the camps with Tamil refugees considering voluntary repatriation. The NGO Organization for Eelam Refugee Rehabilitation had regular access to the camps during the year. The government provided refugees with subsidized rice and other essential goods. As of December 28, a total of 73,300 Sri Lankan refugees resided in 117 refugee camps in Tamil Nadu.

The central government and that of Tamil Nadu jointly provided monthly cash payments (up to $10 per person) and food subsidies to the refugees. The refugees were free to move in and out of the camps, but they must return for periodic roll calls. The refugees were subject to surveillance by police, and housing and sanitation were very poor. Refugee children were generally enrolled in local schools. Those living in the country not formally recognized as refugees included approximately 80,000 Chakmas and approximately 200,000 Santhals, both from Bangladesh, who remained in Arunachal Pradesh, Mizoram, and Assam. In addition, there were Afghans, Iraqis, and Iranians without valid national passports living in the country. The government chose not to deport them, issued them renewable residence permits, or ignored their presence. Due to financial and other reasons, many refugees were unable or unwilling to obtain or renew their national passports and could not regularize their status.

UNHCR provided refugee status and assistance to approximately 1,800 Chins from Burma living in New Delhi. However, UNHCR did not have access to the larger population of ethnic Chin living in the northeastern states. An estimated 80,000 Chins lived and worked illegally in Mizoram. NGOs estimated that, in 2005, 10,000 Chins with alleged ties to Burmese insurgent groups were expelled to Burma, where the military government reportedly jailed them. Mizoram human rights groups estimated that approximately 31,000 Reangs, a tribal group from Mizoram displaced by sectarian conflict, remained in six camps in North Tripura. Conditions in these camps were poor, and the Tripura government asked the central government to allot funds for their care. More than 1,000 Hmar refugees, one of the numerous tribes that belonged to the Chin-Kuku-Mizo tribe, were reportedly displaced in and around Mizoram, some of them from Manipur.

In 2005 the Supreme Court ordered the Ministry of Home

Affairs, the election commission, and the governments of Mizoram and Tripura to resettle approximately 40,000 displaced Reangs and add them to the electoral rolls. To date, approximately 1,000 Reangs have been resettled in Mizoram. The Bru National Liberation Front (BNLF) and Mizoram government agreed on a $6.3 million (277.9 million rupees) financial package and paved the way for the return of Reang IDPs in North Tripura. Section 3 Respect for Political Rights: The Right of Citizens to Change Their Government. The constitution provides citizens with the right to change their government peacefully, and citizens exercised this right in practice through periodic, free, and fair elections based on universal suffrage.

Elections and Political Participation

The country has a democratic, parliamentary system of government, with representatives elected in multiparty elections. The government changed hands following free and fair national parliamentary elections in April and May 2004. Parliament sits for five years unless dissolved earlier for new elections, except under constitutionally defined emergency situations. Citizens elected state governments at regular intervals, except in states under the president's rule. On May 11, elections in Uttar Pradesh resulted in Dalits winning a majority of seats in the State Assembly. Political parties could operate without restriction or outside interference. In July Pratibha Patil became the country's first female President. There were 73 women in the 784-seat national legislature, two in the 32-member cabinet of ministers, and eight among the 47 Ministers of State.

Numerous women were represented in all major parties in the national and state legislatures. The constitution reserves 33 percent of seats for women in elected village councils. The constitution reserves seats in parliament and state legislatures for scheduled tribes and scheduled castes in proportion to their population. Indigenous peoples actively participated in national and local politics.

CORRUPTION AND TRANSPARENCY

The law provides criminal penalties for official corruption; however, the government did not implement the law effectively, and officials frequently engaged in corrupt practices with impunity. The World Bank's worldwide governance indicators reflect that corruption was a severe problem. Both the Election Commission and Supreme Court upheld mandatory disclosures of criminal and financial records for election candidates. However, election campaigns for parliament and state legislatures often were funded with unreported money, and the government failed to combat the problem. In 2005 the media highlighted a videotape showing 11 members of parliament accepting bribes. No one faced legal action related to that bribery.

In July 2006 the government launched a national antiburglary campaign to raise public awareness of the right to information. The 2005 Right to Information Act (RTI) mandates stringent penalties for failure to provide information or affecting its flow and requires agencies to self-reveal sensitive information. While the government took extended periods of time to reply to information requests, local community members as well as noncitizens could access the RTI online portal to get information on personal documentation, city plans, and other public records. Nine state governments have right to information laws.

Section 4 Governmental Attitude Regarding Intranational and Nongovernmental Investigation of Alleged Violations of Human Rights:

A wide variety of domestic and international human rights groups generally operated without government restriction, investigating abuses and publishing their findings on human rights cases; however, in a few circumstances, groups faced restrictions. Government officials were somewhat cooperative and responsive to their views. In February 2006 the Ministry of Home Affairs barred 8,673 organizations from seeking foreign funds under the Foreign Contribution and Regulation Act (FCRA), reportedly for failing to provide the proper paperwork. NGOs called the FCRA restrictive and claimed that the government failed to notify organizations when the requisite paperwork was needed.

Some domestic NGOs and human rights organizations faced intimidation and harassment by local authorities, such as in May 2006 when the Maharashtra Home Ministry placed 57 NGOs under investigation for allegedly assisting Maoist groups. Human rights monitors in Jammu and Kashmir were able to move around the state to document human rights violations, but they were at times restrained or harassed by security forces, counterinsurgents, and police. HRW visited Kashmir in 2006 and was able to meet a broad range of civilian and official contacts.

The main domestic human rights organization was the government-appointed NHRC, which acted independently and often voiced strong criticism of government institutions and actions. Some human rights groups claimed the NHRC was nevertheless hampered by institutional and legal weaknesses. The NHRC received 82,233 complaints of human rights abuses during the year. The NHRC did not have the statutory power to investigate allegations and could only request that a state government submit a report, which state governments often ignored. Human rights groups such as ACHR claimed that the NHRC did not register all complaints, dismissed cases on frivolous grounds, did not adequately protect complainants, and did not investigate cases thoroughly.

The NHRC could investigate cases against the military and recommend—but not mandate—compensation to victims of abuse. On January 15, the NHRC announced interim relief of about $700,000 (28,000,000 rupees) to 89 victims of violence committed during the Tamil Nadu and Karnataka joint search operation for a criminal named Veerapan. Many states had their own human rights commissions, and human rights groups alleged that state human rights commissions were more likely than the NHRC to be influenced by local politics and less likely to offer fair judgments.

During the year the NHRC developed guidelines for

handling child rape cases and issued a report and recommendations on missing children. International human rights organizations faced difficulties obtaining visas to visit the country for investigative purposes, and in-country, there was occasional harassment. In March the AHRC reported that the District Magistrate of Leh ordered the arbitrary closure of some NGOs and banned the public use of the materials produced by these organizations. International humanitarian organizations, such as ICRC, had access to most regions, with the exception of the northeast and Naxalite-controlled areas. UNHCR did not have access to the Northeast; Burmese Chin and others refugees had to travel to New Delhi to seek refugee status.

In 1996 the Supreme Court ordered the NHRC to investigate and address all issues that arose from the mass cremations following the Punjab disappearances from the 1980s to mid 1990s. The NHRC recommended that the government should provide compensation of $6,250 (249,600 rupees) to the next of kin for each of the 195 identified deceased persons as well as $4,375 (175,000 rupees) to the next of kin for the remaining 1,103 identified deceased person whose remains were cremated by the Punjab police.

As of October, only 17 of the 28 states had state human rights commissions, as recommended by the 1993 Protection of Human Rights Act (PHRA). The Jammu and Kashmir state legislature established its state human rights commission in 1997. The commission does not have the authority to investigate alleged human rights violations committed by members of the security forces. In August 2006 the government amended the PHRA to strengthen the NHRC by removing the requirement of prior notification and approval for visits to state-managed prisons. However, NGOs stated the government did not address the NHRC's inability to inquire independently into human rights violations by the armed forces, initiate proceedings for prosecution, and grant interim compensation. Further, NGOs argued that the amendment did not guarantee the NHRC's financial independence or the extension of its mandate to investigate abuses more than one year old.

Section 5 Discrimination, Societal Abuses, and Trafficking in Persons:

The law prohibits discrimination on the basis of race, sex, religion, place of birth, or social status, and the government worked to enforce these provisions with varying degrees of success.

WOMEN

The law sets criminal penalties for rape, including spousal rape, but the government did not enforce the law effectively. Although the government prosecuted rape cases during the year, only 10 percent were adjudicated fully by the courts, and police typically failed to arrest rapists, perpetuating a climate of impunity. Rape and other violent attacks against women continued to be a serious problem. While official statistics confirmed a dramatic increase in reported crimes against women, this may have reflected a growing sense of security in reporting such crimes. The 2005-2006 National Family Health Survey (NFHS) reported that only one in four abused women had ever sought help to end the violence they experienced and only two percent of abused women had ever sought help from the police.

According to the NCRB, two rapes took place every hour nationwide, and 19 of 20 victims knew their attackers. NGOs asserted that rape by police, including custodial rape, was common. The 2005-2006 NFHS reported that one-third of women ages 15 to 49 had experienced physical violence and approximately one in ten had been a victim of sexual violence. In May 2005 parliament amended the Code of Criminal Procedure to stipulate mandatory DNA tests in all rape cases. In an effort to protect women from sexual assault by police, the bill also prohibits the arrest of women after sunset and before sunrise except in "exceptional circumstances."

Upper caste gangs used mass rape to intimidate lower castes, and there were reports of gang rape as punishment for alleged adultery or as a means of coercion or revenge in rural property disputes. In response to an NHRC recommendation to investigate a January 2006 incident in which 18 armed insurgents belonging to the United National Liberation Front and Kanglaipak Communist Party raped 25 women in Manipur, the government of Manipur established a Justice Commission to investigate the case. At year's end, the investigation was underway. Dalit women were often singled out for harassment. For example, they were occasionally stripped by mobs and paraded in public for offending persons belonging to higher castes.

In November, an Adivasi (tribal) woman was stripped in public and assaulted during an Adivasi rally in Guwahati, Assam, by local shop-owners in retaliation after the Adivasis ransacked shops. The CBI reported numerous rape and looting incidents that occurred during the Nandigram massacres. There was no response to an NHRC request of state officials to investigate an August 2006 case in which upper caste men raped seven Dalit women in Lakshim-pursarai district. At year's end a district court in Bhandara was hearing the case regarding the September 2006 incident in which Kunbi caste villagers allegedly killed four members of a Dalit family in Khairlanji village of Bhandara district of Maharashtra.

The Protection of Women from Domestic Violence Act, passed in October 2006, recognizes all forms of abuse against women in the home, including physical, sexual, verbal, emotional, and/or economic abuse. Domestic violence includes actual abuse or the threat of abuse. The law recognizes the right of women to reside in a shared household with her spouse or partner even while the dispute continues, although women can be provided with alternative accommodations, to be paid for by the spouse or partner. The law also provides women with the right to police assistance, legal aid, shelter, and access to medical care. The new law bans harassment by way of dowry demands and empowers magistrates to issue protection orders where needed. Under the new Act, spousal rape is also criminalized. Punishment ranges from jail terms of up to one year and/or a fine of approximately $450 (19,800 rupees). As of November the Act had been ratified by four of

28 state governments: Andhra Pradesh, Tamil Nadu, Uttar Pradesh, and Orissa. Citizens registered 8,000 nationwide criminal cases under the Act since it was brought into force.

The law forbids the provision or acceptance of a dowry, but dowries continued to be offered and accepted, and dowry disputes remained a serious problem. The law also provides extensive powers to magistrates to issue protection orders to deal with dowry-related harassment and murder. Andhra Pradesh police reported 541 dowry deaths; Tamil Nadu recorded 208; and the Karnataka State Commission for Women recorded 68 dowry deaths during the year. NCRB reported 11,300 incidents of dowry deaths that occurred from 2004-6 in the country.

Under the law courts must presume that a husband and/or his family are responsible if his wife dies an unnatural death during the first seven years of marriage and if harassment is proven. NGOs claimed that accused in-laws often avoided legal consequences by bribing police officials. According to press reports, the rate of acquittal in dowry death cases was high, and due to court backlogs, cases took an average of six to seven years to conclude. Madhya Pradesh, Kerala, Bihar, and several other states had a chief dowry prevention officer, although it was unclear how effective these officers were. Madhya Pradesh also required that all government servants seeking to marry produce a sworn affidavit by the bride, the groom, and his father that no dowry exchanged hands.

The government banned sati, the practice of burning a widow on the funeral pyre of her husband, and there were few instances of sati in recent years. Honor killings continued to be a problem, especially in the northern states of Punjab and Haryana. Human rights organizations estimated that up to 10 percent of all killings in those two states were honor killings. In July 2006 the Supreme Court condemned honor killings and directed police to take action against anyone harassing couples that married despite objections by their caste and religious communities.

On July 15, police in Punjab arrested three suspects wanted in connection with the killing of a Jat woman, Baljeet Kaur, and her Valmiki husband. Kaur's father and brothers had kidnapped her and her husband and killed them for marrying without familial consent. In August 2006 Delhi police arrested Deep Chand and his three sons for the alleged honor killing of Chand's daughter, Kamlesh, because she refused to marry the man her parents selected. When interrogated, all four assailants confessed to killing the woman and leaving her body by a railway track. At year's end the case was pending in court.

In 2006 there were 20 cases reported in Assam in which informal courts passed death sentences on women labeled witches. Assam Police, in coordination with organizations like the All Bodo Students Union, launched project Prahari in 2000 to create public awareness of the problem.

While the act of prostitution is not illegal, most activities surrounding prostitution are illegal. The law criminalizes the selling, procuring, and exploiting of any person for commercial sex as well as profiting from the prostitution of another individual. Unlike in previous years, Section 8 of the Immoral Trafficking Prevention Act (ITPA), which criminalizes the act of solicitation for prostitution, was infrequently used to arrest and punish women and girls who were victims of trafficking. The country is a significant source, transit point, and destination for trafficked women.

In October the Jammu and Kashmir High Court criticized the CBI's "lax and deficient" handling of the Sabeena case and directed the CBI to redo the investigation. In April 2006 authorities arrested the former state minister for Tourism in Jammu and Kashmir and his wife Sabeena for allegedly trafficking and blackmailing approximately 40 local girls into prostitution. Sexual harassment of women in the workforce included physical and verbal abuse from male supervisors, restricted use of toilets, and the denial of lunch breaks. In January 2006 the Supreme Court instructed all state chief secretaries to comply with its mandate that all state departments and institutions with over 50 employees establish committees to deal with matters of sexual harassment.

The law prohibits discrimination in the workplace; however, enforcement was inadequate. Employers paid women less than men for the same job, discriminated against them in employment and credit applications, and promoted women less frequently than men. State government and NGO-supported microcredit programs for women began to have an impact in many rural districts. In March 2006 the government amended the law to provide flexibility for women to work in factories on the night shift. In 2005 the All-India Muslim Personal Law Board adopted new *talaq* ("divorce" in Urdu) guidelines, which called for the husband to pay compensation to the wife's family in case of divorce, equality in property rights, protection against physical and emotional abuse by husbands, and assurances that remarried women will be able to maintain contact with their families. In November 2006 the All India Shi'a Personal Law Board unanimously approved a model *nikahnama* (marriage contract) that provided women the same divorce rights as men.

In 2005 parliament removed discriminatory clauses from the Hindu Succession Act by giving equal inheritance rights to Hindu, Buddhist, Jain, and Sikh women, including giving married daughters the same inheritance rights as male heirs. In November 2006 the Supreme Court ruled that if a woman remarries after divorce, her custody rights over the child born in wedlock would not be affected. Many tribal land systems, notably in Bihar, denied tribal women the right to own land. Shari'a (Muslim traditional law) determines land inheritance for Muslim women rather than state statutes. Other laws relating to the ownership of assets and land accorded women little control over land use, retention, or sale. However, several exceptions existed, such as in Ladakh and Meghalaya, where women traditionally controlled family property and enjoyed full inheritance rights.

CHILDREN

The Registration of Birth and Death Act, 1969, provides for

state governments to frame rules establishing the registration machinery and procedures in their state. Accor-ding to the National Commission on Population, approximately 55 percent of national births are covered by the registration machinery at present, and the level of registration varies substantially across states. During the year, as part of a pilot program in cooperation with the UNICEF, the government of Kolkata provided birth certificates to 50,000 street and working children belonging to some of the most disadvantaged castes/ classes. The constitution provides free, compulsory education for children between the ages of six and 14 years of age; however, the government did not enforce this provision. In practice, children in poor and rural areas often did not attend school. UNICEF and the National Institute of Educational Planning Administration reported that approximately 60 percent of the 203 million children between the ages of six and 14 were in schools, and net attendance in the primary level was 66 percent of enrollment.

The 2005-6 NFHS indicated that girls are almost as likely to attend primary school as boys. Nationwide, 85 percent of boys and 81 percent of girls ages six to 10 attend primary school. By ages 15 to 17, 49 percent of boys and only 34 percent of girls attend school. The government launched programs to increase literacy among girls from marginalized social groups through the National Program for Education of Girls at Elementary Level and the Kasturba Gandhi Balika Vidyalaya. A January 2006 report commissioned by the Human Resource Development Ministry showed that lower caste and Muslim student attendance rates were much lower than those of children in high caste families. The report noted that nationwide seven percent of children were out of school, although the rate varied widely from one region or social or religious group to another.

While both boys and girls had legal access to state-provided medical care, society and families tended to seek out care more regularly for boys. Abuse of children in both public and private educational institutions was a problem.

Although corporal punishment is banned, schoolteachers often used it on their students. On August 4, Brijesh Prajapati, a sixth grade student at Kakraiya Primary School in Farukhabad, Uttar Pradesh, died after succumbing to injuries sustained by a beating from his teacher, Kishan Singh. Authorities suspended Singh and the school principal for failing to provide the student emergency medical care. Singh was arrested on a murder charge and at year's end, the case was pending.

In August 2006 Parliament passed the Juvenile Justice (Care and Protection of Children) Amendment Bill, which is the primary law for not only the care and protection of children but also for the adjudication and disposition of matters relating to children in conflict with law. In 2005 the juvenile justice court ruled that any failure by school management or teachers to protect students from sexual abuse or provide them with a safe school environment is punishable with a prison term of up to six months. Despite these legal protections, there were societal patterns of neglect and physical, sexual, and emotional abuse of children, and child labour was a problem

In April the Ministry of Women and Child Development released its first study of child abuse; according to the comprehensive two-year survey, two out of three children were physically abused with a higher percentage reported among children aged five to 12. The states of Andhra Pradesh, Assam, Bihar, and Delhi consistently reported the highest rates of abuse in all forms. Sixty five percent of school-going children reported facing corporal punishment. Fifty-three percent of children reported experiencing one or more forms of sexual abuse; and 22 percent experienced severe sexual abuse. Sponsored by the Childline India Foundation, UNICEF, NGOs, the government and private individuals, a toll-free 24-hour help line for children in distress was available in 72 cities. The "Childline" number could be accessed by either a child or an adult to request immediate assistance, including medical care, shelter, restoration, rescue, sponsorship, and counseling.

The 1939 child marriage restraint act prohibits child

marriage, a traditional practice that occurred throughout the country, and sets the legal marriage age for girls at 18 and boys at 21. In December 2006 the government tightened its legislation against child marriage and passed the Prohibition of Child Marriage Bill declaring that existing child marriages were null and void. Despite legal constraints, according to a 2005 Health Ministry report on population and development, half of all women were married by the age of 15. The 2005 NFHS reported that forty-five percent of women (18-24) and 32 percent of men (18-29) marry before the legal age of 18 years and 21 years, respectively. According to another 2005 report from the Office of the Registrar General of India, 240 girls die every day due to pregnancy-related complications in early child marriages.

The International Center for Research on Women (ICRW) concluded that those married under the age of 18 were twice as likely to be abused by their husbands compared with women married later; they were also three times more likely to report marital rape. ICRW reported that child brides often showed signs of child sexual abuse and posttraumatic stress. Child marriages also limited girls' access to education and increased their health risks, since they had higher mortality rates and exposure to HIV/AIDS than girls married after 18. Trafficking and commercial sexual exploitation of children was a serious problem. According to UNICEF, in 2004 the country supplied half of the one million children worldwide who entered the sex trade.

Female feticide was an acute problem in Punjab, Haryana, and Rajasthan. The states of Punjab, Haryana, Gujarat, Uttar Pradesh, Himachal Pradesh, Delhi, parts of Tamil Nadu, Maharashtra, and Karnataka reported particularly low female/male ratios. Nationally, there were only 933 girls per 1,000 boys. In 14 districts of Haryana and Punjab there were fewer than 800 girls per 1,000 boys. The low male/female ratio resulting from female feticide encouraged families in Punjab and Haryana to import brides from Bihar and other northeastern states.

Baby girls were either aborted or, after birth, left in the

cold to contract pneumonia and perish. NGOs alleged that medical practitioners and government workers often were complicit in pushing or persuading women to abort their girl children. Sex determination tests are illegal under the 1994 Pre-Natal Diagnostic Techniques Act. However, NGOs reported that some family planning centers continued to reveal the sex of fetuses. According to the NGO IFES, feticide is a $116 million industry. Officials claim that the practice is prominent among educated and urban sections of society. On June 15, the *Hindustan Times* reported a Haryana Health Department raid on a maternity clinic run by an unlicensed doctor, A.K. Singh. Officials arrested Singh and seized a portable ultrasound machine and equipment used to terminate pregnancies, in addition to a large quantity of fetal remains.

Haryana has registered 35 cases against doctors illegally conducting sex determination tests in the past two years. The Health and Family Welfare Ministry set up a "National Support and Monitoring Cell" to curb the practice of female feticide by targeting and apprehending those who carry out or abet female feticide. The government also encouraged education campaigns to change the social preference for male children and launched a "Save the Girl Child" campaign designed to highlight the achievements of young girls. During the year the New Dehli municipal government sponsored a program that provided every girl born in a government hospital with a gift deposit of $114 (5,000 rupees) that accumulated interest and could be cashed once the girl reached the age of 18. Authorities from the village of Lakhanpal in central Punjab ran a program to end female feticide, and as a result, the latest figures showed 1,400 female and 1,000 male births. Historically, Punjab had the lowest girl-to-boy ratio in the country, at 776 to 1,000.

TRAFFICKING IN PERSONS

The ITPA prohibits trafficking in human beings; however, trafficking in persons remained a significant problem. The law provides for imprisonment for seven years to life for offenses committed against a child (under 16), or seven to 14 years for offenses against minors between 16 and 18. The minimum term of imprisonment for brothel keeping was one year for the brothel offense and seven years' to life imprisonment for detaining a person, with or without consent, for prostitution. The country was a significant source, transit point, and destination for trafficking victims, primarily for the purposes of prostitution and forced labour. Many girls were internally trafficked for the purpose of forced marriages, while other persons, including children, were trafficked for bonded labour. Women and girls were lured into commercial sexual exploitation through deception and expectations of opportunities in other parts of the country.

Tribal women and those from economically depressed areas were particularly vulnerable to sexual exploitation. Extreme poverty, combined with the low social status of women, often resulted in parents handing over their daughters to strangers for what they believed was employment or marriage. In some instances, parents received payments or the promise that their children would send wages home. To a lesser extent, the country was a point of origin for women and children trafficked to other countries in Asia, the Middle East, and the West for forced domestic servitude or commercial sexual exploitation. Men were also trafficked to the Arabian Gulf for involuntary servitude in the construction sector. Women from Kerala reportedly were trafficked into commercial sexual exploitation and abusive domestic employment in the Gulf.

Women and girls as young as seven years of age were trafficked from economically depressed neighborhoods in Nepal, Bangladesh, and rural areas of the country to the major prostitution centers of Mumbai, Kolkata, and New Delhi. In West Bengal, organized traffic in illegal Bangladeshi immigrants was a principal source of bonded labour. Kolkata was a transit point for traffickers sending Bangladeshis to New Delhi, Mumbai, Uttar Pradesh, and the Middle East. The government cooperated with groups in Nepal and Bangladesh to deal with the problem and began to negotiate bilateral antitrafficking agreements, particularly through the

South Asian Association for Regional Cooperation.

Trafficking of children into domestic servitude and sweatshops remained a problem. States in the northeast region (Assam, Meghalaya, Nagaland, Manipur, Mizoram, Tripura, Arunachal Pradesh, Sikkim), and Bihar served as main source areas for domestic servants in Kolkata, Delhi, Hyderabad, Mumbai, and, to a certain extent, Bangalore. The increasing number of domestic servant recruitment agents suggested that large trafficking networks operated in the region. In many cases women and girls were first brought by agents to Siliguri, West Bengal; they then traveled to different destinations with the traffickers. Often traffickers used truck drivers to carry women and girls from the northeast through National Highway 31, which connects the region to the central part of the country.

A survey by the Indian National Trade Union Congress noted that trends in trafficking could be determined by monitoring the reports of "missing girls" filed by parents in northeast states. The report stated that 40 percent of the police officials interviewed were unaware of the growing trade in women and children. Traffickers usually targeted minors and Dalit women. A study prepared by Bhoomika Vihar, an NGO from Bihar, said that out of the 173 identified cases of women who had become victims of the sex trade, 85 percent were minors and half were Dalits. The report claimed that trafficking, although not often reported, occurred almost everywhere. Conflicts in the northeastern states made women and children highly vulnerable.

The National Commission for Women reported that trafficked women and children were frequently subjected to extortion, beatings, and rape. Although a few women were abducted forcibly or drugged, most were trafficked through false offers of marriage, employment, or shelter. Victims of trafficking often did not speak the local language and were subject to threats, including emotional blackmail, violence, and confinement, as well as the threat of apprehension by authorities, detention, prosecution, and deportation. Women involved in prostitution in Mumbai and Kolkata claimed that harassment, extortion, and occasional arrests on soliciting charges usually characterized police intervention. NGOs alleged that corruption at the enforcement level helped perpetuate trafficking.

NGOs knowledgeable about the trafficking situation frequently identified traffickers and the locations of girls being held captive by brothel owners. However, other NGOs were reluctant to trust police with this information, due to their past conduct in brothel raids and the likelihood that many trafficking victims would be arrested and revictimized rather than assisted by such raids. Several NGOs had significant successes, however, in working with police to target brothels with children.

During the year charges were brought against more than 1,400 traffickers in Andhra Pradesh, Bihar, Goa, Tamil Nadu, Uttar Pradesh and West Bengal, and 27 individuals were convicted on trafficking charges in Andhra Pradesh, Delhi, Maharashtra and Tamil Nadu. Eight joint operations between the Andhra Pradesh and Maharashtra police resulted in an additional 107 victims rescued and 77 traffickers arrested. A total of eight police Anti-Human Trafficking Units (AHTU) were created (three in Andhra Pradesh, three in Bihar, one in Goa, and one in West Bengal).

Although arrests and prosecutions under the ITPA increased, the rate of trafficking convictions remained low, and collection of law enforcement data was difficult because there was no national system for collecting arrest information. ITPA's requirement of an inspector-level officer to investigate cases made charges unlikely. Many police officials preferred to use India Penal Code (IPC) provisions to arrest traffickers, both because they claimed to have more success in getting convictions and because many IPC provisions were not bailable.

The ITPA required police to use only female police officers to question girls rescued from brothels. The ITPA also required the government to provide protection and rehabilitation for victims. In the past, the vast majority of arrests made under ITPA were for solicitation rather than for trafficking or trafficking-related crimes, but this is no longer the norm. Most police no longer arrested trafficked women and children for soliciting, and such arrests diminished significantly. The government significantly increased police training and modestly improved interstate coordination of antitrafficking efforts, cooperated with NGOs, supported awareness campaigns, and increased the number of shelter facilities available to rescued trafficking victims. However, NGOs claimed that the conditions of shelters were not always suitable. They also stated that persons claiming to be parents would remove girls and reinsert them into the industry.

The Ministry of Women and Child Development improved coordination with its state counterparts and NGOs to deliver counseling, legal aid, medical care, repatriation and restoration services, as well as awareness generation programs such as peer education, rallies, posters, booklets, and street plays. The Home Ministry, through its Bureau of Police, Research and Development, continued a law enforcement training program, considered a significant achievement by NGOs, to sensitize police and improve trafficking arrests and convictions. In July the West Bengal government allotted $254,712 (10,000,000 rupees) to form a network coordinated by the women and child development and social welfare departments to fight human trafficking. The government of Andhra Pradesh offered $255 (10,000 rupees) in compensation to trafficking victims, similar to that available to victims under the Bonded Labour Act. In September 2006 the Ministry of Home Affairs created a "nodal cell" to coordinate national law enforcement efforts against human trafficking. That office convened quarterly meetings of state representatives and ensured that information on trafficking in persons was shared across the country.

PERSONS WITH DISABILITIES

The constitution does not explicitly mention disability as a prohibited ground for discrimination. The Persons with

Disabilities Act (PDA) provides equal rights to all persons with disabilities; however, advocacy organizations acknowledged that its practical effects were minimal, in part due to a clause that makes the implementation of programs dependent on the "economic capacity" of the government. Widespread discrimination occurred against persons with physical and mental disabilities in employment, education, and access to health care. Neither law nor regulation required accessibility for persons with disabilities. Government buildings, educational establishments, public transportation and public spaces throughout the country had almost no provisions for wheelchair access. According to the 2001 census, there were 22 million persons with disabilities in the country, but NGOs estimated the actual number to be much higher.

A World Bank report noted that eight percent of the population is disabled. The employment rate of disabled individuals decreased from 42.7 percent in the 1990s to 37.6 per cent in the 2000s. Despite the PDA's requirement that three percent of public sector jobs be reserved for people with physical, hearing, and visual disabilities and the government's development of a list of jobs for people with these disabilities, only 0.44 percent of public sector employees are disabled. The government increased funds to NGO partners to implement the national policy. The PDA provides benefits to private companies at which persons with disabilities constitute more than five percent of the workforce. The government recently began implementing these benefits. Private sector employment of persons with disabilities remained low.

According to the Central Coordination Committee established under the PDA, approximately 100,000 children with special needs attended approximately 2,500 schools that provided integrated and inclusive education or nonformal education. The Human Resource Development Ministry reported in January 2006 that children with mental disabilities had the lowest rate of school attendance out of any group at 53 percent, followed by the speech disabled at 57.5 percent and the hearing disabled at 68 percent.

The Equal Opportunities, Protection of Rights and Full Participation Act of 1995 stipulates a three percent reservation in all educational institutions for persons with disabilities; however, statistics showed that only about one percent of students had disabilities. In 2005 the Times Insight Group reported that most colleges and universities were unaware of the law. The Ministry of Social Justice and Empowerment offered 500 educational scholarships to persons with disabilities to pursue higher education. However, university enrollment of students with disabilities was still very low for reasons including inaccessible infrastructure, poor availability of resource materials, non-implementation of the three percent reservation, and harassment. In 2005 the central board for secondary education issued guidelines requiring barrier-free education in schools, colleges, libraries, and hostels. It also took steps to provide Braille books to educational institutions.

Hospitals were overcrowded and often served primarily to house persons with disabilities. Patients generally were ill-fed, denied adequate medical attention, and kept in poorly ventilated halls with inadequate sanitary conditions. At the end of the year, no action was taken on the 2001 NHRC recommendation to remove all persons with mental illness from jails. The disability division of the Ministry of Social Justice and Empowerment delivered rehabilitation services to the rural population through 16 district centers. A national rehabilitation plan committed the government to provide rehabilitation centers to more than 400 districts, but services were concentrated in urban areas. The impact of government programs was limited due to the concentration of funding provided to a few organizations.

NATIONAL/RACIAL/ETHNIC MINORITIES

The law provides that the practice of untouchability, which discriminated against Dalits and others defined as scheduled castes, is a punishable offense; however, such discrimination remained ubiquitous, stratifying almost every segment of society. The law gives the president the authority to identify historically disadvantaged castes, Dalits, and tribal persons (members of indigenous groups historically outside the caste system) for special quotas and benefits. These "scheduled" castes, Dalits, and tribes were entitled to affirmative action and hiring quotas in employment, benefits from special development funds, and special training programs. According to the 2001 census, scheduled castes, including Dalits, made up 16 percent (166.6 million) of the population, and scheduled tribes eight percent (84.3 million). In December 2006 parliament passed a bill to reserve 27 percent of seats at educational institution for scheduled castes and backward classes.

Dalits faced significant discrimination despite laws to protect them; they often were socially prohibited from using the same wells, attending the same temples, and marrying upper-caste Hindus. They faced social segregation in housing, land ownership, and public transport and were the majority of bonded labourers. Many Dalits were malnourished and lacked access to health care and basic education. There were episodes of vigilante retribution against Dalits who tried to assert their rights. While rare in urban settings, examples of intolerance occurred regularly in rural areas. Many rural Dalits worked as agricultural labourers for caste landowners without remuneration. Reports from the UN Committee on the Elimination of Racial Discrimination found systematic abuse against Dalits, including torture and extrajudicial killings, and an "alarming" rate of sexual violence against Dalit women. NGOs reported that crimes committed by upper caste Hindus against Dalits often went unpunished, either because the authorities failed to prosecute such cases or because the crimes were unreported by victims fearing retaliation.

On September 11, villagers of Multai, in Baitul district of Madhya Pradesh, allegedly killed two members of the Pardhi tribe, and destroyed 62 houses of Pardhi tribe members. The villagers suspected some members of the Pardhi community of having raped a higher caste woman. Although police arrested the alleged rapists, the villagers insisted on carrying out reprisals against nearly 300 members of the Pardhi settlement, who fled to Bhopal, the state capital. While the National Commission for Minorities visited the relief camp in Bhopal and the village and urged the Pardhi to return to Multai, villagers remained adamant against the Pardhi's return to their village. At year's end police had registered a complaint about the murder and the destruction of the houses.

There were no updates regarding the January 2006 case in which a high-caste mob in the Vaishali district of Bihar burned alive a man, woman, and five of their children, despite direct involvement from the Bihar Chief Minister. The Scheduled Castes and Scheduled Tribes (Prevention of Atrocities) Act lists offenses against disadvantaged persons and prescribes stiff penalties for offenders; however, the Act had only a modest effect in curbing abuse, and there were very few convictions. Human rights NGOs alleged that caste violence was on the increase. Caste violence was especially pronounced in Uttar Pradesh, Bihar, Rajasthan, Madhya Pradesh, Tamil Nadu, Karnataka, and Andhra Pradesh. In July 2006 the Supreme Court passed a judgment stating that police and government are obliged to help inter-caste couples and prevent social ostracism. In September 2006 the Ministry of Social Justice and Empowerment directed state governments to increase the incentive for intercaste marriage to $1,050 (46,000 rupees). The central government pays 50 percent.

INDIGENOUS PEOPLE

The Innerline Regulations enacted by the British in 1873 provide the basis for safeguarding tribal rights in most of the northeastern border states, and in practice the regulations were followed. These regulations prohibit any nontribal person, including citizens from other states, to cross an inner boundary without a valid permit. No rubber, wax, ivory, or other forest products may be removed from the protected areas without prior authorization. No outsiders were allowed to own land in tribal areas without approval from tribal authorities.

The 2001 census indicated that 8.2 percent of the population belonged to scheduled tribes. According to the Indian Confederation of Indigenous and Tribal Peoples, 80 percent of the tribal population lived below the poverty level, and more than 40,000 tribal women, mainly from Orissa and Bihar, were forced into situations of economic and sexual exploitation.

There was encroachment on tribal land in almost every eastern state, including by illegal Bangladeshi immigrants, and by businesses that illegally removed forest and mineral products. Numerous tribal movements, such as the Jharkhand movement in Bihar and the Bodo movement in Assam, demanded the protection of tribal land and property rights. As a result of complaints, tribal-majority states were created in 2000 from the Jharkhand area of Bihar and the Chhattisgarh region of Madhya Pradesh, and authorities provided local autonomy to some tribal people in the northeast.

On November 26, a CPM operation in Munnar, Kerala, claimed approximately 1,500 acres of land after party cadres forcibly removed 200 tribal families from the area. In Assam, conflict between indigenous Assamese tribals, including the Bodos, and nonnative "tea tribes" or Adivasis increased with the Adivasi demand for Scheduled Tribe (ST) status under the constitution. On November 24, the All Assam Adivasi Students Union organized a violent rally in Guwahati, Assam, to demand ST status. One person died, scores of others were injured and one Adivasi woman was stripped by a local citizen before police arrived and took control of the situation.

Civil rights organizations, working with indigenous people in Kodagu district of Karnataka, accused the state government of actively promoting the establishment of jungle lodges in the Nagarhole National Park at their expense. The groups alleged that 1,600 families had been evicted since 1972, and that individuals removed from the park area were settled in locations that lacked fresh drinking water, electricity, health care, adequate job opportunities and access to forests. During 2006 the court committee found that only 250 of the

1,738 families had been relocated.

OTHER SOCIETAL ABUSES AND DISCRIMINATION

The law punishes acts of sodomy, buggery, and bestiality; however, the law was often used to target, harass, and punish lesbian, gay, bisexual, and transgender persons. Human rights groups argued that gay and lesbian rights were not addressed along with other human rights concerns in the country. Gays and lesbians faced discrimination in all areas of society, including family, work, and education. Activists reported that in most cases, homosexuals who did not hide their orientation were fired from their jobs. Homo-sexuals also faced physical attacks, rape, and blackmail. Police committed crimes against homosexuals and used the threat of arrest to coerce victims into not reporting the incidents.

Voices Against 377, a high-profile campaign to overturn Section 377, which outlaws homosexuality, led by writers Vikram Seth and Amartya Sen, continued at year's end. In February 2006 the Supreme Court ruled that the Delhi High Court should not have dismissed an earlier case brought by two NGOs on behalf of Seth and Sen and referred the case to the Delhi High Court. There were no further developments regarding this case during the year.

In March a new media outlet based in Kolkata, Ananda Bazar Patrika, reported the attack and killing of apparently effeminate men in Kolkata. No police cases were filed.

There were no developments in the January 2006 arrests of gay men in Lucknow through a sting operation in which police officers posed as gay men on the Internet and, after entrapping one man, forced the individual to call other gay men, also arrested. Several NGOs claimed that the arrests were illegal, that evidence against the men was fabricated, and that the police violated the men's right to privacy. There were no developments in the January 2006 complaint against two constables of the Azad Maidan police station for using decoys in a train station public toilet to entrap and extort money from gay men. The Azad Maidan police apprehended the two constables and handed them to railway police.

In March the UN Development Program (UNDP) released a report on "launda dancers", young men and boys hired to dance in women's clothing at marriage ceremonies and Hindu festivals in Bihar and Uttar Pradesh. Dancers were vulnerable to exploitation by orchestra leaders, who cheated them of earnings or forced them into prostitution. Sexual assault and gang rape by intoxicated clients were frequent and dancers were at high risk of contracting HIV/AIDS. Some laundas had illegal castrations to join the hijra (traditional transvestite) community, but they often suffered from post operation complications for which they could not get government medical care.

Authorities estimated that HIV/AIDS had infected approximately 5.1 million persons, and according to the International Labour Organization (ILO), 70 percent of persons suffering from HIV/AIDS faced discrimination. HRW reported that many doctors refused to treat HIV-positive children and that some schools expelled or segregated them because they or their parents were HIV-positive. Many orphanages and other residential institutions rejected HIV-positive children or denied them housing.

In August state government authorities readmitted five HIV-positive children who were denied education at the Mar Dionysius Lower Primary School Pampady, in the Kottayam District of Kerala. The five students were turned out of school in 2005 under pressure from parents of the other students. In 2004 a Mumbai High Court ruled that HIV-positive persons could not be fired on the basis of their medical status. However a July 2006 survey by the National Council for Applied Economic Research, the National AIDS Control Organization, and the UNDP revealed that 29 percent of persons living with HIV were refused loans and nearly 30 percent denied promotions. More than 16 percent were forced to resign from their jobs, and 10 percent forced to take voluntary retirement.

WORKER RIGHTS

a. Right of Association

The law allows workers to form and join unions of their choice without previous authorization or excessive requirements, and the government generally respected this right in practice. More than 400 million persons made up the country's active work force, and some 30 million of these workers were employed in the formal sector. The rest were agricultural workers and, to a lesser extent, urban nonindustrial labourers. While some trade unions represented agricultural workers and informal sector workers, most of the country's estimated 13 to 15 million union members were part of the 30-million-member formal sector. Of these 13 to 15 million, some 80 percent of the unionized workers were members of unions affiliated with one of the five major trade union centrals.

In practice legal protections of worker rights were effective only for the organized industrial sector. Outside the modern industrial sector, laws were difficult to enforce. The authorities generally prosecuted and punished those persons responsible for intimidation or suppression of legitimate trade union activities when the victims were members of nationally organized unions. Unaffiliated unions were not able, in any instance, to secure for themselves the protections and rights provided by law. Union membership was rare in the informal sector.

The Trade Union Act prohibits discrimination against union members and organizers, and employers were penalized if they discriminated against employees engaged in union activities.

b. The Right to Organize and Bargain Collectively

The law allows unions to conduct their activities without interference, and the government protected this right. Collective bargaining is protected by law, but is limited mostly to the private sector. Public service employees have very limited organizing and collective bargaining rights. When parties cannot agree on equitable wages, the government may establish boards of union, management, and government representatives to make a determination. Although a system of specialized labour courts adjudicates labour disputes, there were long delays and a backlog of unresolved cases. Public service employees have very limited organizing and collective bargaining rights.

Trade unions have a limited right to strike, and workers exercised this right. The Essential Services Maintenance Act allows the government to ban strikes in government-owned enterprises and requires conciliation or arbitration in specified essential industries; however, the Act is subject to varying interpretations from state to state. State and local authorities occasionally used their power to declare strikes illegal and force adjudication. The Industrial Disputes Act prohibits retribution by employers against employees involved in legal strike actions, and this prohibition was observed in practice.

The Supreme Court upheld a Kerala High Court verdict declaring all general strikes illegal and making organizers of such protests liable for losses caused by the shutdowns. While it is likely that the ruling was introduced to discourage political strikes, unions stated that it remained a potential threat to their activities. In 2004 the Supreme Court declared all strikes by government employees illegal; however, in practice this was not enforced. The law provides workers in export processing zones (EPZs) the right to join trade unions and bargain collectively, although EPZ workers often did not exercise their full labour rights. The 2001 Trade Union Act designates the EPZs as "public utilities" and requires a 45-day strike notice.

Entry into the EPZs ordinarily was limited to employees, and such entry restrictions applied to union organizers. While workers in the EPZs have the right to organize and to bargain collectively, union activity was rare. In addition, unions did not vigorously pursue efforts to organize private-sector employees in the years since EPZs were established. Most

EPZ workers were women. The International Confederation of Free Trade Unions reported that overtime was compulsory in the EPZs, that workers often were employed on temporary contracts with fictitious contractors rather than directly by the company, and that workers feared that complaints about substandard working conditions would result in their dismissal.

c. Prohibition of Forced or Compulsory Labour

The law prohibits forced or bonded labour, including by children; however, such practices remained widespread. The Bonded Labour System (Abolition) Act prohibits all bonded labour by adults and children. Offenders may be sentenced up to three years in prison, but prosecutions were rare. Enforcement of this statute, which was the responsibility of state and local governments, varied from state to state and generally was not effective due to inadequate resources and societal acceptance of bonded or forced labour. On the occasions when inspectors referred violations for prosecution, long court backlogs and inadequate funding for legal counsel frequently resulted in acquittals. NGOs estimated that there were 20 to 65 million bonded labourers in the country, including a large number of children. According to the Institute for Socio-Economic Development research on bonded labour in Bihar and Uttar Pradesh, the bondage of agricultural labourers was the main form of bondage in these two states. According to NGOs, nonagricultural sectors that had a high incidence of bonded labour were stone quarries, brick kilns, rice factories, jewelry, *beedi*-making (hand-rolled cigarettes), and carpet weaving.

Members of Scheduled Castes and tribes lived and worked under traditional arrangements of servitude in many areas of the country. In Arunachal Pradesh, the Nishi tribe traditionally subjugated the Sulungs or Puroiks as customary slaves who were not in debt to their masters but whose land and homestead were owned by their masters. Complete eradication of slavery remained difficult due to local customs and landlessness. The Ministry of Labour and Employment

(MOLE) partnered with the National Human Rights Commission and NGOs to investigate allegations of bonded labour. MOLE statistics showed a large decrease in the number of bonded labour cases brought before the courts in recent years, although the extent to which this reflected a decrease in incidents of bonded labour was in doubt. In one February rescue in Orissa, 26 persons were rescued from bonded labour in a brick kiln, with three of the owners of the kiln arrested. In May the British Broadcasting Company reported an estimate from a local labour union that 12,000 of the 60,000 people working in silk looms in Kancheepuram district in Tamil Nadu were bonded labourers.

d. Prohibition of Child Labour and Minimum Age for Employment

The law prohibits forced and bonded child labour; however, the prohibition was not effectively enforced, and forced child labour remained a serious problem. Estimates of the number of child labourers varied widely. The 2001 census recorded 12.66 million working children between the ages of five and 14, with 90 percent of child workers hailing from rural areas. The government's 2004 national survey estimated the number of working children in the age group of five to 14 at 16.4 million. However, NGOs reported that the number of child labourers was closer to 60 million.

According to 2001 census figures, out of the 226 million children between the ages of five and 14, 65.3 million (29 percent) did not receive any formal education. Most, if not all, of the 87 million children not in school did housework, worked on family farms, worked alongside their parents as paid agricultural labourers, or worked as domestic servants. Children worked in the informal sector, often in private homes, with the highest rate (15 percent) in Uttar Pradesh. Social acceptance of the practice, ineffective state and federal government enforcement of existing laws, and economic hardships contributed to the continued prevalence of child labour. Children often were sent away to work because their parents could not afford to feed them or to pay off a debt.

Officials claimed they were unable to stop this practice because the children were working with their parents' consent. Working conditions often amounted to bonded labour.

According to UNICEF, private companies in Andhra Pradesh reportedly employed 200,000 children in the hybrid seed industry. Most were girls between the ages of seven and 14 from other parts of the state. The majority were Dalits and members of economically disadvantaged castes and tribal groups forced to work in debt-bondage. They were routinely abused, subjected to dangerous pesticides, and denied access to education. Human rights organizations estimated that there were as many as 300,000 children working in the carpet industry. There was evidence that child labour was also used in the following industries: gemstone polishing, leather goods, sari weaving, beadwork, sporting goods, brassware, fireworks, footwear, hand-blown glass bangles, handmade locks, hand-dipped matches, hand-quarried stones, hand-spun silk thread, hand-loomed silk cloth, handmade bricks, and *beedis* (hand-rolled cigarettes). A number of these industries exposed children to hazardous work conditions.

According to UNICEF and Vikasa, a community-based organization in Magadi, the number of children involved in the silk spinning industry dropped to a handful due to competition from China and concerted action by the state government against employers of child labour. The Government of Karnataka, in partnership with UNICEF, continued to monitor the child labour situation and developed a bridge program to enable former child workers to enter the state-sponsored formal education system. NHRC officials said that implementation of existing child labour laws was inadequate, that administrators were not vigilant, and that children were particularly vulnerable to exploitation. In comparison to the magnitude of the problem, there were fewer prosecutions and convictions under the 1986 Child Labour Act because of administrative lapses and loopholes under the Act's definition of child labour. A child assisting his/her family is exempt from the provisions of the Act, and employers in cottage industries often exploited this to claim that the children were assisting the family.

There is no overall minimum age for child labour; however, work by children under 14 is prohibited in factories, mines, domestic work, roadside eateries, and other hazardous industries. In occupations and processes in which child labour is permitted, work by children was permissible only for six hours between 8 a.m. and 7 p.m. with one day's rest weekly. Those employers who failed to abide by the law were subject to penalties specified in the Bonded Labour System (Abolition) Act (such as fines and imprisonment) and to disciplinary action at the workplace. A ruling, effective October 2006, prohibits labour in domestic work and the hospitality industry for children under the age of 14, although child labour in some other nonhazardous industries is legally permissible. In September 2006 the Delhi High Court ordered the central and state governments to develop a plan to eradicate child labour in the capital area.

The law stipulates a penalty for employers of children in hazardous industries of $430 (20,000 rupees) per child employed, and establishes a welfare fund for formerly employed children. The government is required to find employment for an adult member of the child's family or pay $108 (5,000 rupees) to the family. According to the South Asian Coalition on Child Servitude, authorities were pursuing over 6,000 cases against employers. NGOs noted that requiring the government to pay the family of a child labourer or finding the adult family member a job could be a disincentive to investigating crimes. The government did not effectively implement the 2006 law banning child labour.

The country made moderate progress on child labour over the past year. MOLE began public campaigns to raise awareness and prevent child labour, and conducted video conferences with states to coordinate efforts. The MOLE, through its 250 National Child Labour Projects, rehabilitated more than 400,000 children after withdrawing them from work situations. In three separate operations in December 2006 and January, Delhi police worked with NGOs and the

ILO to rescue a total of 94 children from abusive child labour worksites. Between September and November 2006, New Delhi police rescued 140 children working in zari factories (embroidering or sewing beads and colored threads to fabric) and rice mills, but it was unclear if these children were placed in effective rehabilitation programs. In Maharashtra, a governmental task force freed more than 18,000 children through rescues and voluntary repatriations in the last year and a half, and made 36 slum areas in Mumbai totally child labour free. Spurred by government raids, many employers voluntarily repatriated several thousand child labourers from zari factories, leather workshops, and restaurants.

During the year Haryana and Punjab state governments attempted to ban child labour in their districts. In Punjab, an action plan and directions were sent to all district offices and departments in the state to ensure strict compliance. The Haryana government attempted to enforce its ban on child labour and opened 137 integrated child development projects within the state. In November, New Delhi labour officials conducted raids on sweatshops run by sub-contractors for garment manufacturer the Gap. More than 100 children were rescued, most under the age of 14. Despite a ban, child labour continued in Karnataka. Varying sources estimated the number of child workers to be as high as 150,000. The Ministry of Labour continued efforts to eradicate the practice through regular police raids and work with public schools to integrate rescued children into the mainstream. In January 2006 labour inspectors in Mysore, Karnataka, rescued 12 child workers from garages and roadside eateries. Charges were filed against employers, and rescued children were handed over to district child welfare committees for rehabilitation. Three former employers were awaiting trial at year's end.

Bihar is one of India's leading suppliers of children as cheap labour to other states. An estimated 25,000 children from Bihar are trafficked every year for child labour. Destination states are Delhi, Punjab, Uttar Pradesh, Gujarat, Maharastra, and Haryana. Trafficking for other purposes such as prostitution, begging, and organ trading also occurred. Bihar is the only state to establish a State Child Labour Commission. Twenty-five districts implemented National Child Labour Projects. During the year the Department of Labour formed a task force to rescue children from hazardous work and to prosecute guilty employers.

Employers in some industries took steps to combat child labour. The 2,500 members of the Carpet Export Promotion Council (CEPC), a quasi-governmental organization that received funding from the Ministry of Textiles, agreed to bar producers from purchasing hand-knotted carpets knowingly produced with child labour. The CEPC conducted inspections to insure compliance and allowed members voluntarily to use a government-originated label to signify adherence to the code of conduct. However, the CEPC stated that even with its programs, it was impossible to ensure that a carpet had been produced without child labour, given the difficulties of monitoring a decentralized and geographically dispersed industry.

Government authorities cooperated with various inter-governmental organizations and NGOs to rescue child workers and eliminate child labour. In November the Delhi government cooperated with NGO Bachpan Bachao Andolan and rescued 74 child labourers working in zari embroidery units in the Khanpur area of South Delhi. All of the children were from Bihar and most had been trafficked from their villages.

e. Acceptable Conditions of Work

State government laws set minimum wages, hours of work, and safety and health standards. The Factories Act mandates an eight-hour workday, a 48-hour workweek, and safe working conditions, which include adequate provisions for rest rooms, canteen, medical facilities, and proper ventilation. There was a minimum rest period of 30 minutes after every four hours of work and premium pay for overtime as mandated by law. These standards generally were enforced and accepted in the modern industrial sector; however, they were not observed in less economically stable industries or in the vast informal economy, which includes nearly 93 percent of the work force.

Minimum wages varied according to the state and to the sector of industry. Such wages were inadequate to provide a decent standard of living for a worker and family. Most workers employed in units subject to the Factories Act received more than the minimum wage, including mandated bonuses and other benefits. State governments set a separate minimum wage for agricultural workers but did not enforce it effectively. Some industries, such as apparel and footwear, generally did not adhere to a prescribed minimum wage. The enforcement of safety and health standards also was poor, especially in the informal sector. Industrial accidents continued to occur frequently due to improper enforcement of existing laws. Chemical industries had the highest number of accidents. Workers from scheduled castes and tribes often worked as rag pickers, recycling bits of trash under hazardous and generally deplorable conditions. Workers from these groups also cleaned sewers and drains of human excrement without proper equipment and under extremely unsanitary conditions.

The NHRC called for a report on the condition of tea garden workers in West Bengal, many of whom are women. Media reported in May that 750 workers died in the tea estates in the past year. Owners occasionally abandoned the estates without paying workers their dues, leaving them with no option but starvation and death. According to the media and NGOs, the miserable conditions in the tea estates also contributed to organized trafficking of girls. Safety conditions were better in the EPZs than in the manufacturing sector outside the EPZs. The law does not provide workers with the right to remove themselves from work situations that endanger health and safety without jeopardizing their continued employment. The country's undocumented foreign workers were not extended basic occupational health and safety protections.

5

Women and the Violence

Over the years, tremendous political and social turmoil has been generated in the state by the forces of religious fundamentalism and by an exclusionary nationalism that seeks to erode the cultural syncretism that is part of the ethos of Kashmir. These forces are responsible for the shutting down of dissenters who voice cultural critique, repression of women, political anarchy, economic deprivation, lack of infrastructure, and mass displacements that have been occasioned by these events. Since 1949, the United Nations and Pakistan have consistently demanded that a plebiscite be held in order to determine the wishes of the Kashmiri people. India uses Pakistan's reluctance to withdraw its forces and the decision of the United States government to supply arms to Pakistan in 1954 to justify its denial of plebiscite. Nearly 400,000 Indian army and paramilitary forces have been deployed in the state, in India's most beefed up counterinsurgency operation till date. Financing these operations has taken an enormous toll on the annual administrative budget of the state.

Kashmir lives in the unpleasant reality of Indian and Pakistani dominance, which is full of redoubtable paramilitary troops, barbed wire, and invasive searches; dispossessed youths trained in Pakistani training camps to unleash a reign of disorganized and misguided terror in the state; custodial killings in detention centers and mothers whose faces tell tales of woe waiting outside those gloomy detention centers to catch glimpses of their unfortunate sons (an exercise in futility);

burqa-clad women afraid of the wrath of fundamentalist groups as well as of paramilitary forces bent on undercutting their self-respect. The anarchy that pervades the cultural and political fabric of Kashmir has been stoked by government-sponsored militants and foreign mercenaries. In such an unwieldy situation, women are psychologically incarcerated.

Such occurrences do not enable an autonomous Kashmir life, devoid of the pressures that Kashmiris have been subjected to since 1947. The brutalization of the culture has been rendered more lethal by the socialization of Kashmiri boys and men into military culture. Within such a masculinist discourse and praxis the rigidly entrenched hierarchical relationship between men and women is inextricably linked with sexualized violence. Custodial disappearances, custodial deaths, bestial interrogation methods have indelibly scarred the psyche of the Kashmiri people. Parveena Ahangar is one of many unfortunate mothers whose son was a victim of custodial disappearance. Her son, Javed Ahmad, was picked up by the National Security Guards (NSG) in Batmaloo, Srinagar, Kashmir, on August 18, 1990 and taken to one of the interrogation centers which had reared their ugly heads all over the Valley. Javed was a school-going adolescent when the NSG suspected him of being affiliated with a militant organization and brusquely picked him up without a substantial rationale for questioning.

Parveena, a courageous and forthright woman, chose to shed the veil and the inhibitions imposed by her cultural mores in order to verbalize the agony of a wounded mother. Instead of lamenting voicelessly behind the closed portals of her cultural and societal mores, Parveena formed an organization called Association of Parents of Disappeared Persons (APDP), comprising bereaved mothers whose sons had been victims of custodial disappearances or custodial deaths. Politicians at the helm of affairs in the Valley have only managed to turn the groans of these mothers into screams that cut through the air, laden with pain and an unrequited longing for their children. In early 1999 Amnesty International estimated that since 1990, over eight-hundred people been victims of custodial disappearances; in August 2002 the Kashmir Times, local English daily, estimated the figure at 3,500 (Amnesty International, "If They are Dead Tell Us": Disappearances in Jammu and Kashmir. London: Amnesty International, Feb. 1999; "Militancy in Kashmir Valley Completes Fourteen Years," Kashmir Times, Aug. 2002 internet ed).

The members of the APDP mobilize the concept of protecting the dignity and rights of non-partisan citizens who do not have vested political interests. The APDP is an apolitical organization which doesn't receive funding from any regional or national political organization. The organization hasn't been patronized either by the establishment or by political parties in the opposition. She succeeded in assembling relatives of persons who had been subjected to unwarranted torture, death, solitary confinement, and other brutal methods while in the custody of police or military forces in various parts of the Valley. While foregrounding the trials and tribulations of such parents, Parveena, who hitherto had been unexposed to other political, cultural, and social perspectives, participated in conferences on human rights violations in the Philippines, Thailand, Indonesia, and even organized peaceful demonstrations in the backyard of India's political gurus and masters, New Delhi. She stuck to her convictions in the midst of forceful antagonism and even refused monetary compensation which was offered to her to forget "the unfortunate incident."

Parveena and other mothers like her seek to know the fate of their children who disappeared in the abyss of political and military oppression before life had a chance to beckon them. The unknown fate of their children is a constant presence, like a leaden sky whose clouds are getting lower and lower. The lack of closure in the lives of such parents makes their infernal existences unbearable. Their sagas evoke tragic destinies, unredeemed by justice. "There are many families of disappeared persons who are on the verge of starvation. There are hundreds of half-widows (grass widows), who are in a dilemma whether to remarry or not," says Parveena (Conversation with Parveena at her Residence in Srinagar, Kashmir, 2006). The unflinching courage of marginalized women like Parveena in their fight for justice in an era of rampant corruption symbolizes the self-actualization and intervention of Kashmiri women in patriarchal national history by speaking from their locations about the current political realities.

In contemporary Kashmiri society, the question of the role of women in the nationalist scenario remains a vexed one. As Ann McClintock observes about the role of the subaltern woman in "Third-World" societies, "Excluded from direct action as national citizens, women are subsumed symbolically into the national body politic as its boundary and metaphoric limit" (1997: 345). For instance, the only women's reactionary organization in Kashmir, Dukhtaran-e-Milat, claims that the image of woman as a burqa-clad faceless and voiceless cultural icon, devoid of the agency to pave a path of her own choosing, is sanctioned by the versions of religious scriptures that this vigilante group subscribes to and reinforces her strength and courage of conviction to sacrifice for the family. This vigilante group uses intimidating and questionable tactics to raid houses that allegedly have been converted into brothels and brutally censors romantic liaisons between college-going boys and girls.

The women members of Dukhtaran-e-Milat would perhaps never identify the modern Kashmiri woman with the liberated woman of the Western world. On the contrary, they make a facile attempt to reconstruct historical and cultural discourses in order to inspire the kind of cultural nationalism that fundamentalist politics requires. This organization advocates the creation of a homogeneous culture devoid of the freedoms that Kashmiri women have traditionally enjoyed. Their draconian methods to enforce purdah, reinforce a patriarchal structure in which an un-accompanied woman is rendered vulnerable, and curtail the mobility of the technology savvy youth is an attempt to arabize the syncretic ethos of Kashmir.

There seems to be insensitivity in such reactionary

organizations as well as in former and current regional and national administrations of the diverse interpretations of religious laws regarding the institutions of marriage, divorce, inheritance rights, etc.; of the rich heterogeneity of cultural traditions and to the paradoxes within them. The vociferous members of the Dukhtaran-e-Milat would better serve the female population of the state by campaigning for quotas for women in the legislative assembly, legislative council, parliament, and the judiciary. An increase in the female representation in these institutions of authority would facilitate a cultural shift in terms of gender role expectations, legitimizing a defiance of the normative structure. The intrusion of women in traditionally male domains would cause perceptible erosion in the structural determinants of sexualized violence. This form of empowerment would "frame and facilitate the struggle for social justice and women's equality through a transformation of economic, social, and political structures".

In the present scenario, no thought is given either by the state authorities or by insurgent groups to women who have been victims of the paramilitary forces and/or of militant organizations. Women in Kashmir have borne the brunt of the violence. In the absence of their menfolk, hapless women have been negotiating with officials and military personnel, both materially and sexually. Unfortunately, the innate conservatism of Kashmiri society disables women from overtly describing and condemning sexual exploitation. Kashmiri women are further dehumanized because of the self-denigration that accompanies physical defilement. There is no statistical data of rapes and molestations in the State because of the secrecy with which such bestial acts are shrouded. The validity of these fears were established by an Indian newspaper, which recently reported that, "There can be no two opinions that the women of Kashmir during the past two decades have been in the vanguard and have been fighting battles against all kinds of injustices and crimes against humanity committed by the State and by some dubious non-state actors". A large percentage of rape victims and war widows are afflicted with post traumatic stress disorder and are prone to suicidal tendencies.

Educated Kashmiri women like Dr. Hameeda Naeem, reader at the University of Kashmir, are unable to relate to the ideology of the Dukhtaran-e-Milat. Hameeda Naeem had articulately delineated the brutal human rights violations occurring in Jammu and Kashmir at the United Nations Conference in Geneva in 1996, after which the Government of India had impounded her passport, rendering it impossible to speak at other international for a. In the enlightening conversation that I had with Hameeda at my parents' house in Srinagar, Kashmir, she described the Dukhtaran-e-Milat as self-styled custodians of the Islamic faith, who had caricaturized Islam by reducing it to the veil. She categorically stated that the Dukhtaran-e-Milat did not represent all Kashmiri women and lacked the authority to enforce a code of conduct. I asked Hameeda how sixteen years of armed insurgency and counter insurgency had pervaded the social fabric, and what measures, if any, had been taken to redress the grievances of women adversely affected by militancy. Hameeda expressed an adverse judgment on the government of Jammu and Kashmir for having facilitated the psychological, sexual, economic, and emotional violation of women, particularly in insulated rural areas. The law of the jungle which prevails in those areas leaves no scope for the rehabilitation of the victims of violence.

The desecration of the political, social, and cultural landscape looms large in the lovely face of nature in its pure undesecrated majesty. The grievances of these lacerated hearts and aggrieved souls are, inevitably, not redressed. The unalloyed purity of nature and the spiritual illumination it inspires are indelibly tarnished. Although educated women desire persistently full participation in professional and political life, the damaging nexus between patriarchy and militarism has insidiously indoctrinated women to the extent of making a virtue of helplessness and destitution. Women in Kashmir now live in an unendurable atmosphere created by the acrimonious implementation of draconian laws. Indian paramilitary forces, militants, and mercenaries have unleashed indiscriminate violence in J & K which has metamorphosed the legendary beauty of Kashmir into an intolerable inferno of molten bodies and bottomless perdition.

No stringent and timely measures are taken to redress those wrongs. In effect, the Kashmiri woman is constructed as a parchment on which the discourses of religious nationalism, secular nationalism, and ethnonationalism are inscribed, and the most barbaric acts are justified by Indian paramilitary forces as means to rein in uncontrollable separatist forces and by militant organizations as means to restore the lost dignity of the "women." Women politicos in the current legislative assembly and legislative council of Jammu and Kashmir played the role of tokens who bolstered the social, cultural, and moral institutions that maintain a male-dominated power structure. Even those with access to the echelons of power refuse to engage "more effectively with the politics of affiliation, and the currently calamitous dispensations of power".

Despite its firm promise, the current state government has been unable to incorporate the Special Operations Group, a paramilitary division of the police accused of heinous human rights violations, entirely into the regular police force. The SOG continues to run amok and functions as an entity that only obeys the law of the jungle. Alongside the SOG, the Special Task Force, a militia group comprising renegade militants, has been incorporated into the regular police force as well but has not been disbanded. These forces have been deployed to handle extrajudicial matters in arbitrary ways and are responsible for gross misdemeanors against women. Why is gender violence such a consistent feature of the insurgency and counter-insurgency that have wrenched the Indian subcontinent for about decades? In nationalist rhetoric the equation of the native woman to the motherland has in recent days become more forceful. In effect, the native woman is constructed as a trough within which male aspirations are nurtured, and the most barbaric acts are justified as means to restore the lost dignity of the "women."

The story of the partition of India in 1947 into two separate nation-states, India and Pakistan, is replete with instances of fathers slaughtering their daughters in order to prevent them from being violated by the enemy; and women resorting to mass suicide to preserve the "honour" of the community. If a woman's body belongs not to herself but to her community, then the violation of that body purportedly signifies an attack upon the honour (izzat) of the whole community. In one instance, the crime of a boy from a lower social caste against a woman from a higher upper caste in the Meerawala village in the central province of Punjab in Pakistan in 2002 was punished in a revealing way by the "sagacious" tribal jury. After days of thoughtful consideration, this jury gave the verdict that the culprit's teenage sister, Mai, should be gang-raped by a group of goons from the wronged social group: The tribal jury ruled that to save the honor of the upper caste Mastoi clan, Mai's brother, Shakoor, should marry the woman with whom he was accused of having an illicit relationship while Mai was to be given away in marriage to a Mastoi man. "The prosecution said that when she rejected the decision she was gang-raped by four Mastoi men and made to walk home semi-naked in front of hundreds of people. The lawyer for one of the accused argued the rape charge was invalid because Mai was technically married to the defendant at the time of the incident". Such acts of violence do occur on the Indian subcontinent and bear testimony to the intersecting notions of nation, family, and community.

My attempt to theorize women's agency involves framing the concept in cognitive, psychological, economic, and political aspects. I borrow eminent educationist, Nelly Stromquist's assertion regarding agency which involves taking decisions that deconstruct cultural and social norms, and beliefs that structure seemingly intransigent traditional gender ideologies; the psychological aspect refers to developing self-esteem for which some form of financial autonomy is a basis; the political aspect involves the ability to organize and mobilize for social change, which requires the creation of awareness not just at the individual level but at the collective level as well (1995).

For me, empowerment is a process which enables the marginalized to make strategic life choices regarding education, livelihood, marriage, childbirth, sexuality, etc., which are critical for people to lead the sort of lives they want to lead and constitute life's defining parameters. It is important to keep in mind, however, that women are constrained by and grapple with the normative structures through which societies create gender roles. Do women embody the history of a culture and community only as it is remembered in the murky corridors of official-dom? In order to diligently study groundbreaking work accomplished by local agencies, cadres, and social networks, a distinction between traditional praxes that conscript the role of women and progressive roles prescribed for women within Islamic norms needs to be highlighted by a responsible scholarship and social work.

The western preoccupation with empirical observation had led to the inaccurate conflation of Islamic norms with practices. Western feminist epistemologies can impair the research paradigms, hypotheses, and field work on women in Islamic societies. The articulation of the fervent patriotism of Kashmiri women, which manifested itself in their emboldened personae in 1931, 1947, 1950, and 1975 until the dawn of insurgency and counterinsurgency in 1989-90, requires research paradigms and hypotheses that give as much credence to the path-paving work of women within religious, familial, and communal frameworks and to the work of those women who deconstructed well-established frameworks in order to lead subaltern movements, motivate minority education as opposed to state-controlled education, and recognize culture and history as sites of struggle. Power relations within the prevalent discourses of patriarchy and fundamentalism mediate the Kashmiri woman's identity. The valorization of her subordination is underwritten by praxes that legitimize gender identities, which are necessary to patriarchal and fundamentalist dominance. Can women step out of their ascribed gender role to significantly impact sociopolitical developments in Jammu and Kashmir? Can the political and social exigencies of Kashmiri women be addressed in nuanced and purposeful ways?

Culture inscribes a wide range of experiences, which centralizing institutions attempt to render invisible and homogeneous.

Women in Kashmir, as in other postcolonial countries, are positioned in relation to their own class and cultural realities, their own histories, their sensitivity to the diversity of cultural traditions and to the questions and conflicts within them, the legacies of Sufi Islam, their own struggles not just with the devastating effects of Indian occupation and Pakistani infiltration, but also with the discourses of cultural nationalism and religious fundamentalism propagated in the valley, their own relations to the West, their interpretations of religious law, their beliefs in the different schools of Islamic and Hindu thought, and their concepts of the role of women in contemporary societies.

THE STATUS OF WOMEN

Different groups of people contribute to the building of society in different ways. This diversity carries a special significance for the social structure as a whole. If diversity had not existed, human society would not have advanced even as far as the Stone Age, let alone the present stage of civilization. So we have to impartially consider and support all the diverse ideas, forms and colours which are conducive to fostering personal growth and social development among human beings. If we fail to do so, that section of society which has been built around a particular idea, form or colour will wither and die. I direct this not only to those who think deeply about social welfare, but to all members of society, to impress upon them that no one, through their thoughts, words or actions, should ever condone injustice.

If any physical, psychic, social, moral or spiritual weakness becomes apparent in a particular activity or in any sphere of individual or social life, it is the duty of the other members of society to eradicate that weakness with all the sweetness of their hearts. However, due to a lack of genuine humanism or spiritual outlook, people do just the opposite. The moment opportunists discover a weakness in somebody, they exploit that weakness and devour all the vitality of the person. They even consider it a weakness on their part if they reflect on the sufferings and heartaches of those who are weak.

As in the societies of most other species, in human society also females are physically weaker than males. Because their nervous systems are weaker, their minds are also slightly weak. Nevertheless women have no less value in human society than men. Selfish men, however, have disregarded the value of women; they have taken full advantage, and are continuing to take full advantage, of their weakness. Although men have publicly declared that women should be respected as the mothers of society, they have actually relegated them to the status of domestic cattle and sheep.

In every sphere of life men have either substantially limited the rights of women, or made the ability of women to exercise their rights subject to the whims and caprices of men. Such an attitude never existed among the primitive human beings who lived at the dawn of human history. Nor had primitive men conceived of the deceitful practice of establishing their supremacy by keeping women in bondage in the name of social purity. Even today among primitive races we do not find significant lack of magnanimity concerning the freedom of women.

By nature human beings are not wicked; rather most people are peace-loving and thus inclined towards personal purity. This inclination of the individual keeps the collective mind pure. Although women enjoy freedom in so-called underdeveloped races, we can observe that there is not even one per cent of the social purity in so-called developed races that there is among those races. When freedom is forcibly curbed a hostile reaction is produced in the mind, and purity rapidly disappears as a result. This is one of the causes of the lack of social purity in the so-called developed societies of today. To try to camouflage this impurity with high-sounding rhetoric or ostentatious religious rituals cannot do any real good for society. Those who want to keep women subservient to men by holding out false hopes or the illusory prospect of heavenly enjoyment in the afterlife, fail to understand that although such false hopes or the lure of heaven may be sufficient to keep women passive or in servitude, no real good can ever come to human society from this. The reason is that if, due to dogma and superstition, half of society is bogged down in a state of inertia, the other half will undoubtedly find progress difficult carrying a heavy, inert burden. In individual life purity is equally necessary for both men and women, and to make this possible real spiritual vision is essential. As long as injustices against either sex exist, purity is impossible.

Everyone should realize that to construct or preserve anything, there must be close cooperative action among the constituent parts. Human beings are not lifeless matter, so not only should all of their collective structures be based on cooperation, but that cooperation must be of a special type. It should not be based on the relation of master and servant, but on mutual cordiality. It should be a coordinated cooperation and not a subordinated one.

What sort of treatment have women received so far? It is very true that women have gradually lost their rights or freedom in certain cases due to lack of competence. There are those who think that, because of this, special abilities are the only criteria for having rights. Such people, however, actually want women to be wageless slaves under the strict supervision of men. But is it merely due to their lack of competence that women have lost their rights? Have not the overflowing sentiments of their hearts also been partly responsible? Have not women, swayed by their emotions, ignored their own petty interests and gradually given everything even the high social status that fascinates them to their husbands, sons and brothers? Is it not reasonable to expect human beings (certainly human beings are not animals) to pay proper respect to such humility and large-heartedness? If a guest arrives unexpectedly, who volunteers to forgo a meal to feed the guest? Who deprives herself first when a delicious dish is prepared? Who leaves home to keep house for others, giving up her paternal property rights (regardless of what the law says)? Are not these observations applicable throughout most of the world? I do not say that men are ordinary human beings and that women are angels; I have only focused on women as human beings and mentioned their special qualities. Does a husband, when his wife is ill, nurse her with as much care as she nurses him when he is ill?

If men wish to prevent helpless widows from remarrying by taking advantage of their sentimental female hearts, they convince those widows that they will be reunited with their late husbands after their deaths so how can they consider remarrying? Shame on such men! Perhaps such tales may make women, already sentimental, even more so. The prospect of being reunited with the spirit of their deceased husband after their death may induce helpless widows to undertake rigorous lifelong penance, and to fast on every ekadashi [the eleventh day after each new moon and full moon]. Are not those who want to keep women slaves to dogmatic ideas guilty of acting against the dictates of their consciences?

The very idea of heaven and hell is sheer nonsense anyway. Such stupid ideas thrived in the minds of those who popularized ancient myths, but they have no capacity to find a foundation in the solid ground of rationality. If, however, in order to humour such fools, I accept the existence of heaven and hell, I might ask, If the spirit of a wicked husband goes to hell and grazes in the fields as a bull, should his virtuous wife also go to hell after her death, become a cow and start grazing beside him?

Let us end this digression. The main point of the discussion is this: those who take advantage of people's simplicity or ignorance are veritable demons in human form, and those who deceive people by exploiting their sentiments of sacrifice are even worse than demons. Freedom is attained through struggle. No one offers it on a platter, because freedom is not a gift; it is one's birthright. But as far as the rights which women have lost today, at least so it seems in most countries of the world, proper socio-psycho-analysis shows that women have not really lost their freedom; rather, they have trustingly placed their destiny in the hands of men. This is the plain truth.

Actually, when there is no question of women's rights having been snatched away, there is no need for a movement styled on the trade-union movement. Whatever responsibility there may be in this regard, it is entirely that of men. If at all a movement is required, it must be implemented by men themselves. Today men should consider the needs of women and gradually restore to women the rights which women once entrusted to men out of feelings of helplessness or in response to their heartfelt sentiments. It must always be remembered that freedom, or liberty, and license are not the same thing. The concept of women's freedom is good, but license should not be encouraged in the name of liberty. Giving license to either men or women could destroy the social structure in a short time. Hence those who are the most vocal in proposing the freedom of women must carefully consider the form this proposed freedom shall take.

When we pay recognition to any simple truth, we should not be carried away by sentimentality. Only rationality based on humanism is acceptable. As children of nature, women should have the same access as men to light, air, earth and water. In fact, it is not a matter of granting rights to women, but rather a case of recognizing their rights. If, however, the recognition of women's rights is treated sentimentally, it may result in great social disaster. The law of inheritance: For example, take the right of inheritance. There are diverse views on the subject among different sections of society around the world. Some people favour women having the sole right of inheritance to the complete exclusion of men; others favour equal distribution between men and women; still others give women only some tiny leftovers and in reality keep everything in men's hands. Behind all these systems there is clearly an attempt to maintain the influence and supremacy of one gender or the other, rather than to demonstrate rational judgement and humanitarian concern.

In fact, a final decision on this issue should be based on the fundamental principle that we will not deprive anyone; we will give equal opportunities to both men and women concerning the right of inheritance. At the same time we will enact laws to ensure the orderly administration and preservation of property in order to reduce the possibility of a breach of domestic peace. In most countries society is patrilineal. The patrilineal system has some advantage over the matrilineal one. There are two main advantages.

The first advantage stems from the fact that it is not as easy to determine the identity of the father as that of the mother, and in the absence of any direct blood relationship(2) the mother's affection for her children is generally greater than the father's. Under these circumstances the patrilineal system is much better, for it awakens in the father a proper sense of responsibility for his children and precludes the possibility of the children's identity remaining unknown or concealed. And the father is compelled by circumstantial pressure to take responsibility for bringing up his children; and therefore makes an effort to properly preserve the structure of the family. (Among less-developed creatures, fathers rarely take care of their offspring due to the absence of this sort of circumstantial pressure.)

The second advantage of the patrilineal system complements the first. Since the relationship between the father and the child is known, the mother naturally does not feel so very alone in rearing the child. The physical and mental structure of a woman is such that even though she may have all the requisite ability to take care of her children, it is extremely difficult for her to bring them up properly and to adequately provide for food, clothing, education and medical care all alone; at the same time she has to keep her children with her or near her, or else it becomes difficult for the children to survive. Therefore if men, instead of women, take the main responsibility for providing food and clothing, while women, after duly attending to the needs of the children, where possible or in cases of necessity earn money by working either at home or outside, neither the children nor society will be adversely affected in any way.

I do not support the supposed wisdom of those who advise women to spend their lives with ladles, [[tongs]] and spatulas, because this is unrealistic. Necessity often compels women to discard this convention. Such a system may suit a handful of rich or upper middle-class people, but it has no value for day-labourers or the poor. Many of those who loudly advocate equal rights and the freedom of women, in reality keep their women behind a purdah or covered with a burka. Even among such families I have noticed poor housewives going to the market with their husbands to buy and sell, or to the fields, farms or coal mines, voluntarily taking on light work. Evidently, they cannot afford to behave ostentatiously and live indolently behind a lace curtain.

However, there are people who, in the name of giving equal rights to women in all spheres of life, want them to engage in heavy physical and mental labour which is unsuitable for them. Such an outlook is deplorable. It must be accepted that the physical bodies and nervous systems of women are not as strong as those of men, so men and women cannot work in identical areas. Apart from this, for physical reasons women cannot work in the same way every day of the month, and during pregnancy and the post-delivery period the ability to work strenuously is severely restricted. These points must not be overlooked.

There are many people who sentimentally think that if a few women are made ministers or members of parliament they will serve as shining examples of equal rights and the progress of women. But is this the correct attitude? Will it not be detrimental to society as a whole if rights are granted, or a principle of accelerating progress is adopted, at the expense of competence? The recognition of rights is a legal matter as well as a collective psychological phenomenon, and the only way to expedite progress is to establish a progressive education system. A woman who becomes a minister or an ambassador in any country is not an index of the real status of the women in that country. To raise the standard of women in society is neither so easy nor so cheap.

Since rational analysis leads us to the conclusion that the patrilineal system is better than the matrilineal, the system of inheritance should be structured accordingly. Of course, at the time of drafting the law of inheritance, special precautions must be taken so that nothing is framed in the name of the patrilineal system that will make women slaves fighting for their very survival in the houses of their brothers or brothers-in-law. In other words, after recognizing the equal rights of women to use family property as long as they live and to enjoy a lifelong income from such property, the law of inheritance should be based on the patrilineal system. The dowry system: Many people regard the dowry system, which is followed in various countries today, as being unfair and unjust towards women. But actually this is not so. The question of justice or injustice to women [[does not arise in relation to the dowry system]].

The problem is primarily economic, although there are secondary causes as well. In some societies, where women do not earn money, they are considered an economic liability once they are married. At the time of marriage the parents of the groom therefore extract a substantial amount of money or goods from the parents of the bride in order to maintain the wife for the rest of her life. These are the actual facts behind the dowry system. Similarly, in societies where men do not earn money, the parents of the bride receive a substantial dowry from the parents of the bridegroom. Of course a secondary cause of the dowry system arises when there is a disparity between the number of men and women in a particular country or section of society. So in fact, the parents of the bride give a dowry in a particular society only when the subsistence of the woman is dependent on the income of her husband, or where the number of men is less than the number of women. If it is mainly the women who earn the money or if the number of women is less than the number of men, the situation is reversed.

There are those who mistakenly think that the dowry system will cease once the equal rights of daughters to paternal property are recognized. However, it has been noticed that even in societies where daughters are heirs to paternal property, the dowry system has gradually gained prominence for economic and other reasons. Generally very few daughters these days inherit alluring amounts of property from their parents, so it is completely unrealistic to expect that the parents of the groom will relinquish their claim to a dowry in the hope of receiving inherited property. A few daughters from rich or upper middle-class families inherit very substantial properties and therefore do not have any cause for worry, whether the dowry system exists or not. Even the most unattractive daughter of rich parents gets married very easily due to the power of money.

Social interaction: There are diverse views among those who formulate social codes concerning the free mixing of men and women. It does not require much logic to convince people that the final outcome of free mixing in an undisciplined society is unhealthy. It is also true, however, that the absence of social interaction creates a suppressed longing, a special attraction or an unhealthy curiosity, as does the denial of other desires. This may lead to illicit mixing, which eventually undermines social purity. A system that thwarts social interaction is nothing but an attempt to suppress the mind. Where there is illicit mixing, the only harm done to men is that they degenerate morally, but the damage to women is far greater, because they may be cast out of society in disgrace. Thus on the one hand, men and women will have to be free to mix together socially, while on the other hand, a well-thought-out code of self-control will have to guide their social interaction.

Those who want to keep their daughters away from the influence of modernism, and are therefore reluctant to send them to school and college, perhaps do not realize that long ago the waves of modernism intruded into the privacy of their homes without their knowledge. So their efforts to protect their daughters and themselves by following the custom of purdah and making women wear burkas, are entirely farcical. The trend of the age is irresistible, for in this too there is dynamism. It is the duty of intelligent people to channelize the trend of the age towards the path of benevolence by applying their intellect. Neither the individual nor the society as a whole is capable of resisting the powerful spirit of the age. It knocks down anyone who tries to thwart it, and proceeds ahead with irresistible speed. Those knocked down and sprawled on the ground stare at it in utter helplessness, with dazed minds and vacant eyes, as it marches by.

MUSLIM WOMEN

The Institute of Islamic Studies and the Minority Research Group, London, recently organised here a seminar on 'Problems of Indian Muslim Women'. A large number of academics and social activists participated in the event. The seminar was inaugurated by film actress Ms. Shabana Azmi. She stressed the need for concrete steps to be taken to improve the lot of Muslim women in the country. In his opening paper on 'Islam, Women and Gender Justice', noted Leftist expert on Islam Dr. Asghar Ali Engineer of the Institute of Islamic Studies said that the basic core of the Qur'anic message was that of justice, a comprehensive concept that included gender justice as well. Hence, he said, injustice to women went completely against the grain of the Qur'an's teachings.

Economist Dr. Abusaleh Shariff, in his paper on 'Relative Economic and Social Deprivation in India', pointed out that Muslims were among the most marginalised communities in the country, and that the position of Muslim women was, pathetic. He made the distressing revelation that over the past few years, the enrolment rate in elementary schools among Muslim females in India has actually been witnessing a considerable decline. Dr. Ramala Baxamusa of the Research Centre for Women's Studies, SNDT Women's University, Mumbai, spoke at length on 'The Economic Status of Muslim Women in Maharashtra'. Based on official data, she showed how Muslim women are in economic and educational terms one of the most backward groups in the entire state. Thus, in rural Maharashtra, 40 per cent of Muslim households are without any land, and 42 per cent had a holding of between .01 to 1.0 hectares only. Only some 25 per cent of rural Maharashtrian Muslim women are literate, and the dropout rate among them is particularly high. Dr. Baxamusa provided a case study of two projects that have recently been started to impart education to Muslim girls in Maharashtra, and made an analysis of their achievements.

These are the Saboo Siddiq Open University Scheme in Mumbai for drop-out girls and women, started in 1997, and the community project run by the Department of Post-Graduate Home Science Studies and Research, SNDT Women's University, in Gilbert Hill, a Muslim dominated slum in Mumbai. Dr. Malika Mistry, a Pune-based demographer, focused in her paper on the economic and educational backwardness of Muslims in India, particularly Muslim women. She noted that while the 34.7 per cent of Hindu women were illiterate, the figure for Muslim women was 52.1 per cent. While only 2.7 per cent of Muslim women had studied beyond high school, the corresponding figures for Hindu, Christian, Sikh and Jain women were 11.7 per cent, 16 per cent, 16.6 per cent and 30.5 per cent respectively.

Dr. Mandakini Pant, also of the SNDT Women's University, Mumbai, presented an interesting paper on the Bandheria of Jaipur. These are a group of Muslim women, belonging largely to the Kaimkhani Rajput Muslim community, who depend for their livelihood on tying knots in cloths for the tie-and-die handicrafts industry. These women, she pointed out, are desperately poor and, having little bargaining power, are at the mercy of unscrupulous middlemen who pay them just a pittance. Several speakers dwelt on the Qur'anic injunctions that pertain to women and pointed out how despite the rights that the Qur'an had granted women, these have been effectively denied to them. Noted political scientist Imtiaz Ahmed of the Jawaharlal Nehru University, New Delhi, spoke on the issue of unilateral triple divorce. He said that the Qur'an had actually provided for a system of arbitration for divorce, but that this was not being followed in India.

Diane D'Souza, a research student from Hyderabad, spoke on the growing recognition among Muslims today about the right of women to pray in the mosques. This author presented a paper on the role of Muslim women in the Tablighi Jama'at, an Islamic reformist movement. Others who spoke on the occasion included Dr. Mumtaz Ali Khan from Bangalore, Dr. Mahmooda, lecturer in the Department of English, Kashmir University, Srinagar, Sonia Khan, an Ahme-dabad-based lawyer, as well as activists of the Mumbai-based Muslim women's organisation, Awaz-i-Niswan. Several recommendations emerged at the conclusion of the seminar. Many speakers called for reservation for Muslim women in educational institutions and public sector jobs within the OBC quota. Others stressed the urgent need for preparing model nikah-namahs or marriage contracts to properly safeguard the interests of Muslim women. It was also decided that a regular newsletter will soon be launched to document the efforts of various individuals and groups engaged in promoting social reform and development among Muslims all over India.

MUSLIM WOMEN IN INDIA

Huma, a Muslim woman from Faizabad, describes the contradictions and pressures of the interface between her Muslim religious identity and Indian citizenship. 'My family has had a communist history, though it later leaned towards the Congress [Party]. Some cousins did leave for Pakistan, it was never a choice open to us. Despite slogans to the contrary, the family has never considered itself marginalized or oppressed. The Babri Masjid [Mosque] demolition taught us a different lesson.

By mid-November '92, lakhs [many thousands] of people began coming into Faizabad even as the Chief Minister continued to claim that the situation was under control. Some of us [the girls] were studying outside, in Lucknow and Aligarh. We received telegrams from our parents telling us not to come home. I can still recall the insecurity - being told our homes were not safe for us. My father moved just one day before the demolition, and he had to leave by the stairs at the back of the house. The feeling of being vulnerable in your own house is one that is etched in my family's memory. It was worse than partition. Much worse. Then at least one had claimed another land and could go there. We had nowhere else to go. Where could we go? Then of course, there was this ongoing refrain that we must remember that we are a minority. Why should we? Does that make us in some way lesser citizens? What is it that the Hindus have done for this country that we have not? Don't we have equal rights? Women were the ones who suffered the most. Due to the rhetoric of the majority community, the pressure to be the bearers of one's own community has further intensified. We are the ones who are controlled; we are told that we are supporting the BJP [the pro-Hindu Bhartiya Janata Party] if we demand our rights.'

There exist 110 million Muslims in India - which, with the exception of Indonesia - is the largest population of Muslims in a single country in the world. Muslim communities in India are geographically scattered, culturally diverse and economically disparate. A majority of Muslims in India live in Uttar Pradesh, Bihar and West Bengal. According to the 1991 Government of India Census, there are over 48 million Muslim women in India. Like women from other communities, Muslim women are differentiated across gender, class, caste and community, and are subject to the interface between gender and community within the Indian social, political and economic context.

At the same time, Muslim women's location in modern India also derives from their status as a minority which colours their life experience and self-perception in distinct ways, and in this respect they differ from women belonging to other communities. After five decades of independence the majority of Muslim women are among the most disadvantaged, least literate, economically impoverished and politically marginalized sections of Indian society. The social and economic issues confronting women in Muslim communities mandate attention as does the violation of their rights as citizens of India.

MUSLIM WOMEN IN INDIAN SOCIETY

Women in India do not constitute an undifferentiated, homogenous category, yet, little information exists on Indian Muslim women. However, the perception that Muslim women's social status in India can be ascribed to a certain intrinsic, immutable feature of Islam or that their legal status derives solely from reference to Muslim laws is widely prevalent. As a result of this misconception, Muslim women are often considered as 'separate' or 'different' from Indian society, reinforcing cultural stereotypes and obscuring their contemporary realities. Mainstream historical narrative with its emphasis on the rise and fall of the Muslim empire excludes Muslim women. Although Muslim women were generally absent from public life during this period, several women from royalty were authors and poets - or even a Sultan as in the case of Raziya Sultana.

At the turn of the twentieth century the topic of female education was taken up by Muslim communities. Several Muslim women made pioneering contributions to female education. Figures for Muslim girls' participation in educational institutions during the early decades of the twentieth century surpassed figures for the national average. Muslim women also participated in campaigns against female seclusion and legal discrimination, and played an active part in the emerging women's movement. This trend suffered a setback due to the social, political and economic upheavals in, during and after the partition of India in 1947. In the wake of the trauma and large-scale migrations during 1947, and a subsequent lack of political presence, it was extremely difficult for Muslim women to articulate their concerns, both within the community and as citizens of India.

THE RISE OF COMMUNAL POLITICS

The rise of communal politics with its inherent link between politics and religion, privileging 'minority' (or community) interests over gender interests, and the appropriation of Muslim women's experiences and aspirations by a (male) Muslim constituency, rendered the possibility of re-negotiating their position vis-a-vis Muslim men even more difficult. Muslim obscurantism coupled with Hindu right-wing prejudice made the possibility of Muslim women raising their concerns harder still, as was seen during the passage of the Muslim Women's Bill in 1986. The Bill subordinated the rights of Muslim women to the demands of community identity, denying them their constitutional rights as Indian citizens. The issue was simultaneously used by the Hindu right-wing to incite anti-Muslim prejudice.

The political preeminence of the Hindu right-wing and the subsequent demolition of the Babri Mosque at Ayodhya in 1992 undermined secular law and seriously questioned the commitment of the Indian state to protect the human rights of its Muslim citizens. Communal violence in the aftermath of the Ayodhya demolition highlighted the collabourative role of the state and its agencies in inflicting grave human rights violations against Muslim communities - including Muslim women. This was in violation of the constitutional ideals of religious nondiscrimination, protection of human rights, implementation of social justice and the equality of all Indian citizens, as well as principles of international human rights law. Numerous reports have documented these human rights violations, although prosecutions have yet to take place.

MUSLIM WOMEN' S SOCIO-ECONOMIC AND POLITICAL STATUS

In modern-day India, the socio-economic status of women in Muslim communities, along with their political participation rates and the need for legal reform, are causes for concern and need attention. This point cannot be overstated in a context where, in 1983, the Gopal Singh Committee instituted by the government, declared Muslims as a 'backward' community in India. A central feature of this 'backwardness' is the appalling educational and socio-economic status of Muslims in India, particularly Muslim women. In a study of 39 districts in 1981 - where the population of Muslims ranged from 20 per cent to 95 per cent (which could be considered a fairly representative sample of the Muslims in India) - the literacy rate of Muslim women was found to be 21.91 per cent, which was lower than the average of 24.82 per cent for the whole country. Muslims' share in public employment in All-India and Central Services is less than 3 per cent. Within this picture of poor overall employment statistics, it is a predictable certainty that the corresponding figures for Muslim women are lower still.

The impoverished status of a large number of Muslim women in India underlines the urgency for further inquiry in this area and also the need for active intervention by state agencies to implement policies to redress this imbalance - and ensure Muslim women's full and equal participation as Indian citizens. Equally importantly, it is crucial for members of Muslim communities - Muslim women and men - to introspect and debate among themselves as to the reasons and remedies for their economic vulnerability and poor educational and employment status, and to consider possible remedies. There is also a need for debate and mobilization by Muslim women on legal reform in order to overcome patriarchal structures with Muslim communities. The debate on legal reform is linked to debates on women and Islam. Muslim women in India need to participate in the contemporary debate on Islam and women's rights. It is imperative for Indian Muslim women to reclaim their right to religious knowledge, enter the discourse on the Shari'a and challenge their historic marginalization from religious knowledge as well as its discriminatory interpretations.

6

Equity to Women in India

WOMEN WITH DISABILITIES

Women with disabilities are multiply disadvantaged through their status as women, as persons with disabilities, and majority numbers as persons living in poverty. In May 2002, ESCAP adopted the resolution "Promoting an inclusive, barrier-free and rights-based society for people with disabilities in the Asian and Pacific region in the twenty-first century". The resolution also proclaimed the extension of the Asian and Pacific Decade of Disabled Persons, 1993-2002, for another decade, 2003-2012. "There are currently some 5.6 billion different people in the world. Some have a difference called disability." —Disability Dimension in Development Action: Manual on Inclusive Planning, United Nations. The 1970s marked a new approach to disability. The concept of human rights for disabled persons began to become more accepted internationally.

The Declaration on the Rights of Disabled Persons, adopted by the General Assembly on 9 December 1975, encouraged national and international protection of the rights of the disabled. Recognition was given to the fact that disabled persons were entitled to the same political and civil rights as others, including measures necessary to enable them to become self-sufficient. The declaration reiterated the rights of disabled persons to education, medical services, and placement service. It further recognized their right to economic and social security, to employment, to live with their families, to participate in social and creative events, to be protected against all exploitation, abuse or degrading behaviour, and to avail themselves of legal aid. Realizing the need to promote the full participation of the disabled in the social life and development of their societies, on 16 December 1976, the General Assembly declared the year 1981 International Year of Disabled Persons (IYDP), stipulating that it be devoted to integrating disabled persons fully into society.

"Around the world, women make up just over 51% of the population. Women with disabilities are the most marginalized in Indian society. They are deprived of political, Social, Economic, and health opportunities. The problems of women with disabilities become very complex with other factors such as social stigma and poverty. Women with disabilities have been largely neglected when it comes to research, state policies, the disability and women's movements, and rehabilitation programmes, and this has become a widely accepted fact in recent years. Also, "due to numerous societal standards, they continue to be left out of the decision-making processes. This reality is especially true of women with disabilities in cultures where the role of wife and mother is considered to be the primary role for a female." Irene Feika, Deputy Chairperson of Underrepresented Groups, Disabled People International. Although this may seem to be of minor importance, the pattern of ignoring and isolating disabled women is repeated throughout national and international publications and websites of people with disabilities.

EDUCATION

Women with disabilities do not form a homogeneous group. For example, the mentally ill and mentally retarded, the visually, hearing and speech impaired and those with restricted mobility or with so-called "medical disabilities" all encounter different barriers, of different kinds, which have to be overcome in different ways. Throughout the Asian and Pacific region, public attitudes are changing regarding the value of educating and training women with disabilities. The prejudice surrounding their ability and value continues to perpetuate the view that educating them is futile. Opportunities for girls with disabilities to receive an education or to attend training courses are available to only a few. For example, the then International Council on Education of the Visually Handicapped estimated that only two per cent of visually-impaired children in developing countries receive any formal schooling. In China, where there are some 5 million disabled children aged between 7 and 15 years, only 6 per cent are enrolled in schools. It is reasonable to expect that the number of girls included in those estimates is significantly less than half.

One report on women with disabilities in the Raichur district of Karnataka State, India, indicated that the literacy rate of such women was 7 per cent compared to a general literacy rate for the State of 46 per cent. Traditionally, schools for disabled children are most commonly segregated institutions for those with visual, hearing and intellectual impairments. Girls with extensive physical disabilities have even less opportunity for schooling. The few special schools, concentrated in large cities, have residential facilities; the residential system discriminates against access by girls. So long as education for people with disabilities is largely confined to a segregated system, only a few disabled girls and women will be benefited. Evidence also indicates that a predominantly segregated school system for disabled children is unlikely to be adequate and accessible for this group of children, and that it is also educationally inferior. A study of disabled girls, both in special (usually residential) schools and in regular schools, found that those in special schools were less proficient in basic literacy and numeracy skills, had lower expectations about their own capabilities and lacked confidence in social settings. Thus, it is obvious that mainstreaming girls with disabilities into society must begin at school.

Education is the key to the advancement of women and girls with disabilities as it provides access to information, enables them to communicate their needs, interests and experiences, brings them into contact with other students, increases their confidence and encourages them to assert their rights. Without a basic education, their chances for employment are almost nil. Hence, there is an urgent need to consider policies and programmes that will place greater emphasis on the participation of women with disabilities in the mainstream education system. Certainly the challenges are great. In the year 2003 Ministry of social justice and empowerment has introduced novel scheme of providing scholarships for people with disabilities to pursue higher education. The important feature of this programme is it reserves 50% of scholarships for women with disabilities.

EMPLOYMENT

Women in general face discrimination in employment. For women with disabilities, this discrimination is far greater. In situations where there is high unemployment, opportunities for remunerative work tend to be severely limited. When disabled women do find jobs, they receive considerably lower wages. For example, even for an industrialized country, studies have shown that a disabled woman working full-time earns only 56 per cent of the salary of a full-time employed disabled man. In fact, disabled women earn the lowest wages compared to disabled men or non-disabled women. Furthermore, in addition to the prejudice and discrimination barrier, the inaccessibility of the physical environment (e.g., buildings, roads, transport and toilet facilities) is a serious obstacle to disabled women working outside their homes.

Since the lack of mobility limits disabled women from obtaining raw materials and marketing their products themselves, engaging in piece-work is the most common form of income-generation available to them. Examples of piecework by disabled women and girls include labour-intensive and poorly paid activities such as weaving, sewing, basket making, the assembling of toys and production of handicraft items. The materials are delivered to their homes and finished products are collected by agents. There is no legal or social protection. Disabled women and girls may be exposed to unsafe materials and subjected to excessive hours of work under harsh conditions. Even where disabled women have jobs, their rights as workers may be over-looked. Faced with discrimination, little job mobility and few skills, disabled women workers may be forced to endure oppressive working conditions.

SOCIAL EXCLUSION

Women with disabilities, especially from rural areas, are likely to be left out of family interactions and community activities. In addition, they are exposed to social stigma and stereotyping within their communities, which lead them to feel devalued, isolated, and ashamed. A study conducted (Emily.et.al 2002) demonstrated culturally appropriate form independent group living to have a beneficial impact on the women's levels of sociability and their confidence to venture out in public or to social functions. Living among other women with disabilities and in a non-judgmental environment helped in raising self-esteem and in developing social skills. All of the women who resided in the group house felt accepted, sociable, and confident to venture. Together, confidence in their abilities was strengthened and they could carry out their business with mutual support. Thus, independent group living helps in Social Development (Increased sociability, public confidence and ability to support) and Personal Development (improved self-image, independence and professional motivation).

Despite the most optimistic outlook for change in employment opportunities for women with disabilities, the present reality is that the best hope for productive work may lie in self-employment or group employment probably on a cooperative basis. While numerous projects exist which provide skills training for disabled women, they frequently fall short of meeting the ultimate goal of providing a means of adequate income. A critical need remains for programmes such as credit schemes, entrepreneurial skills training and advisory services for disabled women and to develop a niche in the market for the goods and services they can offer. For women with disabilities in rural communities more attention has to be paid to developing options for productive and remunerative work, and the requisite training.

Incest is very common in India. Women with disabilities are the easy prey for the exploitation within the family. We also do not discuss these issues in public. The large demand of parents of mentally retarded daughters for compulsory sterilization speak volumes. There is a need to tackle this issue by creating awareness and strengthening the existing laws to punish the offenders severely. Abandoning girls with disability is another issue that needs strengthening. The measures required are to prevent abandoning by creating awareness and to improve homes for them, which are often the centers of exploitation. Adoption of children with disabilities is another issue, without which these children stay homeless. There is a need to start SOS homes for these children instead of allowing them stay in orp-hanages forever. Apart from economic independence, work is an essential means of enabling a person to develop a sense of identity and self-esteem. Thus, gainful employment is an important means of promoting the social integration of disabled women. From the perspective of the State, investing in the education and training of women with disabilities, and promoting opportunities for their employment, is sound economic and social policy. Gainfully employed women with disabilities contribute actively to the economy.

HEALTH

Health problems of older women will become an increasingly important issue in developing countries partially because of the sheer increase in absolute numbers. Today, two out of three of the world's 469 million women older than 50 already reside in developing countries. By 2020 three out of four will reside in developing countries, an absolute increase of 408 million. It is imperative to keep in mind the heterogeneity of developing countries. Aging and disability have close association. Older women constitute a distinct population that requires interventions very different from a population of younger women, who need an emphasis on maternity care. Obviously health problems of women are not homogeneous and cannot all be addressed through the traditional maternal and child health services. The pattern of the health problems older women face reflects to a large extent the level of development of their region and country.

Additionally, a woman's well being is a result of all her previous experiences, including factors such as urban or rural residence, marital status, number of children, education, income, and nutrition. Furthermore work has a tremendous influence on women's physical and mental health. Indeed, occupational health problems are emerging as a result of the increased number of women in urban industrial jobs. Two other issues that emerge as critical, but that are rarely discussed by disabled women's groups are terrorism /riots and its impact on disabled women and AIDS among disabled women. AIDS poses a bigger threat to disabled women. It is estimated that as much as 10 percent of the population in many Asian countries is already infected by AIDS. Given the extremely poor health care and lack of appropriate AIDS prevention information received by women with disabilities all over the world, the AIDS rates are expected to be very high. Policy directions and programs towards prevention of mortality and morbidity among women older than 50, and major causes of disease burden are required.

ADVOCACY

In general, the burden of work for women with disabilities falls squarely on the shoulders of disabled women themselves so that disabled women's issues can be addressed and information and resources shared. Women with disabilities have been an integral part of the history of movements for disability rights. In spite of their contributions, however, disabled women's issues were largely ignored and their accomplishments minimized. In addition, within disabled women's organizations the focus seems to be on organizing and advocating for women with physical or visual disabilities.

There is very little attention paid to women with other disabilities such as women with mental retardation, cerebral palsy, and mental illness even to the point of lack of access to these organizations. With the realization that their future lies firmly in their own hands, women with disabilities around the world are focusing on their enormous strength and emerging resources to directly change the picture. Since the beginning of this current movement for Independent Living, women with disabilities have been active organizers and advocates for the rights of all people with disabilities.

A BBC report states that "War, poverty, lack of health care and lack of decent working conditions and safety regulations are the fundamental causes of most disabling impairments. The problem is circular: poverty means few resources; few resources perpetuate poverty at the same time as they cause disability." Disabled women in India face numerous challenges. "In the absence of well coordinated government policies aimed at integrating disabled people in mainstream activities, disabled women live under extremely difficult conditions, for not only are they women but most of them are in the rural areas. The women with disabilities in India are discriminated against equality. Discrimination deprives disabled women of vital life experiences, and therefore by denying them the opportunity to participate fully in community affairs they are deprived of equality of opportunity." Without effective remedial action, the consequences of disability will add to the obstacles to the development of women with disabilities. Hence it is essential that we include immediate, adequate and appropriate measures for the equalization of opportunities for girls and women with disabilities in the following areas:

- Some of the key areas of concern to disabled women include:
- Awareness: to highlight the plight of women with disabilities, especially in rural areas
- Education: Disabled girls are less likely to attend school than disabled boys.

- Training: Professional and Vocational- limited access into training programmes.
- Employment: Disabled women are less likely to be granted loan facilities or be employed
- Violence: Women and girls with disabilities are particularly vulnerable to violence, especially within the home situation. Sexual abuse is quite common, especially among women with mental and/or hearing disabilities. Abuse by physicians and caregivers, e.g. forced sterilization, is common.
- Health services: Refusal of health workers to advise disabled women and girls on appropriate family planning services and methods
- Empowerment

Some of the needs to be addressed:

- Public education and awareness programmes to promote positive perceptions on the potential of disabled women in society
- Career-oriented education for disabled women
- The right to control their own fertility
- Legislative provisions to promote and protect the human rights of disa.-help organizations of disabled persons. Twenty of these organizations are nation-wide cross-disability organizations. One Indian disabled woman frames the situation this way: "The issues of women with disabilities are same as other women in India plus more [complex] as they lack access to education, resulting in all the problems linked with illiteracy such as poverty, lack of decision making power and lack of available options. Because of disability they are not considered to be women who can fulfill the traditional roles of Indian women. Worst of all I have seen that most women with disabilities who are leaders themselves really believe in this notion. So the issue, which needs attention, is lack of recognition of rights. The concept that a woman has rights is well adopted by the women in India, however not by women with disabilities."

An Indian disability activist says: "In a society where the practice of gender inequality has become a convention, disabled women are the most isolated and marginalized. After years of struggle, disabled men have succeeded to some extent in making their voice heard. A special initiative is required to make sure that disabled women are also heard."

Tools for Empowerment:

Non-governmental organizations can play a powerful role in counteracting the cycle of oppression through which disabled women are denied access to support and resources that would empower them to reach their potential and contribute to the community. The need for funding support presents a critical challenge for women with disabilities. One survey respondent summed it up: "there is much to be done and not enough resources to do it with."

Some of the recommendations to NGOs to more effectively include women with disabilities:

- Disability organizations, leadership training projects and independent living services must collect data on involvement of women and girls with disabilities and conduct specific outreach efforts to include women with disabilities.
- Mainstream organizations must support and work in partnership with organizations led by women with disabilities.
- Women with disabilities must be involved in all policy and decision making processes, and at every level of the projects: as staff, volunteers, participants, and evaluators.
- Education, vocational training and rehabilitation programs must include women with disabilities, to prepare women and girls for careers and gainful employment.
- Rehabilitation and adaptive technology must be available for women with disabilities, and women with disabilities must be involved in the development and production of adaptive devices.
- Health service personnel must be trained to offer informed

and sensitive service and education addressing the health needs of girls and women with disabilities.

Non-governmental organizations must work with women with disabilities to pressure governments to effectively implement the recommendations, which have been made over the years by various UN bodies and non-governmental organizations, particularly at the Fourth World Conference on Women in Beijing in 1995.

- Entrepreneurship development cum pre vocational training cum Vocational Training cum placement multipurpose centers to promote self and group employment (with a cross disability approach) for women need to establish at least one in each Taluk/block level with hostel facilities. After successful training and placement in the open employment/self or group employment independent living houses need to be supported by the government. Such houses should be identified from the government housing projects and houses in the ground floor with accessibility should be provided in addition to providing loans to purchase accessible taxi/auto rickshaw/cycle rickshaws for commuting to the work place. NGO's who are interested in building such housing facility for working women with disabilities need to be supported with grants.
- Women with disabilities working in the agriculture related work needs extra support.

Other Recommendations:

Aligning with the Biwako Millennium Framework for action: towards an inclusive, barrier-free and rights-based society for persons with disabilities in Asia and the Pacific

The Commission has to set the following targets:

1. By 2005, Governments should ensure antidiscrimination measures by forming special task forces to protect women with disabilities.

2. By 2005, self-help organizations adopt policies to promote full representation of women with disabilities,
3. By 2005, women with disabilities should be included in all the policy making bodies from panchayath to parliament levels
4. Set up state wise task force to prepare white paper on the quality of services available for girls/women with disabilities and all the institutions managed or supported by the government and other donors.
5. The Commission should insist on 50% Reservations for girls with disabilities in schools and colleges (out of the existing quota) as well as 50% of the total of job opportunities, reserved for persons with disabilities, ranging from a minimum of 30% and to a maximum of 50% as per the PWD Act, 1995.
6. In order to improve the quality of life of women with disabilities in the rural and urban India, district CBR Societies for women with disabilities should function in cooperation with CBR societies for persons with disabilities at the district level, with the District Commissioner as the Chairman of the and the Deputy Director, Women & Child Development as the Secretary. All organizations working for women with disabilities and all organizations of women with disabilities and Self-Help Groups of Parents of adolescent girls with disabilities should become members of the society. A sample of the Byelaws of the District CBR Society for persons with disabilities is enclosed and Byelaws for district CBR Society for Women with Disabilities need to be developed.
7. In urban areas in addition to the reservation, women with disabilities are finding it extremely difficult to get hostel facilities. Therefore, a 3% reservation should be made in all existing women's hostels for women with disabilities.
8. There is a need for a scheme to support Self help mutual aid groups of women with disabilities on the lines of

Stree Shakthi in Karnataka and the DFID Velugu programme in Andhra Pradesh for women with disabilities and this should include a seed money to start both self and group employment. In addition to promoting self and group employment, there is a need for EDP programmes, both rural and urban, for women with disabilities to start their own cooperatives on the lines of SEWA, both in Khadi Commission and all the poverty alleviation programmes. Industrial development corporations. Women's development cooperatives should provide skill development, financial support and marketing linkages. In all the shops and malls owned by government or cooperatives or quasi government, out of the 3% reservation, 50% reservation should be made for women with disabilities and it should be allotted at 50% of the cost.

9. Finally, about movies and media, initiatives should be taken to regulate the media, which are mainly focusing on women's external beauty to promote the brands and nothing beyond. We can promote this on the lines of the Erikson Company, Finland which states women with disabilities should also promote the popular brands. This will help to fight for the age-old image about women and help people to appreciate inner beauty.

10. Under Sarva shisha Abhiyan a special programme for the inclusion of girls with disability in ICDS and elementary schools should be launched on the lines of Joyful inclusion and Udisha Portage programme launched by the Women and child Development Department, Government of Karnataka in cooperation with CBR NETWORK (South Asia)

11. The existing practices of discrimination based on degree of disability or economic criterion should be removed for children with disability up to the age of 0-14 years for the educational purpose to scale up the access to basic educational services.

7

Social Justice and the Issues of Rights and Freedom

The consultation paper entitled Pace of Socioeconomic Change under the Constitution released by the NCRWC takes a critical look at India's development experience since 1950, when the Constitution came into force. This chapter evaluates the successes and failures of the State in fulfilling its Constitutional obligation of assuring every citizen a life with dignity. The main concern of the chapter is whether socioeconomic progress made since independence has been fair, fast and equitable, particularly to those belonging to the vulnerable sections of the society like the Dalits, adivasis, women and children. The paper notes that the Indian economy has grown considerably since independence with the introduction of new technologies, modernization of agriculture, rapid industrialization and the production of a whole new range of goods and services. The initiation of economic reforms in 1991, such as the abolition of the license-quota raj, privatization of several government owned enterprises, reducing restrictions on exports and imports and reforms in the banking and the financial sectors have led to further economic growth. Statistics pertaining to the size of the economy, the monetary value of the goods and services produced and growth in per capita income are provided in the chapter. Inspired by the ideas of the Nobel Laureate economist Amartya Sen, the paper considers the level of human development as the criterion for evaluating progress, rather than considering development merely in terms of economic growth and rising levels of per capita income. Human development means the expansion of freedom and rights of the people so that they may have the capacity to lead the kind of life they value.

Human development therefore implies attaining freedom from fear, repression, discrimination and exploitation, freedom to lead a life of dignity, freedom from hunger and freedom to participate in decision-making in an informed and intelligent manner. The paper notes that though the aim of the State has been to achieve overall economic stability, the experience of the past 50 years has shown that this growth has not trickled down. This is made worse by the persistence of social disabilities such as the caste system, untouchability, religious taboos, and discrimination against women. Development, therefore, has not benefited the poorer sections of the society, including the Scheduled Castes and Tribes and backward classes. The paper thus points out, that the only way to ensure sustained development and socio-economic change is to have a rights-based approach to development, founded upon the principles of equity and justice for all. Indeed this is the very foundation upon which the founding fathers have erected the Constitution of India. The rights based approach means: the consideration of human rights, equity, equality, social justice and accommodation of diversity as being central to the conceptualization, design, implementation, delivery, monitoring and evaluation of all developmental processes. It was believed that the noble values of justice, liberty, equality and fraternity would serve to unify the diversity of India by dissolving the social inequities and assuring the dignity of the individual.

Recognizing pluralism as the core of democracy, the paper points out that the Constitution seeks humanism, endurance and higher values as its ultimate goals, which can be achieved by ensuring its citizens a free and just world. The paper states that the Constitution of India, reflects an "uncompromising" respect for human dignity, an "unquestioning" commitment to equality and an "overriding" concern for the poorest and weakest in society. This triad of concerns is enabled by the embodiment of a charter of fundamental rights and the directive principles of state policy. The constitution makers therefore embodied the principles of social justice in two parts of the constitution, i.e. Chapters III and IV. It is in fact the Constitutional mechanism for the realization of socio economic goals, which is mandatory for the promotion of freedom and ensuring every citizen a decent standard of living. This views a regime of rights where the social and economic rights are interdependent with political and civil rights. Over the years, the Supreme Court has progressively widened the scope of the right to life to include several social and economic rights. The paper, however, comes to the firm conclusion that the social and economic justice guaranteed to all citizens by the Constitution still eludes majority of the people comprising of women, the Scheduled Castes, the Scheduled Tribes, backward classes, unorganized workers and the poor.

RIGHT AND FREEDOM

A review of the fifty years reveals that the humanistic ideals of the Constitution have remained largely unrealized. The paper holds that the social and economic rights conferred upon the citizens by the Constitution of India have been systematically denied to them. The denial of rights has led to a condition of non-freedom. This conclusion is arrived at by the persistence of human deprivation over the last 50 years and by the existence of a series of non-freedoms, which has led to a condition of human poverty. In order to redress these deprivations, the paper has identified five major areas of socio-economic rights, which need to be instituted for the eradication of poverty. These socio-economic rights are the essential attributes of the right to life as guaranteed under Article 21 of the Constitution. The Supreme Court has emphasized this on many occasions. In its words, "we think that the right to life includes the right to live with human dignity and all that goes along with it, namely the bare necessities of life such as adequate nutrition, clothing and shelter over the head and facilities for reading, writing and expressing oneself in diverse forms." These basic socio-economic rights of food, water, shelter, clothing, education and a clean environment has eluded the vast majority of Indians despite 50 years of industrial growth and Constitutional assurance.

With the help of statistics and tables, the paper portrays, that even after considerable growth in the economy and the liberalization of the market, India falls short, even below Sub-Saharan Africa (the entire continent of Africa excluding Egypt, Tunisia, Libya, Algeria and Morocco which constitute the Maghreb region) in terms of health and literacy. In all cases, rural areas have suffered more than urban areas, the Scheduled Castes and Tribes more than the upper castes, women more than men and states like Madhya Pradesh, Bihar and Orissa have on an average fared worse than the rest of the country. The statistics show that Kerala has the least socio-economic disparity in all aspects compared to the other states of India. It is necessary to recognise the importance of political rights alongside social and economic rights. The relationship between the two sets of rights is important. Realisation of one is dependent on the availability of the other. The following sections will discuss the status of each of these socio-economic rights as enumerated in the above table.

RIGHT TO SURVIVAL

The paper looks at the right to survival from the point of view of life expectancy at birth and infant and maternal mortality. Life expectancy means the number of years an individual may expect to live in good health. Life expectancy increases when a safe and healthy living environment is available. This includes the availability of a good public health system, sanitation, access to safe drinking water and an adequate standard of living (which includes sufficient resources to buy these commodities and services and their availability at affordable prices). When the State fails to provide these basic civic amenities, the standard of living falls and the life expectancy of the citizens deteriorates. The paper shows that the rural poor, the lower castes and tribal communities, large numbers of women and children do not have access to these facilities, which the State has a responsibility to provide. This has contributed to their low standard of living, ill health and untimely and avoidable deaths. In 1999, WHO (World Health Organization) scientists developed a new indicator to measure life expectancy, called DALE or Disability Adjusted Life Expectancy. DALE estimates the expected number of years to be lived, which is equivalent of full health. The years of ill health are measured according to severity and subtracted from the expected overall life expectancy to give the equivalent years of healthy life.

The years lost in disability or ill health is substantially higher in poorer countries because of injuries, blindness, paralysis and tropical diseases like malaria and tuberculosis. People in the healthiest nations lose 9% of their lives to ill health as compared to 14% in worse off countries. In 24 countries, DALE equals or exceeds 70 years and is less than 40 years in 32 countries. Japan tops the list with a life expectancy of 74.5 years and Sierra Leone is in the bottom of the rung with a life expectancy of 25.9 years. The bottom 10 countries are in Sub-Saharan Africa where HIV-AIDS epidemic is rampant and is the leading cause of death. Life expectancy in India has increased from 32 years in 1950-51 to 63 years in 2000, yet it is less than that of Japan, China, Sri Lanka, Bangladesh and Nepal. The lowest life expectancy is in Madhya Pradesh with 57 years and the highest in Kerala with 75 years. Female life expectancy in Madhya Pradesh is one of the lowest in the world, 26 years lower than the life expectancy of Japan. In fact apart from Sub-Saharan Africa, only Sudan (56.4 years), Cambodia (55.2 years) and Lao P.D.R (55 years) have lower life expectancy than Madhya Pradesh does. It is believed that if women and men have equal access to care, nutrition, medical and other health facilities, women tend to outlive men, as they are biologically stronger. They are also more health conscious, more active and less prone to diseases. Even female fetuses have greater chances of being born; i.e. they have a lower probability of miscarriage than male fetuses.

Universally, though more male babies are born, as they increase in age, their proportion in the overall population begins to fall due to lesser chances of survival. As countries get richer, female mortality tends to decline faster than male mortality. In the industrialized nations, in the 1900s, the gap between female and male mortality was 2-3 years but by 1999 this gap had increased to 7-8 years. However, on a global scale as a whole, women do not outnumber men. This 'shortfall' of women is largely observed in Asia and North Africa. In the OECD countries, the life expectancy of women exceed that of men by 5 years, while in India, it exceeds by only a year. In Bihar, U.P. and Orissa, the situation is worse as the trend is reversed with the men outliving the women. Amartya Sen has spoken of the concept of 'missing women' to describe the phenomenon of "women who are simply not there, due to unusually high mortality compared with male mortality rates." This would refer to the increased number of women one would expect to find in a given country if both men and women received equal benefits from the public health care system. In his study of 1986, Sen had estimated 37 million missing women in India. This occurs when there is unchecked discrimination against women, as they receive much less attention and health care than men do. Women tend to work twice as much as men as they are active both within the domestic space as well as outside it, helping the men in their livelihood, particularly in the agricultural field. They clean, cook, wash, look after the children, fetch water, as well as weed, thresh, weaving etc. Their intake of food both in terms of quantity and nutrition is far less than the male members of the household and they suffer regularly from a deficiency of protein, iron and iodine.

Their decisions to undertake health care are usually governed and very often vetoed by their husbands and other seniour male members of the household. So even if the State provides adequate health care, women very often are denied access to it. The situation of missing women is enforced by the prevalence of female foeticide and infanticide. The paper presents statistics to show that Punjab, Haryana, Maharashtra,

Uttar Pradesh, Gujarat, Rajasthan and Andhra Pradesh, all have a female infant mortality rate that is higher than the male infant mortality rate. The Prenatal Diagnostics Techniques (Prevention and Misuse) Act, 1994, make sex selective abortions illegal. Despite the existence of such laws, public authorities continue to condone these inherent biases against women. Numerous women are made to go through it, as they are repeatedly humiliated at home for producing female babies. In a judgement delivered on 10th July, 2001, the Consumer Disputes Redressal Commission, Ahmedabad has observed that "the male child is always a precious child for the mother...to her it is of more value". This judgement serves to legitimize the inhuman gender bias against the girl child in our country and violates all norms of gender justice and equality. It is especially surprising as Gujarat has a high female IMR and the Commissioner has admitted that it is due to the sex selective abortions of female foetuses. The Consumer Commission's judgement reflects the social attitude towards women in India and particularly, the girl child to the extent it reveals the mindset of government officials.

The Supreme Court, in a recent judgement, has served notices on the Union and State Governments to enforce the existing law forbidding sex determination and selection procedures and subsequent abortion. These procedures have been criminally misused in collusion with medicos and clinics, which have mushroomed all over the country. The apex court has also directed that Pre-natal Diagnostics Techniques Act, 1994 be implemented and even amended, if necessary, to plug any loopholes. Infant Mortality Rate (IMR) is the probability of dying between birth and exactly one year of age expressed per 1,000 live births. India has one of the highest infant mortality rates (IMR) in South Asia at 70 per 1000, although her per capita income may be higher than some of her neighbouring countries. This is despite the fact that the number of infants dying at birth or soon after birth has reduced by half since independence. The rate of improvement of child survival in India is very slow, in fact, slower than that of other South Asian countries.

The first 28 days after a child is born, or the neonatal period, is critical. This is the time when fundamental health and feeding practices are established. It is during this time that the child is at the highest risk of death and requires protection against illnesses, including malnutrition and infections. One million children die each year from lack of breast-feeding. The paper states that IMR is a comprehensive development indicator, as it reflects the quality of people's lives, specially, the income and education of the parents, the prevalence of malnutrition and disease, availability of sanitation and health facilities and the position of women. Most importantly, it reflects the unequal opportunities for survival faced by the child. In India, the rate of maternal mortality (MMR) or the number of mothers dying while giving birth to children or soon after paints an even grimmer picture. Maternal death is the death of a woman while pregnant or within 42 days of termination of pregnancy, from any cause related to or aggravated by the pregnancy. Direct maternal deaths can result from medical complexities such as hemorrhage, unsafe abortion, obstructed labour, interventions, incorrect treatment etc. Indirect deaths occur from previously existing diseases such as malaria, anaemia or HIV/AIDS. Often diseases occur during pregnancy.

The MMR measures the obstetric risk and the frequency with which they are exposed to this risk. It is calculated as the number of maternal deaths in a given period per 100,000 women of reproductive age (15-49 years). Maternal mortality rate was first estimated in 1980. In 1996, WHO and UNICEF discovered that the problem was significantly greater than they had calculated. They estimated that 600,000 maternal deaths occurred each year, with the overwhelming majority of them in developing countries. In developing regions, one woman in 12 die compared to one in 4000 in industrialized countries. Of these deaths in the developing countries, 25% is from hemorrhage or excessive bleeding and 20% is from preexisting diseases, significant of which is anaemia, an indicator of under nourishment and iron deficiency. According to official estimates, the maternal mortality rate in India in

2000 was 408 per 100,000 live births. Not only is maternal mortality extremely high but it is 100 times higher than in the developed countries of the West. It is also higher than most other less developed countries. The maternal survival rate is so low in Uttar Pradesh that only five countries in the world claim to have a survival rate, which is higher. Poor access to safe reproductive health, emergency obstetric assistance and inadequate health care and nutrition for women is some of the main reasons for this high rate of mothers dying due to childbirth related complications. The death of woman during pregnancy is not only a health issue but also a matter of social justice.

Governments are not only required to ensure appropriate health care during pregnancy and childbirth, but women have rights to decide whether, when and how often to bear children. Governments must address these factors within the legal and health systems, which deny women these rights. These rights can be provided through the primary health care system and include information on reproductive health issues, include family planning, abortion and sex education. Government'' health care should be non-discriminatory, in that women should not be required to obtain consent of husbands or parental authorization in healthcare interventions. Laws should be reformed to bring about such change.

RIGHT TO GOOD HEALTH

Low life expectancy and high infant and maternal mortality rates reflect the status of health of citizens' in the country. Hence, the above discussion on the right to survival would remain incomplete unless it is linked to the debate on the right to good health. The paper states that there is a lack of systematic and reliable data on the state of citizens health in India, so it has relied on what it terms as 'surrogate' (or stand in) indicators. These include child malnutrition, low birth weight babies, anaemia and access to safe drinking water and sanitation as markers for identifying the status of health. Bangladesh and India have the highest level of child malnutrition in the world. Despite a remarkable expansion in food production and good stock of food grains, 53% of children less than 5 years in India suffer from lack of appropriate, adequate and nutritious food. The level of malnutrition is twice that of Sub-Saharan Africa. The reduction in the level of child malnutrition has been painfully slow, with estimates showing that it reduced by 5% between 1992-3 and 1998-99. The reduction in the level of 'wasted' children was less than 4%. This sordid situation calls for an improvement in child health care, improved knowledge of childcare practices and better health care for mothers.

Even primary health care like immunization is not accessible to all in India. The official survey of 1998-99 reveals that merely 42% babies were immunized against life threatening diseases, of which Bihar and Rajasthan have negligible records. The child in India begins its life by being malnourished in the womb and therefore is born with low birth weight. The child continues to remain malnourished, as the mother may not be able to nurse the newborn baby with her own milk adequately, due to her own weak condition. This is because women in India do not get the required nutritious diet and rest, especially during pregnancy after childbirth. Data shows that only 1/3 of deliveries in the rural areas are attended by medical professionals. After 6 months, when the child is due to be weaned and introduced to eat solid food, the mother leaves the baby in the care of its elder siblings as she has to go to work in order to feed the whole family. The siblings being young themselves are unable to tend to the child, who thus continue to remain under nourished without any proper food or care. Hence it is not surprising that the proportion of low birth weight babies in India is 33%, making the level of child malnutrition in India twice that of Sub-Saharan Africa. This child is born malnourished and continues to remain unfed even during periods of bumper harvests, let alone during famine and droughts. The paper observes that the root of child malnutrition therefore, does not lie in income levels or food availability but in the manner in which society treats its women and cares for its children.

An indicator of the poor health of women is the existence of anaemia. Anaemia or chronic iron deficiency is the most prevalent kind of malnutrition in India. It is caused by low intake of food among the poor. Severe anaemia leads to the birth of premature babies, low birth weights and still births and causes 34.5% of maternal deaths. The National Family Health Survey in 1998-99 states that 52% married women aged 15-49 years and 74% children below 3 years suffer from anaemia. Andhra Pradesh has 50% anaemia. A study done by James, Aitken and Subramaniam claim that anaemia in India is 88% and this has remained constant for a long time. Amartya Sen holds, that the gender bias reflected in the neglect of the girl child and women in general lead to under nourishment of pregnant women, which in turn leads to deprivation of nutrition to the foetus, the birth of underweight babies and subsequent child malnutrition. The child ultimately grows up to live in poor health and if a girl child, the vicious cycle is repeated. Therefore, Sen states that, the deprivation faced by women also adversely affects men. Apart from medical facilities, access to safe drinking water and proper and adequate sanitation facilities are the pressing needs for the health of a nation. According to official estimates 90% of India's population have access to safe drinking water but the paper states that this is a mirage and not ground reality.

Large numbers of people in both rural and urban areas do not have access to safe drinking water. This is due to lack of physical access for geographical reasons (such as the distant location of dwellings from water sources), social reasons (such as exclusion of dalits, tribals and other social outcastes) and contamination from chemical poisoning like arsenic or from industrial wastes being disposed into water bodies, prevalence of waterborne diseases and the gradual depletion of the water table due to indiscriminate drilling of borewells for water supply in urban areas and agricultural purposes in rural areas. The combination of the above mentioned facts indicate that though there is an extensive network of public health care and sanitation system in India, it is poor in quality, inefficient and inaccessible to the vast majority of the population. Public health care has not been able to tackle widespread infectious diseases like Malaria, Tuberculosis, Hepatitis, HIV/AIDS. Thousands succumb to these diseases every year. The consultation paper holds that the spread of these infectious diseases cannot be contained without the active participation of civil society. Government run public hospitals have serious logistic and administrative problems which make them inefficient, while the honesty and integrity of government officials are also doubtful. As a result, people are losing faith in them. In such situations, civil society interventions appear to be the only way out of the imbroglio.

The Alma Ata Declaration which was signed by a majority of countries of the world including India, in 1978 had promised "health for all" by the year 2000. It was expected that with adequate investments in health infrastructures and an appropriate mix of public health strategies, the countries would be able to meet this goal. Despite the setting up of complex medical and health infrastructures involving teaching, training and research, drugs and medical instrument production in India, the general public remains dissatisfied with the services they receive in terms of both cost and quality. The truth of the matter is that a disproportionately large amount of health expenditure remains concentrated in urban, technologically intensive, curative medicare. There has been a proliferation of private medicare facilities and the setting up of super specialty hospitals in big cities and towns, while the primary and secondary health care systems, which are mainly found in rural areas, have declined steadily. The growing private sector has attracted more and more doctors and medical professionals trained using public funds, at the cost of the public health system. The bottom line is that access to both general and specialty health care, especially in the rural areas, remains unavailable to a large majority. The Bhore Committee in 1946 had advocated a focus on preventive heath, i.e. nutrition and clean drinking water, control of communicable diseases and the establishment of a rural medicare system. This was reiterated by the ICSSR (Indian Council of Social Science Research)-ICMR (Indian Council of

Medical Research) Health for All Report of 1978.

There has also been innumerable low cost, community based health care experiments conducted by voluntary organizations that have been successful, models from which the government could have drawn inspiration and lessons. Structures of inequality and inequity within the system are being persistently ignored. State policy has remained obsessed with family planning and population control. The nomenclature may have changed in recent years to reproductive and child health and safe motherhood and child survival, but the underlying focus continues to be population control rather than a holistic approach to public health. A holistic approach can also profitably accommodate the non-allopathic systems of medicine, such as ayurveda, unani, homeopathy, folk and tribal medicine, which is still followed by the majority of the people in our country. These non-allopathic systems use medicinal plants and herbs available in plenty throughout India and are used in traditional ways. These indigenous systems of medicine have existed since time immemorial and the knowledge has been handed down over several generations. The rural poor, who comprise the majority of the country's population, are dependent on these traditional and folk systems of medicine for their primary health care. The Draft National Health Policy 2001 released by the Ministry of Health and family Planning, Government of India, recognizes the lacunae in state policy as mentioned above.

It has identified Kerala, Maharashtra and Tamil Nadu as the better performing states and Orissa, Bihar, Rajasthan, Uttar Pradesh and Madhya Pradesh as the low performing states as far as health is concerned. It advocates strongly, the role of civil society intervention and the complementary use of traditional medical systems such as Ayurveda and Unani. Most significantly, it focuses on the wide interstate and rural/urban disparity in accessing public health care. The Policy observes that this implies that "for vulnerable sections of society in several states, access to public health services is nominal and health standards are grossly inadequate." This persistence on social inequity is the message of the new Health Policy. In the words of the Policy as stated in Para 2.2.3, "it is a principal objective of NHP 2001 to evolve a policy structure which reduces these inequities and allows the disadvantaged sections of society a fairer access to public health services."

FREEDOM FROM HUNGER

The most fundamental of all socio-economic rights is an individual's right to food. Food constitutes an essential need and a basic right for all individuals. Without food the right to life loses meaning, as human lives are dependent on the consumption of food on a daily basis. In this sense, the right to food can be said to be centrally embedded in the most fundamental of all human rights namely, the right to life. While human society has achieved unprecedented scientific and technological progress during the last few centuries, millions of people around the world remain hungry every night. The gravity of the situation is put into perspective by a recent FAO (Food and Agricultural Organization) estimate. More than 800 million people face chronic undernutrition and 200 million children under the age of five suffer from chronic calorie and protein deficiencies in developing countries alone. In spite of the fact that the "right to food" has been frequently endorsed by nations with both unanimity and urgency, economists have pointed out that no other human right has been as comprehensively violated on such a wide scale in recent decades.

Right to food, as laid down in Article 11.2 of the International Covenant on Economic, Social and Cultural Rights refers to the "fundamental right of everyone to be free from hunger." Hunger not only means absence of food but also an inadequacy of food. To be free from hunger is to be adequately fed. For food to be adequate, it must be nutritious, safe and accessible. It must have sufficient nutritional content, be readily available and affordable and be free from harmful content like poisons. The state therefore has a duty to protect and ensure the food adequacy and food security of its citizens. Basic needs such as the need to eat in order to survive must be fulfilled and the state has a mandate to do so. Unless that right is first fulfilled, the protection of other human rights becomes a mockery for those who must spend all their energy to feed themselves in order to survive another day. Therefore citizens in such countries enjoy the right to food as a freedom which is justifiable. Even after 50 years of independence and a tremendous increase in food production levels and the 'successful' ushering in of a Green Revolution, India has 260 million people living below the poverty line.

According to official statistics, poverty has reduced from 47% to 27.09%, between the years 1951-2000, but this pace is too slow to ensure socio-economic justice to the entire population. The paper holds that the quality and reliability of official statistics regarding poverty levels in India is doubtful. The use of different methodologies to determine poverty levels by different government and statistical survey agencies throw up a variety of data that are difficult to compare with each other. Hence though the Planning Commission's Report shows there has been a reduction in the number of people living below the poverty line, other estimates arrived at by economists such as Suresh D. Ten-dulkar and S. P. Gupta show an increase between 1989-90 and 1998 which includes the first phase of economic reforms beginning in 1991. Newspaper reportage and independent studies show that states like Orissa, Bihar and Rajasthan harbor starvation deaths, although officially it has been denied. In Orissa, the horror stories of parents selling their children in order to feed themselves have been prominent in the national dailies in recent times.

The reduction in the level of income poverty has not only been slow but uneven among the states. In the last three decades, although Kerala, Punjab and Haryana have managed to reduce income poverty by 75%, Orissa and Bihar have achieved less than 32%. The government has tried to reduce poverty levels through it's Anti Poverty programme, an important component of which is the Public Distribution System (PDS). The PDS is a food subsidy programme for the poor, where essential commodities like wheat, rice, sugar, edible oil and kerosene are distributed through a network of

Fair Price Shops. There are 4.6 lakh Fair Price Shops across India, which serve 180 million Ration Cardholders. The PDS however has failed to deliver with Fair Price Shops largely remaining inoperative and one third of the food supply diverted to other channels flouting all ethical norms. Yet at the same time the Food Corporation of India hoards huge stocks of food grains in its godowns as the people do not have the money to buy them. To counter the failure of the PDS, the system of Food Coupons had been introduced as an experimental measure in some areas. It has also been suggested that a percentage of Fair Price Shops be reserved for members of the Scheduled Castes and Scheduled Tribes.

The consensus arrived at by the consultation paper is that the PDS benefitted the urban areas and failed to serve the population that lives below the poverty line. It did not succeed in reaching out to the poorest of the poor and instead catered to those who live above the poverty line. Subsequently, the Chief Ministers' conference held in July 1996, recommended that the PDS should be revamped as the Targeted Public Distribution System (TPDS). The TPDS, which was adopted in June 1997, is a two tier subsidized pricing structure for families living below the poverty line (BPL) and those living above the poverty line (APL). The thrust of the TPDS is to include only the really poor and vulnerable sections of the society such as the agricultural labourers, marginal farmers, rural artisans/ craftsmen, potters, tappers, weavers, blacksmiths, carpenters, porters, rickshaw-pullers, handcart pullers, and fruit and flower sellers on the pavement. In the BPL scheme, the government is committed to issue 10 kg. of food grain per month per family at 50% of the economic cost of the Food Corporation of India (FCI). In practice, this works out to be much less. Under the APL, foodgrain is available at 90% of the FCI cost. The amount of food grain currently in need per annum is 156. 49 kilo tonnes for BPL families and 106.31 kilo tonnes for APL families. The states have the option of providing additional allocation of foodgrain in case there is a shortage. The budgeted provision for TPDS for 2000-2001 is Rs. 12.50 crores. In fact, the Union Budget for 2000-2001 doubled the monthly allocation of foodgrain for BPL families.

To make TPDS more targeted towards the poor, the Antyodaya Anna Yojana was launched in December, 2000. It aims at identifying 10 million poor families and providing them with 25 kg. of foodgrain per family per month at Rs. 2/kg. for wheat and Rs. 3/kg. for rice. The estimated annual allocation under this programme is 30 lakh tonnes of foodgrain involving a subsidy of Rs. 2315 crores. Despite these efforts, the quantity of foodgrain is insufficient. The supplies are not timely and the quality is often poor and nutritionally inadequate. The PDS and the system of food coupons and midday meals are seen as temporary measures to overcome what is a more systemic problem. Eradication of poverty can only be achieved with food security, which is associated with a more ecologically oriented agricultural policy. The question needs to be addressed as to why the producer of food is the first to be denied his right to his basic need. The small farmer in India, who is the actual tiller of the soil, has remained marginalities, barely eking out an existence for himself and his family. This is the result of the unequal land holding pattern, which was brought about during the British rule. It created big landlords who own large tracts of land, which were then leased to middle farmers.

The middle farmers, in turn, lease it out to the tillers who are the small and marginal farmers, at an extremely high rate of rent. Sometimes, when they cannot afford the rent, they are employed as labourers by the middle and big farmers to till their land. The small farmers therefore often remain landless or are weighed under the burden of debt to the moneylender, the big and middle farmers. These marginal farmers, who are either tenants or landless agricultural labourers, are the actual tillers of the soil, who toil day and night to produce the crops and vegetables for the nation. Unfortunately, being caught in a vicious cycle of poverty and debt traps, they remain the poorest of the poor and very often, unfed. So, the provider of food is denied his right to food security. In July 2001, PUCL filed a petition in the Supreme Court against the state governments of Orissa,

Rajasthan, Chattisgarh, Maharashtra, Gujarat and Himachal Pradesh, alleging them responsible for starvation deaths in their respective states. PUCL raised the question whether or not the scope of right to life as provided in Article 21 of the Constitution of India, included the right to food. Right to food implies that the State has a duty to provide food, especially in situations of draught, to people who are affected by it and are not in a position to purchase food. The petition drew the Courts attention to the fact that a surplus of 50 million tons of food grain was lying unused and rotting in the godowns of the FCI, while the poor continued to starve because of lack of food.

The Supreme Court, appalled and concerned, said that the government's priority should be to provide food to the aged, infirm, disabled, destitute, pregnant and lactating women in draught-prone areas and asked the state governments to devise schemes to tackle the situation. The Bench observed that though there was plenty of food, lack of distribution among the poor and an inefficient officialdom were responsible for creating a situation of scarcity. The Court asked the state governments to reopen closed public distribution shops within a week and to identify the poor families for food grain distribution under the Antyodaya scheme, which is reserved for the poorest of the poor. Most state governments not only failed to comply but those who did were unable to provide evidence of it to the Court. The Supreme Court took strong exception to this and described the situation as callous and horrendous. The matter is pending in the Court and is the first time that the right to food was discussed so substantively in the apex body as a necessary extension of the right to life.

RIGHT TO EDUCATION

A very essential socio-economic right is the right to education and together with the rights to shelter, food and health falls within the scope of right to life. Although most of the international covenants on human rights speak about the duty of the state to provide free and compulsory elementary education to all, right to education was originally not a part of the fundamental rights included in the Constitution of India. The founding fathers however, did endow the State with some responsibilities for the education of the nation. Article 45, which is a part of the Directive Principles of State Policy and hence is non-justifiable, gives the space to the State to attempt and provide free and compulsory education to all children until they complete the age of 14 years. This task was to be completed by 1960 but universal elementary education remains an unfulfilled dream. According to official statistics in 2001, India has a literacy rate of 65.38%. As many as 350 million people are still unable to either read or write. While the literacy rate for men is 75.96% it is a dismal 54.28% for women. The consultation paper throws up some more shocking facts. India' overall adult literacy rate of 52% (1991) and female literacy rate of 38% (1991) are lower than that of Sub-Saharan Africa and East Asia. The average years of schooling and completion of elementary education are considerably lower in India than other South Asian countries such as Sri Lanka, Indonesia, and Malawi in Africa. The literacy rate for Indian women is perhaps one of the lowest in the world, with further disparities across states and communities.

Typically, the worst affected are women from rural areas. The literacy rate among Scheduled Tribe women in Rajasthan is an appalling 4% (1991). Bihar, one of the states with the lowest literacy level has 50% of female children attending schools (1998-99). Only 15 countries in the world have a lower literacy level among women than Bihar. This, despite the fact, that Article 46 of the Constitution directs the state to take special care of the educational interests of the weaker sections of the society, especially the Scheduled Castes and Scheduled Tribes. Interestingly, almost 95% villages in India have a school within a walking distance of one kilometer, yet the national survey of 1997 reveal that half the proportion of Indian women and one-third of the men are illiterate. The paper notes that in many single teacher based village schools, the teacher appoints deputies, agents or seniour students to do the teaching on his behalf, which contributes to the poor quality of education in these schools and lead to dropouts. Quality in compulsory elementary education is of essence. The qualified and well-trained teaching personnel prefer to be employed in the better known schools in cities, rather than teach in village schools. The quality of education in wealthy schools located in urban areas is consequently, far superior than in rural educational institutions. This increases the hiatus between the 'better-educated-urban-rich' and 'poorly-educated- rural-poor'.

The paper therefore suggests that civil society participation through voluntary organizations, self-help groups, neighbourhood committees, is necessary to address a task of this magnitude, rather than leaving it in the hands of the administrative officials who are usually perceived to be corrupt and inefficient. Education does not merely train students to acquire skills so that they may secure jobs for a living. Education has many social benefits. Improved levels of education and awareness can be directly linked to improvement in hygiene, reduction in infant mortality rates, decline in population growth rates, increase in labour productivity, greater political empowerment and democratization. Yet, despite numerous commissions and experiments, universal education looks like a distant dream. The Shiksha Karmi project in Rajasthan, which involved community and voluntary organizations, has shown that both quantitative and qualitative retention has been high. Even in rural and 'socially backward' areas, parents are keen to send their children to school, but these schools should be within walking distance, should have flexible timings to suit life cycles characteristic of specific communities for example those dependent on agriculture or those who migrate to nearby towns in search of jobs during the lean season, should have textbooks in local languages/ dialects and at least one female teacher.

Children from poor families often cannot afford to attend school, as they have to supplement the family income by working in the fields, in brick kilns, tending cattle or shepherding or simply looking after the household in the absence of parents especially if the girl child happens to be the eldest sibling. Keeping this is mind, many states initiated a mid-day meal programme to encourage parents to send their children to school. But these schemes have had varying degrees of success in increasing enrolment and reducing dropout rates. The debate finally has led to the question of education as a fundamental human right by the Supreme Court. The Universal Declaration of Human Rights in Article 26 and 15 states unambiguously that "everyone has a right to education" and that elementary education should be free and compulsory. The Convention on the Rights of the Child states in Article 28 and 16, that every child has a right to education and that such education should be free and compulsory. The International Covenant on Economic, Social and Cultural Rights, recognizes in Article 13 and 17, the right of everyone to education and that 14 The Shiksha Karmi project hired young middle school educated youngsters to teach working children in accessible night schools by involving the community and local NGOs. Article 26.1 "Everyone has the right to education. Education shall be free, a least in the elementary and fundamental stages. Elementary education shall be compulsory.

Teaching and professional education shall be made generally available and higher education shall be equally accessible to all on the basis of merit." Article 28.1 "State Parties recognize the right of the child to education, and with a view to achieving this right progressively and on the basis of equal opportunity, they shall, in particular: (a) Make primary education compulsory and available free to all; (b) Encourage the development of different forms of secondary education, including general and vocational education, make them available and accessible to every child, and take appropriate measures such as the introduction of free education and offering financial assistance in case of need; (c) Make higher education accessible to all on the basis of capacity by every appropriate means; (d) Make educational and vocational information and guidance available and accessible to all children; (e) Take measures to encourage regular attendance at schools and the reduction of dropout rates." Article 13.1 "The State Parties to the present Covenant recognize the right of everyone to education. They agree that education shall be directed to the full development of the human personality and the sense of its dignity, and shall strengthen the respect for human rights and fundamental freedoms. They further agree that education shall enable all persons to participate effectively in a free society, promote understanding, tolerance and friendship among all nations and all racial, ethnic or religious groups, and further the activities of the United Nations for the maintenance of peace.

The State Parties to the present Covenant recognize that, with a view to achieving the full realization of this right: primary education should be compulsory and free to all. Though the constitution makers recognized the importance of providing universal primary education they did not go to the extent of making it a fundamental right, as they were aware of the meager volume of financial resources that India possessed at the time of independence. Yet they made the State responsible for providing free and universal elementary education to all children up to the age of 14 years within a decade by incorporating a guideline in the Directive Principles of State Policy. But citizens could not approach the courts demanding that the State honour its obligation, as the directive was not justiciable like a fundamental right. Despite the passage of more than four decades since the inauguration of the constitution this promise was not fulfilled. Hence it is not surprising that the Supreme Court of India in Unnikrishnan's case, said, that education upto the age of 14 years should be considered a fundamental right. The 83rd Constitution Amendment Bill was introduced in the Rajya Sabha for that express purpose, but only as late as July 1997. The Bill was referred to the Parliamentary Standing Committee on Human Resource Development, which placed its recommendations in front of both Houses within three months but and yet the government did not act upon it.

Educationists and voluntary organizations lobbied strongly for making education a fundamental right given the alarming levels of illiteracy and ignorance within the country.

The National Alliance for Fundamental Right to Education (NAFRE), a coalition of hundreds of NGOs, was formed. These voluntary groups argued that constitutional commitment is a firm necessity in order to bring the school to the child. Without this commitment, political will remains ineffective despite promises ritualistically made by almost all parties at the time of every general election. Opinions vary on this point, the main criticism being that the State cannot take the burden of proving free education to all as it is difficult for it to marshall the necessary financial resources for quality education. However, it is indisputable that unless the State is compelled to live upto its Constitutional commitment, the excuses for non-performances will continue to exist. Finally, in September 2001, the Parliament incorporated the recommendations of the Parliamentary Standing Committee and adopted the 93rd Amendment Bill. The Bill was passed on 28th November, 2001. The 93rd Amendment expanded the scope of right to life under Article 21 by including right to education as one of its essential components. It inserted Article 21A which provides that all children between the age of 6-14 years shall enjoy the fundamental right to free and compulsory education, especially those who were dropouts or were not enrolled at all.

A majority of these children belonged to the Scheduled Castes and Tribes and other Backward Classes. It also amended Article 45 to include Early Childhood Care and Education (ECCE) which would be provided to all children between age 0-6 years. The 93rd Amendment however has been severely criticized by educationists and voluntary organisations. They claim that the Amendment dilutes Unnikrishnan's judgement, which speaks of a fundamental right to education for all, whereas the Amendment has granted it only to those between the age of 6-14 years. The crucial age group of 0-6 years has been left out. Educationists also feel that ECCE or early childhood care should be made a part of the fundamental right to education and not made part of the Directive Principles of State Policy. The Amendment has not made any provisions for financial allocation, which will have a bearing upon the quality of the education. Finally, the concept of free education is limited, as the parents in poor families will have to bear the costs of uniforms and textbooks. The 10th Five Year Plan claimed that Universal Elementary Education will be achieved by 2007 but the Union Human Resource Development Ministry has said that it will not be possible to attain this before 2010. It is indeed laudable that the scope of right to life in the Constitution of India has been expanded to incorporate this integral socio-economic right to education, but it remains to be seen how the people exercise it and the duration it will take the Government to act upon it.

FREEDOM FROM GENDER-BASED DISCRIMINATION

Of all the disadvantaged groups, women have been denied their socio-economic rights the most severely. This has taken the form of gender-based discrimination and has prevented women from participating in the process of development. In India, there are several forms of gender-based discrimination such as a discrepancy in the male and female levels of literacy, anti-female bias in mortality as expressed in rising levels of female foeticide and infanticide, a lack of freedom to make choices to a lack of decision making power. There is also the denial of a whole range of socio- economic rights from no equal opportunity to work to domestic violence and sexual harassment at the workplace. Following Amartya Sen, the paper holds that the crucial aspect of development is the political, economic and social participation as well as leadership of women. Female infanticide and foeticide is one of the most appalling aspects of gender discrimination.

The occurrence of these practices has increased with the advent of sex determination tests. The low female ratio in India's population was detected as early as 1951, when the first post independence census was undertaken. This deficit in the female population has increased over the years. While the cause of the earlier gender deficit was due to female infanticide traditionally prevalent in many States, the recent deficiency begins from the womb itself, soon after conception, after the sex of the foetus is identified in a labouratory. In

European countries, USA, and Japan, there are 95-97 males per 100 females indicating a marginally higher proportion of women in the population. The obsessive preference for sons and a deeply entrenched patriarchal system has given South Asia one of the most distorted sex ratios in the world - 940 females for every 1000 males. Only in the SAARC countries and China is the ratio unfavourable for the female. In some Indian States, the ratio is as low as 800 females/1,000 males. Kerala is the only State in India, where the gender ratio is comparable to that in European countries and USA.

It is commendable, more so, as the state relates it to the highest female literacy rate. Kerala has the lowest birth rate in India despite having a very high population density. This confirms what specialists have always indicated that female literacy goes hand in hand with population control. When women are educated, they are more aware of the choices that are before them and their consequences. They are conversant with health and family issues and have access to the necessary information about reproductive health and can therefore exercise their discretion and chose wisely. The NSSO estimates of 1997 show that half of the women population in India is illiterate while in the case of men it is only a quarter. The 2001 estimates quoted above reveal that of the total number of illiterates, approximately 76% are men, while only 54% are women. The number of dropouts among women is higher. The male-female ratio is higher in Rajasthan, Madhya Pradesh, Bihar, Uttar Pradesh and Orissa, crossing a differential gap of 25%. Rajasthan has a differential ratio of 38%, lower than all other countries of the world except Guinea-Bissau and Yemen.

If women are the worst sufferers of human deprivation in India, one of the main reasons has been their invisibility in the economy. Economic independence is significant as it enhances the social status of women, especially in rewarding occupations. This improves their lot in life considerably, enabling them to break out of discriminatory conditions voluntarily. There is a lack of economic empowerment of women as they are denied the freedom to work as well as equal opportunities at and to work. Among women belonging to the working age of 18-45 years, only 34% have jobs of which 75% is in the agricultural sector. Mechanization in the agriculture sector has marginalised women. In the organised sector, women work under contracts, which give them no rights. In the small industries, the hours of work are long and the income miserable. Women's salary is usually less than the prescribed minimum wages and they are denied maternity leave and crèche facilities. A small section of urban women have access to higher education, while the bulk of the work done by the women in the country remains unnoticed and unrecognized.

This has been recognised by ILO recently as they realize that a large and silent majority of the labour force are women and is seeking to redefine 'work' as 'decent work', which is altogether a new concept. The trend so far has been to overlook and not see women as primary earners, their working conditions and rights as workers, the importance of informal work, the issue of sexual division of labour and the link between women's work, status and the market. Reproductive labour is another form of discrimination and is not accounted for while calculating national income figures. Sri Lanka includes it while computing GDP figures. Sexual harassment at the workplace has become a common source of violence against women and a tool whereby they are denied equal opportunities at work. People who enjoy a certain position of power in a place of employment often try to coerce and intimidate those in a subordinate position, for sexual favour in exchange of employment benefits. The Supreme Court's landmark judgement in Vishaka 19, states that,

- "Sexual harassment of women in the workplace results in the violation of the fundamental rights of gender equality and the right to life and liberty.
- It is a clear violation of the rights under Articles 14, 15, 21...and 19(1)(g)...
- Gender equality includes protection from sexual

harassment and the right to work with dignity, which is a universally recognised basic human right."

The judgement has lain down, that in the absence of domestic laws dealing with women's rights and protection from sexual harassment, the judicial process would intervene to facilitate the process. Judicial activism is to be supplemented by international conventions and norms which guarantee these abovementioned rights of gender equality and the right to work in dignity such as the Convention on the Elimination of All Forms of Discrimination Against Women (CEDAW). The judgement also draws attention to the commitment made by the Government of India at the Fourth World Conference on Women in Beijing, to operationalise a national policy on women and to set up a Commission for Women's Rights to "act as a public defender of women's human rights... (and) therefore reliance can be placed (on it)...for the purpose of construing the nature and ambit of Constitutional guarantee of gender equality in our Constitution."

The judgement observes repeatedly, "the absence of enacted law to provide for the effective enforcement of the basic human right of gender equality and guarantee against sexual harassment...particularly at workplaces...". The Court for the first time in India lay down guidelines and norms in *Vishaka,*

- "for strict observance...until a legislation is enacted for the purpose...and (the Vishaka guidelines are to be) treated as the law declared by the Supreme Court."
- It expanded the scope of the definition of "sexual harassment" by including indirect and implied sexually determined behaviour and sexually coloured remarks.
- It considered it discrimination when a woman's work or employment is disadvantaged due to a hostile work environment.
- "That appropriate work conditions should be provided in respect of work, leisure, health and hygiene to ensure...that no woman employee...is disadvantaged in

connection with her employment."

The Vishaka judgment is therefore symbolic in ushering in judicial activism in the arena of gender justice. Sexual harassment falls under the general rubric of crimes against women, which also includes another very large sector where there is gross discrimination against women, namely, domestic violence. In 1992, the Government of India coined the term "Crimes against Women" as a distinct category which includes, along with sexual harassment, rape, abduction, dowry deaths, torture and molestation. The term now used increasingly is domestic violence. The paper, citing the National Crimes Records Bureau states that there are almost 7000 complaints of domestic violence reported to the Delhi Police every year, out of which FIRs have been filed in only 10% of the cases.

The paper holds that it is only in the political sphere that women's participation has been observed and where there has been significant gain. This has been enabled by the 73rd and 74th Amendments to the Constitution, which have created new institutions for local governance. These Panchayati Raj institutions have opened new possibilities for women's participation in political decision-making, especially for the rural women. It has facilitated the building of linkages between voluntary organisations and the poor, rural women as well as the women's groups in the urban areas. The Panchayat Raj institutions have seen the creation of 227,698-Gram Panchayats, 5906 Panchayat Samitis and 474 Zilla Parishads, where nearly 3 million members have been elected. The Constitution amendments have ensured that one third of the seats are reserved for women at all levels.

The paper states that the impact of this has been phenomenal as by 1999, nearly 8,11,194 women had been elected as members of these bodies. Contrarily, women have never been adequately represented at higher levels of policy and decision making namely, parliament, state legislatures, council of ministers and the cabinet at the state and central levels, and the civil services. The presence of women in Parliament is lower than the global average. Women are better represented in the parliaments of Bangladesh and Sub-Saharan African countries. Even neighbouring Sri Lanka has a higher representation of women in its cabinet. The participation of women in the judiciary is even worse where against 500 odd male high court judges, there are only 15 women judges. The Supreme Court, occasionally, has one woman judge amongst its 25 members.

The involvement of women in the three central services namely, the Indian Administrative Service, IPS and IFS and those serving in the Government of India at the higher levels is abysmally low. The paper points out that even after 50 years of the working of the Constitution, women remain underrepresented at various levels of government services, denying them not only their share of income but also the space to enhance their status. The paper states, that although women have begun to enjoy decision-making power in the political arena, at least at the rural level, there is a range of sociocultural factors, which curb the freedom of women. Women on the whole do not enjoy the freedom to make decisions about their lives and live within the grip of a patriarchal culture. They do not enjoy the freedom of choosing whom to marry and when to marry or whether to pursue a career or education. The paper states that 50% of women in India are married before the legal age of 18 years. The National Family Health Survey-2 of 1998-99 show that in Uttar Pradesh, Andhra Pradesh, Madhya Pradesh, Rajasthan and Bihar, over 62% women are married below the age of 18 years.

Women are also denied their reproductive rights, in that they do not make decisions regarding their health and bodies, especially when, where and how many children they should conceive or whether or not they choose to abort their pregnancies. Women cannot leave their houses without the permission of their husbands, fathers or brothers. The paper cites statistics to show that in Uttar Pradesh, Madhya Pradesh, Bihar and Haryana, 80-85% women require permission even to go to the market, let alone to visit friends or relatives. It therefore points to a need for an attitudinal change towards and among women, without which women cannot free themselves from discrimination. This may be judged from the level of autonomy they enjoy and their share in the decision making of their own lives and their household, their freedom to decide their destiny and their freedom to make choices. It speaks of breaking out from a certain socio-cultural mindset, from the threshold of patriarchy towards true gender equality.

The focus of the government has now gradually changed from viewing women within the framework of family welfare to gender equity and oppression faced by women belonging to a wide spectrum of class/caste. The focus is on rape and wife battering, maintenance and child custody, legislative reform, opposing sexist curriculum in education and towards equal opportunity at work with equal pay. This shift in focus has been largely due to relentless lobbying and pressure from the voluntary organizations and the women's movement who have challenged as well as informed state policy, very often through the judicial process.

They have also begun to enter into partnership with the government in order to bring about change from within. Women's groups have pointed out that the government's initiatives perceive women's empowerment as instrumental for development and not as gender equality per se. The ultimate aim is to see women's rights as human rights, which is what the Constitution delineated in the first place 50 years ago, but which remains unrealized.

It is clear from the above discussions on socio-economic rights, that the majority of the population of our country does not enjoy the basic amenities of a dignified life, namely food, shelter, clothing, health and education. This majority consists of the poorest of the poor, tribal communities, *Dalits*, lower and backward castes and women and children. In all areas, the poor have suffered more than the affluent, the rural regions fared far worse than the urban ones and women as a rule have borne the brunt of deprivation and discrimination. There is interstate, inter-region and interclass disparity, and it is this gross social inequity which has marked the history of economic development in India. To redress this social inequity a strong regime of rights is a primary prerequisite, for political empowerment can hasten the process of economic alleviation. The Constitution, as always, remains the modus operandi par excellence for strengthening and operationalising this regime of rights.

8

Human Rights Education for Social Transformation

HUMAN RIGHT AND GENDER EQUITY

Women's human rights and the international laws, declarations, platforms and mechanisms mandate respect, protection and fulfilment of all human rights for all women worldwide. However, the reality for millions of girls and women today remains exclusion, abject poverty, systemic violence and discrimination as well as other fundamental violations of their human rights. In many spheres, systems, structures and institutions of power, decision making remains intrinsically patriarchal. Transforming the rhetoric of human rights into realities for women remains a critical issue.

Denied access to and ownership of productive resources and property, sexual abuse and domestic violence, the patriarchal nature of traditional cultural and religious beliefs, discrimination in education, particularly in conflict and informal settlement areas are but a few of the pressing matters facing women. New challenges like globalization and HIV/AIDS have wreaked further havoc, dramatically increasing the poverty, burden, violence and insecurity that women experience. Such exposure always has a multiplier effect on existing inequalities, highlighting again the urgency of achieving gender equality in all societies, where both women and men can take their rightful place in influencing their own development.

Many struggle relentlessly within the women's movement for gender equality, fighting to ensure that voices from the ground are heard at national and international levels. They employ multiple strategies to negotiate and wrest power from the powerful to secure women's access to and ownership of resources, services, opportunities and social, economic, political and cultural spaces. These groups engage diverse means to advance women's rights in a manner that is inclusive and reflects respect for the fundamental human rights to equality and non discrimination.

The World Social Forum (WSF)– a venue for exploring strategies for social justice, international solidarity, women's rights, peace and environment protection– is a key opportunity to further this struggle. As in previous WSF editions, the Human Dignity and Human Rights Caucus (HDHRC) would like to contribute to the coordination and visibility of human rights activities within the Forum, to be held in Belem do Para (Brazilian amazonian region) in January 2009.

At WSF 2009, the HDHRC will provide a platform for sharing information and ideas about human rights related activities and for networking with other organisations to organise joint activities. The Caucus will offer an open and inclusive space for different groups, movements, organisations, and people. It will provide an opportunity to: share experiences and voice concerns; analyze our actions, and their implications; discuss alternative strategies; mobilize; and engage and learn from different practices around the world. The goal is: to build on joint strategies and, in the long term, to strengthen the process for ensuring gender equity, equality, and justice in all areas of the lives of women and men, girls and boys. In order to ensure some continuity with past WSF editions, HDHRC plans to organize activities on the following issues:

- Human rights and struggles for social and economic justice
- Human rights and struggles for gender equity

- Human rights and struggles over habitat, land and environment
- Human rights, mobility and citizenship gap
- Human rights and conflict, militarization and culture of impunity
- Human rights and faith and cultural diversity

Equalin rights (The Netherlands) and PWESCR - The Programme for Women's Economic, Social and Cultural Rights (India) have taken responsibility within the HDHRC for mobilising a group focused on human rights and struggles for gender equity in preparation for the upcoming WSF in Belem. Through extensive outreach several organizations globally have come together to strategize on how best to use Belem to advance women's rights and bring visibility to the struggles faced by women within three broad subthematic areas:

- Livelihood, Development and Displacement
- Gender Based Violence
- Culture, Religion and Fundamentalisms

LIVELIHOOD, DEVELOPMENT AND DISPLACEMENT

In today's social economic and political environment, livelihoods of people are being threatened in various ways: Several development projects such as dams and extractive activities result in mass displacements, environmental degradation and the destruction of natural resources. In addition, sustainable forms of agriculture are disappearing, and so are traditional forms of sustenance. Disaster—both manmade and natural with climate crisis, is getting worse. As a result, people, especially women including women from marginalized communities such as Dalits, indigenous are daily pushed away from self-reliant sources of livelihood to welfare dependency, sexual exploitation, trafficking and poverty. Losing livelihood options and breaking up of socio-cultural fabric of the society brings about new forms of violence and exploitation - and women are the worst sufferers. This also leads to massive migration, vulnerable to trafficking and exploitation and extreme hardship.

The global phenomena of using women's labour as a cheap option to substitute development investment and the targeting women through promotion of micro-finance as a means to access women's resources for development and profit is rapidly increasing. This is consciously kept an integral component in the development package. The impacts of laws, policies and acts in various countries have little to do with protecting women's right to live with dignity. The capitalist and globalisation paradigms have created new kinds of violence and exploitation including cultural genocide which need be better understood and a collective voice needs to emerge much more strongly across the globe to impress upon the world the severity of the situation and the dire circumstances faced by many women across the globe, particularly its devastating effects on marginalities women.

The right to livelihood is identified as a key right to the realization of all other rights. Livelihoods for people are a means to live a life with dignity. However, the critical issue of livelihoods is not adequately addressed by current the human rights framework International human rights instruments recognize the right to adequate standard of living, including right to food and housing, the right to work, the right to social security and the right to health. While the protection and promotion of these rights may to a certain extent afford minimum protection of people's livelihood, still there are protection gaps. In most circumstances, issues connected with livelihood security are not sufficiently addressed.

The activities under Livelihood, Development and Displacement subtheme will aim at:

- To exchange experiences and information regarding development-induced displacement and loss of livelihood to draw commonalities to have clear understanding of what women's right to livelihood means.
- To strengthen coalition and build alliance with diverse groups working globally on this issue.
- To develop appropriate and effective collective strategies to address these issues.

- To explore how to use International human rights framework to address these issues.

GENDER BASED VIOLENCE

Gender-based violence is a major human rights, social and public health problem throughout the world. Gender-based violence refers to all forms of violence that happen to women and men because of the unequal power relations between them. Gender-based violence in most cases is systematically directed at women, because women have less power and status in most parts of the world due to the prevalence and history of patriarchal societies, making women generally more vulnerable to acts of violence. The overall goal of the perpetrator of GBV is to control and dominate. GBV usually involves a pattern of abuse. This is particularly true when the perpetrator knows the victim, which has been documented to be true in the majority of the cases of GBV.

Prolonged exposure to violence tends to normalise it; for example in post-conflict situations Gender Based Violence often continues as a means to discharge tensions. Stopping the impunity of GBV is crucial to stop the cycle of violence and it is crucial for the healing process. Gender Based Violence takes many forms ranging from domestic violence to violence in the workplace and violence in post-conflict zones. In the Democratic Republic of Congo sexual violence has been a weapon during the conflict up to 2003 and in current post-conflict situations violence against women by community members and police or still present military forces is still common.

One of the main obstacles to both preventing and punishing Gender Based Violence is the high degree of stigmatisation of the victims, who then become reluctant to raise the issue with the authorities or even with their families out of fear for repercussions due to the stigmatization. In Central and Latin-America the issue of 'Femicide' is brought forward: violence against women which culminates into murder. In many countries domestic violence is a major but hidden problem, which receives insufficient attention from the state and private actors. During the World Social Forum in 2007, women and men present at the gender equity seminars decided to give follow up on the issue of widespread impunity especially for violent crimes against women. The need for awareness raising, networking and information sharing on gender based violence was also stressed. During Skype-meetings and D-group discussions with the WSF-gender equity group, GBV has been identified as one of the three main themes by NGOs and individuals from different countries to be put on the agenda at the WSF.

Objectives of the workshop:

- To exchange information and experiences with regard to approaches applied in GBV-programs between partner organisations to learn from each other.
- To exchange lessons learned and challenges with regard to working against GBV and/or impunity.
- To raise awareness of the international framework with regard to GBV such as UN-resolution 1820 (2008) and the uses of CEDAW in addressing GBV.
- Increase networking between women's and gender organizations, especially in relation to GBV.

CULTURE, RELIGION AND FUNDAMENTALISMS

In a period of sensitivities and political correctness, cultural defensiveness prevails as a condition that undermines the universality of human rights, particularly those of a woman. In India, for example, preference for a son results in anything from foetal or female infanticide to neglect of the girl child over her brother in terms of essential needs such as nutrition, health care and education. Women's rights are non-negotiable. However, one of the biggest obstacles human rights face in terms of implementation, particularly in context of gender, is cultural relativism. The conflict arises when universal rights of women are claimed to be in conflict with what are seen as religious or cultural obligations. This objection is subsumed in the larger question of whether 'international' organisations and / or communities are fit to 'judge' or 'criticise' cultural or religious practices and that this judgementalism smacks of a neo-imperialist agenda in the hope of making inroads into policy-making in the formerly colonised communities.

As a result, any arguments pertaining to the violation of the woman's 'human rights' are viewed as an unwarranted external intervention. Religious practices and culture become the private spheres that we cannot touch or see but only respect and protect. This view is further supported by the claim that to interfere with cultural and religious practices is tantamount to interfering with the freedom of religion and the right to cultural practice, both in terms of the individual's right and the group right. Culture and religion become the closets where governments put everything that they don't want to discuss. In some countries, the State ensures that women and men have equal rights to access the land, with the exception of the indigenous communities where the land is distributed according to traditional uses. This policy of noninterference with the customs of indigenous populations is resulting in a harmful practice that is impeding women's access to land resources and livelihood, thereby condemning them to a life of poverty.

A further issue of critical concern which arises within this theme is the question of communal violence and interethnic conflict and the different sites in which this manifests itself. First and foremost, the violence and conflict manifest themselves mostly in the form of violence against a woman or a group of women of the warring factions, whereby their bodies become the battleground and they are raped, mutilated or their wombs taken out as a measure to violate and limit their capacities as mothers and morally upright women within the community. The second manifestation of this conflict takes root in interfaith marriages where willing partners to such marriages are persistently harassed either by the communities or other organizations 'policing' this alleged act of impurity. In these instances, both men and the women who are parties to the marriage are either kidnapped, forced to divorce each other or abandon their spouses, failing which they are killed and often made an example of to ensure others do not have the courage to take similar steps.

One of the key areas of intervention that have been clearly identified by women advocates is in the area of culture and cultural rights. Women feel that culture shapes all aspects of their lives and women all over the world face oppression in the name of culture and religion. Human rights advocates however, have stayed shy of both religion and culture given the murky waters they represent and the increasingly fundamentalist manifestations that have sprung in the name of culture and religion today. There is a need to develop conceptual frameworks as well as practical strategies to address these concerns in a fruitful manner that enables gender equality to be more visibly instituted in these systems and also to further gender equity overall.

Some questions to explore are:

- What kind of obstacles do groups working on women's rights face in context of religion and culture? How are they working through these barriers?
- How can we develop strategies to move the conversation from a position of protecting religion, customs, beliefs and practices to a conversation co-opting the human rights framework to ensures women's rights are non negotiable?
- If the main obstacle is cultural imperialism, as alleged, is there a way to work through the customs and religious practices from within communities to inculcate greater ownership of values and help secure a sustained commitment to equality between the sexes and the abolition of harmful and degrading practices?
- What can we learn from individual experiences of various countries to help alleviate certain harmful and discriminatory practices, i.e. from India, Kenya, etc.

ORGANISING FOR WOMEN'S ECONOMIC AND SOCIAL

This was provoked by our experiences, as academics and feminist activists, taking part in international meetings in the

1990s in which women increasingly articulated their economic and social objectives in terms of claims for the fulfilment of economic and social rights. This took place in a context in which women were making gains in terms of political rights in many countries, but at the same time were experiencing deterioration in their standard of living. Here we explore the potential strengths and weaknesses of the International Covenant on Economic, Social and Cultural Rights (ICESCR) as a focus for women's international orga-nising to claim economic and social rights. The ICESCR (adopted in 1966 and entered into force in 1976) is a central pillar of human rights law.

Together with the Universal Declaration of Human Rights and the International Covenant on Civil and Political Rights (ICCPR) (which was adopted in 1966, entering into force as a treaty in 1976), it forms the International Bill of Rights. In the 1970s and 1980s, civil and political rights were frequently referred to as "first generation rights" while economic and social rights were referred to as "second generation rights," implying a hierarchy in the development of human rights within the UN system. However, the inclusion of economic and social rights in core human rights treaties shows that in international law, they are rights on a par with civil and political rights. Their equal status has been reinforced by the articulation of the principle of the indivisibility of human rights at the UN conference on human rights in Vienna in 1993; and further strengthened by rulings from the Committee on Economic, Social and Cultural Rights on the ICESCR obligations.

The challenge, as with all human rights, is to bring about their realisation in practice. Our point of departure is a recognition that despite limitations and ambiguities, rights language retains considerable rhetorical and mobilising power, reminding us "that people have justified and urgent claims; rights confer agency and enable women in particular to articulate strong claims for equality". In our view, the invocation of claims to economic and social rights does not necessarily imply an adherence to liberal feminism. The hallmark of liberal feminism is not a focus on rights per se, but a belief that women's emancipation comes through equal rights to own private property and participate on an equal basis in the markets of the capitalist system. Many women campaigning for economic and social rights do not share that liberal feminist view. Instead, they are using such claims to challenge the Operation of contemporary capitalism. They focus on rights to use collective property, such as public health systems, rather than on rights to own private property.

International Organising around Women's Human Rights Women's rights have been an important focus for women's organising since the beginning of feminist movements. In the last quarter of the twentieth century many women's organisations in all parts of the world undertook a critical evaluation of the UN human rights system, its treaties and practices, and campaigned to ensure that it started to recognise violations of women's rights as violations of human rights even if they took place in the private sphere. Successive UN conferences, beginning with the First World Conference on Women in 1975, were an important focus for their campaigns. The first fruit of this campaigning was the Convention of the Elimination of all Forms of Discrimination against Women (CEDAW) (adopted in 1979, entering into force as a treaty in 1981).

By early 2004 one hundred and seventy five states had ratified CEDAW, although a substantial minority of states has entered reservations limiting their obligations with respect to particular articles, often where they anticipate conflict between CEDAW and customary or religious law. Women's organisations in many countries proactively used this treaty to influence the courts and the legislatures and to 'name and shame' governments that were failing to implement CEDAW. CEDAW has had an impact where women have been proactive in using it. It has been used as a guide in producing new, more equitable, constitutions (for instance in South Africa, Brazil and Uganda), in guide in courts decisions an issues like sexual harassment (India) and women's property rights (Tanzania), and in reforming national laws.

Moreover, elsewhere NGOs have used the CEDAW reporting process to publicize their demands. For example in 1998 in Croatia, after presenting their second report to the CEDAW Committee the Government did not publicize the results of the meeting as they had promised. A coalition of Croatian women's NGOs (who had also presented a Shadow Report) organised a widespread publicity campaign to pressure the Government to fulfill their commitment, to keep the Government accountable, and also to help develop the public's understanding of the international women's human rights entitlements Croatia had endorsed.

Attention then turned to the International Covenant on Civil and Political Rights (ICCPR). The ICCPR includes the right of all human beings not to be subjected to "torture or to cruel, inhuman or degrading treatment" but the interpretation of the treaty failed to recognise domestic violence as coming within its ambit, as domestic violence is not committed by the state. Women's groups in many countries organised to change this. A Global Campaign for Women's Human Rights was created to transform the outcome of 1993 World Conference on Human Rights in Vienna. The Campaign was successful in ensuring that the Vienna Declaration and Programme of Action stated that "the human right of women and the girl-child are an .inalienable, integral and indivisible part of human rights".

The Conference also initiated the Declaration on the Elimination of Violence against Women which was subsequently adopted by the UN General Assembly in 1993. Although such Declarations are not legally binding, many women's groups across the world used their governments' acceptance of the Declarations to campaign for improved rights for women. For example, they inspired one of the most effective campaigns promoted by the Latin American Women's Movement, the Violence against Women (VAW) campaign, in nineteen different countries across the region, including Brazil, Bolivia, Peru and Nicaragua. NGOs working with rights-based agendas joined organisations pressuring the state for legal reform and were able to collabourate productively on there issues. The campaign enabled groups normally opposed to one another, such as feminist organisations and the churches, to form strategic alliances to bring about change.

The campaign resulted in changes to legislation and the introduction of a range of policies in different countries to deal with domestic violence. For example the 1998 Law against Violence towards Women and the Family in Venezuela (the only Andean country without a VAW law until then) and the adoption of the legal procedures for implementing the existing VAW legislation in Bolivia have been attributed to the campaign. In the ten years since the Vienna Conference, there has been a widening of the enjoyment of civil and political rights for millions of women, with democratisation in many countries, both in the developing world and in the formerly communist states of the former Soviet Union and Eastern Europe. Yet concurrently there has been a limitation of the enjoyment of the economic and social rights set out in the ICESCR. The fall of state socialism across Eastern Europe signified an end of guaranteed universal access to social services, and in many developing countries the ongoing reduction and privatisation of public services (generally a condition for IMF and World Bank loans) has removed much of the more limited access their citizens had.

The established welfare states of the OECD countries have also been under pressure from the forces of economic globalisation. The implications have been somewhat different for women in rich and poor countries. While in many developed countries the decline of the welfare state, together with market deregulation and globalisation, has resulted in the erosion of workers' rights and a rise in unemployment; in contrast in many developing countries, the creation of new forms of employment has actually increased individual autonomy for many women workers, even though at the same time they are subject to discrimination and exploitative working conditions. These contradictory trends have lead to an increasing concern with claiming women's economic and social rights. Since the late 1990s the language of women's human rights has been adopted by organisations that focus on gender and development and draw mainly upon economic and social analysis since they believe it offers considerable potential for improving the context of many women's lives.

In addition, women's human rights activists and scholars, often drawing upon legal analysis, have begun to focus on women's economic and social rights in the context of the UN human rights system. Some of this work has culminated in the drawing up of the Montreal Principles on Women's Economic, Social and Cultural Rights, which are discussed in more detail below. Symptomatic of the former is the change in focus of the Association for Women in Development (AWID), founded in 1982 primarily as a US organization bringing together US academics, voluntary organisations and development policy practitioner. AWID became a global membership organization in the 1990s, embracing the "gender and development" approach, which sought to transform development, not merely to integrate women into development. In 2001 it changed its name to Association for Women's Rights in Development, signalling a further shift in thinking and practice.

As explained by its Executive Director, Joanna Kerr, AWID sought: to bridge the gap between the fields of women's human rights and gender and development. Women's rights provides the powerful language and monitoring System to assert that women's rights are an inherent part of all women's lives and gender and development is an enabling tool for overcoming the social realities that violate those rights. One of the four thematic programs of the new AWID is "Women's Rights and Economic Change" focusing on how best to guarantee women's human rights in a global economy. It builds capacity to meet this challenge through its international forums, website, publications and through electronic networking.

Among the strategies it identifies is "using the ICESCR as a tool for social and economic justice". Similarly the European NGO, Women in Development Europe (WIDE), had already identified this human rights instrument as one that needed further consideration, particularly from a gender perspective and devoted its Annual Assembly in June 1998 to this topic. Assessments of the status of women's economic and social rights in different regions were given by leading international women's rights activists. Both AWID and WIDE point to the advantages of a discourse of economic and social rights. AWID highlights its "powerful vocabulary of legal and moral accountability, which is backed up by international recognition".

WIDE author, Mariama Williams (1998), points to its ability to limit the freedom of markets to turn people into commodities, providing a basis for challenging the dominance of market- led development strategies. At the same time, Williams and other WIDE members have been critical of various aspects of the ICESCR. Feminist lawyers Day and Brodsky (1998) make three important points about why women should be interested in the ICESCR as well as in CEDAW. Firstly, its subject matter is practical, material conditions, and it articulates the responsibility of governments for ensuring those conditions is adequate. Secondly, because for women "a division between rights to economic security and rights to personal liberty is purely artificial. In the circumstances of women who have violent or psychologically abusive male partners, for example, the indivisibility of economic issues from violence issues is clear".

Thirdly, because the ICESCR precludes equalising downwards (that is narrowing gender gaps in ways that reduce the standard of living of both women and men). CEDAW, with its focus on eliminating discrimination, is not so well-equipped as the ICESCR to provide a basis for resistance to the erosion of living standards in neo-liberal economic restructuring. However, Day and Brodsky are not uncritical of the ICESCR and have been active in setting up the Canadian-based Women's Economic Equality Project (WEEP) which develops more effective ways in which the human rights framework and human rights instruments can be used to promote women's economic and social rights.

Thirty global women leaders in the economic and social rights movement attended a WEEP consultation in Cape Town in December 2000, where papers were presented on different issues in the interpretation and implementation of women's economic and social rights. WEEP has now been superseded by the Women's Working Group of the International Network for Economic and Social Rights (ESRC- Net). This Working Group has focused an developing a set of principles to guide interpretation of the guarantees of equal enjoyment of rights contained in the ICESCR, and in December 2002 held a meeting in Montreal, resulting in the Montreal Principles on Women's Economic, Social and Cultural Rights. In particular the Principles point to the failure of the ICESCR to acknowledge the context of many women's lives and the disadvantaged position resulting from their caring responsibilities. They also point to the need to move beyond gender-neutral language, to recognise women's autonomy and see women not merely as dependants of men.

The Group is currently seeking endorsement of these principles by individuals or organisations. The International Covenant on Economic, Social and Cultural Rights What does the Covenant actually say, and how is it opera-tionalised? The Covenant states that men and women have equal right to the enjoyment of all the rights it sets out. These rights include the right to work, including the opportunity to gain a living by work which is freely chosen (Article 6); the right to just and favourable conditions of work, including fair and equal remuneration (Article 7); the right to form and join trade unions (Article 8); the right to social security (Article 9); the right to an adequate standard of living, including adequate food, clothing and housing (Article 11); the right to the highest attainable standard of physical and mental health (Article 12); the right to education and the right to take part in cultural life (Article 13).

Special mention is made of the family, which should be accorded "the widest possible protection and assistance", while "marriage must be entered into with the free consent of intending spouses" (Article 10 (1)). This Covenant, like the ICCPR, is considered to impose three types of different obligations on states that are party to it (termed "States Parties" within human rights treaties): the obligations to respect, protect and fulfil the rights enumerated in it. As of July 2003, 147 states had ratified this treaty, with the USA being one of the few that had not. The obligations on States Parties are qualified in article 2 (1) of the ICESCR, which says: "Each State party to the present Covenant undertakes to take steps, individually and through international assistance and co-operation, especially economic and technical, to the maximum of available resources, with a view to achieving progressively the fall realisation of the rights recognised in the present Covenant."

Article 2(2) sets out the principles of equality and non-discrimination in relation to the provision of covenant rights. The implication of the phrases "to the maximum of available resources" and "with a view to achieving progressively" is to allow a state to realize its obligations over an (indefinite) period of time. This wording is in contrast to Article 2 of the ICCPR, in which State party have en immediate obligation to respect and ensure all enumerated rights. Considerable debate surrounds the question of the nature of States Parties' obligations and the broader question of justicability of economic and social rights. Some critics have suggested that the nature of the obligation set out in the ICESCR is so onerous that virtually no government will be able to comply. Others have argued that the concept of progressive realisation, particularly in the light of the qualification related to the availability of resources, renders the obligation devoid of any meaningful content, so that governments can present themselves as defenders of economic and social rights without their polices and behaviour being constrained in any way.

Political theorist David Beetham (1995, 54) argues that it is relatively easy to demonstrate that economic and social rights are firmly anchored in corresponding duties. He asserts that the general duty to aid those in need falls in the first instance on national governments, from societal resources, to ensure basic rights are realized where individuals, families or groups are not able to do so. Where governments, particularly from developing countries, do not have sufficient resources it is the responsibility of inter-national organisations to support national governments. In determining how far these duties are realisable in practice he suggests that one can divide the arguments into two distinct categories—technical-economic and politico- economic. Beetham maintains that numerous technical studies, including from the World Bank and United Nations Development Programme, have shown that there are sufficient resources and economic and technical expertise to ensure that the basic rights of the global population could be guaranteed within the next decade.

Where the feasibility of such a project begins to look more doubtful is when one considers the politico-economic standpoint. From this perspective such an achievement seems impossible since any such guarantee of basic economic and social rights would essentially require a large-scale redistribution of resources which the majority of international financial institutions and governments would be unwilling to undertake. However, this is not to say that populations cannot mobilise against this. Beetham concludes that perhaps the most important point of the ICESCR and human rights discourse is that it "offers internationally authorised discourse to the deprived to legitimate their own struggles for their realization" (1995, 60). States Parties' compliance with the Covenant is monitored by the Committee on Economic, Social and Cultural Rights (CESCR). The CESCR was set up by the Economic and Social Council of the UN in 1985 and has eighteen members (in July 2003, only three members were women), elected by the UN Economic and Social Council, who serve a four year term.

Decisions made by the CESCR are not legally binding and it lacks the authority to drive any political reform to ensure States Parties' commitments to the ICESCR are upheld. The Committee issues General Comments intermittently which provide an authoritative substantive interpretation of the Covenant and its application to issues of concern. They clarify the contours and content of the rights set out in the Covenant and the resulting obligations on States Parties; and they also clarify procedural rights, including the right to participate, the right to information, and the right to effective remedies from domestic courts. In General Comment 3 it was clarified that the concept of "progressive realization" does not permit the perpetuation of economic injustice and disparity. States are required to take steps continuously to improve people's enjoyment of economic, social and cultural rights. Two particularly important principles have been established. The fast is the principle of minimum core content, which means that policies that deprive people of a basic level of subsistence are violations of the Covenant.

The second is the principle of non-regression, which means that measures that actually worsen enjoyment of economic, social and cultural rights are violations of the Covenant. Moreover, it has been clarified that "progressive realization" does not apply to discrimination. There is an immediate duty to end discrimination in the enjoyment of the rights, including unintended as well as deliberate discrimination. The principles set out in General Comment 3 in theory prohibit a government from reducing basic public services if this policy is assessed to be detrimental to the enjoyment of the rights in question. Some commentators are hopeful that they will thus provide states that are party to the treaty with some defence against the imposition of neoliberal economic reforms as conditions of loans from the IMF and World Bank. Pillay (2002) argues that when a government is required to implement an economic reform program, it can object to certain elements of the program if it can Show that it would entail measures that are contrary to the obligations in the ICESCR.

The idea is that if countries ratify the ICESCR they can use this as a bargaining chip to ensure that the conditions set by financial institutions are compatible with the country's obligations under the Covenant. There is currently an open-ended UN Working Group responsible for looking at the relationship between Structural Adjustment Programs and

Economic, Social and Cultural Rights. However, there is no International Court that can hold states (or international financial institutions) accountable for violations of economic, social and cultural rights. The only international implementation mechanism is via the system of reporting to the Committee. Those states that have ratified the Covenant are expected to submit a report to the Committee within two years of ratifying the Covenant, and then provide a follow up report every five years.

States are expected to provide detailed information on the degree to which rights are implemented and areas where difficulties have occurred. The reports should provide a general profile of each country, as well as details of the legal status and specific implementation of the ICESCR within the country and the role of international cooperation in the implementation of the Covenant. There are specific guidelines structured on an article-by-article basis, for reporting and the substantive provisions, and the information requested generally consists of a mix of descriptive information and statistical data. Critics have argued for more gender-sensitive methodologies, targets, and indicators as well as gender- disaggregated data to be required in the compilation of the reports.

An evaluation that we conducted in 1999 of four reports submitted from four countries in different regions of the world certainly supports this argument. 5 The reports undergo a review process by members of the Committee, who then issue "concluding observations" regarding compliance with the Covenant in the reporting state. These are made public at the end of each Session, but are not legally binding. National and international non-governmental organisations (NGOs) and community-based organisations (CBOs) can submit information to the Committee on the extent to which a state has complied with the Covenant (so called "shadow reports") and can present their views an the first day of the Committee meeting.

The active participation of NGOs and CBOs can ensure that there is widespread publicity for the concluding observations issued by the Committee in the country to which they pertain, so that even if the concluding observations are not legally binding there may be social and political pressure to respond to them. An example of NGO use of the ICESCR reporting system is the submission of Canadian NGOs concerning the impact of the 1995 Canadian Budget Implementation Act (BIN. The National Action Committee an the Status of Women joined together with other Canadian NGOs such as the Charter Committee on Poverty Issues and the National Anti-Poverty Organisation to make representations to the ICESCR Committee, requesting that the government of Canada be called to account to explain how the BIA was consistent with the terms of the Covenant. The ICESCR Committee subsequently called upon the government of Canada to provide an account in its third periodic report in 1998.

The concluding observations of the Committee included the judgement that the BIA, by replacing the Canada Assistance Plan with the Canada Health and Social Transfer "entails a range of adverse consequences for the enjoyment of covenant rights by disadvantaged groups in Canada" (para 19) and specifically noted that this had had a particularly harsh impact on women. (para 23). Only a limited number of NGOs currently submit reports to the Committee. Williams believes that this is because many are unaware of this process or only have an imprecise or vague understanding of the rights. AWID does encourage women's groups to submit shadow reports to the Committee. Women's groups have done this very effectively in relation to the Convention on the Elimination of Discrimination Against Women (CEDAW), which has a similar reporting process, but we are not aware of any women's group that has submitted a shadow report on compliance with ICESRC, though some have played an important role in coalitions of NGOs which have jointly submitted a shadow report, as in the case of Canada discussed above.

At present it is not possible for individuals or groups who feel that their rights under the Covenant have been violated to submit formal complaints to the ICESRC Committee. The adoption of an Optional Protocol which would make this possible has been discussed by the Com-mittee at as number of meetings, and is called for in the Maastricht Guidelines (point 31), but as yet has not been put into practice. A working group is currently looking into options for the development of an Optional Protocol. An Optional Protocol to CEDAW was adopted in 2000. Where national procedures have been exhausted, the Optional Protocol offers an international procedure that could potentially help women secure their rights. However, it is important to note that a woman cannot make use of the Optional Protocol unless it has been ratified by the state under whose jurisdiction she lives, and in February 2004 only sixty states had ratified. Molyneux (2001) has shown how women's groups in Peru were able to use international campaigns for women's rights to bring about local level changes around women's reproductive rights when they failed to make any progress at the national level.

The Optional Protocol could offer similar possibilities. Women's Human Rights Net (WHRN), an NGO working within AWID argues that the Optional Protocol can be of use to women when it is used as part of a broader set of strategies to secure women's rights. While any recommendations made by the CEDAW committee are not legally binding and their enforcement depends upon the commitment of the State party and pressure by civil society, the Committee and the international community, the Optional Protocol does offer the possibility of redress for victims who would otherwise have none. WHRN argue that the main advantage of using the Optional Protocol is that CEDAW provides a conceptual and legal framework capable of encompassing a wide range of the rights indispensable to women's lives and it creates relatively specific obligations for States. Feminist Evaluations of the ICESCR In an assessment of human rights over the last fifty years, Peterson and Parisi (1998, 148) contend that human rights are typically conceptualised as mainly applicable to the public sphere of the market and state.

Within this understanding, the identification of women as primarily mothers and dependants of male providers limits their claims to socio-economic rights. Because male breadwinners are expected to provide for the basic needs of their dependants, women are less able to claim such rights on their own behalf. The wording of the Convention certainly reflects such a view of the world. For instance, Article 11 refers to "the right of everyone to an adequate standard of living for himself and his family." Charlesworth (1994, 106) makes a similar point, contending that many human rights principles are inherently biased against women since they operate primarily in the public sphere and ignore what takes place in the private sphere, where many abuses of women's rights actually take place. While it may seem that economic and social rights transcend this public-private dichotomy, this is not the case. Instead, she believes that the definition of these rights, as set out in the ICESCR, indicates the tenacity of the distinction between public and private worlds in human rights law.

The ICESCR does not touch upon the economic, social and cultural contexts in which most women live, since the crucial economic and social power relationship for many women is not one directly with the state but with individual men, whose authority is supported by patriarchal state structures. This reflects the fact that the ICESCR was drafted in the 1950s and early 1960s before the reemergence of feminism as an international current of thought. Similarly Neuhold (1998, 7) draws attention to the fact that the Covenant (and other human rights instruments) affirms the principle of nondiscrimination while simultaneously asserting the importance of the family (described as the "natural and fundamental unit of society"). She indicates how the patriarchal organisation of families may hinder the equal enjoyment of economic rights: for instance when there are shortages of food, men will be fed first.

Williams (1998) points to other shortcomings, arguing that although the Covenant does refer to the equal rights of both men and women to enjoy all economic and social rights, supports equal wages for work of equal value without discrimination of any kind, and also recognises the right of women to paid maternity leave, these rights are only applicable to women who are already integrated into the paid economy as independent earners. The ICESCR fails to recognise the needs of the many women who do not participate in the paid economy, or participate as unpaid family labour in family businesses and who are thus not covered by the rights that are conferred on workers who earn wages in the paid economy. The CESCR has recognised some of the anomalies in the wording of the Covenant.

In its general comment 4 on the right to adequate housing, the Committee states: "The right to adequate housing applies to everyone. While reference to `himself and his family' (in article 11 (1) of the Covenant) reflects assumptions as to gender roles and economic activity patterns commonly accepted in 1966 when the Covenant was adopted, the phrase cannot be read today as implying any limitations upon the applicability of the right to individuals or to female-headed households or other such groups. Thus, the concept of `family' must be understood in a wide sense. Further, individuals, as well as families, are entitled to adequate housing regardless of age, eco- nomic status, group or other affiliation or status and other such factors. In particular, enjoyment of this right must, in accordance with article 2 (2) of the Covenant, not be subject to any form of discrimination." In response to some of the criticisms and limitations raised here, an Expert Group was set up by the UN Division for the Advancement of Women (DAW) in 1997 in an attempt to consider how to advance women's social and economic rights.

Many of the fundamental concerns raised by women's rights theorists and activists were addressed by the Expert Group at their meeting in Finland in 1997. The Expert Group acknowledged the debates around economic and social rights and concluded that the failure to develop concrete standards and remedies for the enforcement of economic and social rights made it difficult to hold states accountable for violations of women's economic and social rights (point 23). The group also identified as a priority the need for developing gender-sensitive indicators of economic and social rights and urged that gender factors should be fully integrated at all three levels of state dunes in relation to socio-economic rights—the duty to respect, to protect and to promote and fulfil (point 32).

Furthermore, the group emphasised the importance of mainstreaming a gender perspective into legislation, policies and programs designed to realize economic and social rights. These points were reiterated in the Montreal Principles. Following the Expert Group Meeting, the question of women's real enjoyment of their economic, social and cultural rights was addressed by the Fifty Fourth Session of the Commission on Human Rights. Yet while some of the issues raised by die Expert Group were addressed and the UN commitment to improving women's access to economic and social rights (point 11, op.cit) reiterated, many of the issues raised by die Expert Group were not incorporated into this document. The CESCR has been considering issuing a General Comment on women's economic, social and cultural rights, and has consulted the Women's Economic Equality Project and its successor, the Women's Working Group of the International Network for Economic, Social and Cultural Rights, about the possible content of such a General Comment.

WEEP submitted their views on the General Comment on Women to the CESCR in April 2001 and restated, among other things, the importance of moving beyond gender-neutral language in any analysis and discussion of economic and social rights and highlighted the importance of removing systemic barriers to women's enjoyment of their rights. The periodic reporting System remains the principle mechanism of supervision for economic and social rights and consequently a General Comment can play a vital role and has been used effectively by other UN Committees such as the Committee on the Elimination of Racial Discrimination. As rights activist Dianne Otto (2002, 11) argues "general comments have become `distinct juridical instruments' whereby treaty committees set out, in detail, their evolving interpretations of the treaties they supervise ... [and are] ... of immense importance to the UN human rights treaty System."

Nevertheless, there are some limitations to the general comments, most importantly that while carrying enormous political and moral weight they are not legally binding. Beyond Legal Approaches to Women's Economic and Social Rights In developing strategies for the realisation of women's economic and social rights, some feminist analysts are stressing that it is important to move beyond a purely legalistic approach. Their concern is supported by the findings of a recent study of the judgements of national high courts in Canada, New Zealand and Israel: [J]udicial interpretations of constitutional rights appear to possess a very limited capacity to advance progressive notions of social justice in areas such as employment, health, housing, and education, which require greater state intervention and more public expenditure. A discourse of economic and social rights can, of course, be mobilized without any specific reference to the ICESCR. For instance, the Women's International Coalition for Economic Justice (WICEJ) mobilises around the commitments made at the UN conferences of the decade 1990-2000. WICEJ is an international coalition representing 35 organizations from all regions of the globe, including AWID and WIDE.

It seeks to build bridges between the issues of women's rights, women's economic justice, the multiple forms of discrimination against women, and the issues of peace and security. It focuses on intervention in global forums, both those which are intergovernmental (such as the UN Financing for Development conference in 2001) and those organized by civil society. WICEJ specialises in the critique of macroeconomic and trade policy and does not focus on specifically on the ICESCR. Rather it uses a discourse of economic and social rights to contest the abdication of government responsibility for provision of the services women need in their daily lives. One of the resources that WICEJ draws upon is feminist economics. This offers, for instance, an analysis of economies as "gendered structures" that operate in ways that disadvantage women even if there is no overt discrimination against women.

The starting point for looking at the economy as a gendered structure is recognition of "the unpaid care economy" organised in neighbourhoods and communities that support social reproduction and human development through the provision of care for family and community members—rare that is overwhelmingly provided by women and girls. The unpaid care economy produces labour, the crucial input into the paid economy, and it maintains the daily well-being of the population through activities such as housework, water collection and food preparation. The Out- put of goods and services is only included in the GNP if it involves market transactions, so that the unpaid care economy is invisible to economic policy makers. The economic efficiency that neoliberal economic policy makers seek is generally defined in market-based terms and ignores the implications for resources which are not bought and Sold in markets. Broadening the vision of the economy makes the interaction of paid and unpaid activities central. Using this perspective it is easy to see how economic policies which purport to improve the efficiency of resource use may instead shift costs from the paid economy to the unpaid economy.

It makes it easy to ask the question—"efficiency for whom?" and to challenge supposedly "efficient" policies which in reality simply transfer costs from the visible part of the economy to the invisible. The way in which much of women's work is rendered invisible because it is unpaid is but one example of the many ways in which economic institutions, both public and private are "gendered" in the Sense of operating according to norms that reflect men's lives. For instance, the organisation of private sector business and public sector services is structured on the assumption that workers have someone else at home taking care of the household, and is structured according to the rhythms and norms of men's lives. Neither public nor private sector economic institutions value and recognise unpaid care work; they marginalise women as workers, beneficiaries, and clients; they treat the household as if it were an integrated harmonious unit and treat women as dependants of men within the household.

This institutionalised bias hinders women's ability to participate fully in decision-making processes. The exclusion of women from key economic institutions, or their subordinate position within them, means that they are hindered from being able to articulate and claim their economic and social rights. For example, the absence of women from key decision making and the persistence of gender-biased norms in the allocation of public expenditure tends to result in patterns of expenditure that reproduce rather than diminish gender inequality. Women in a growing number of countries are challenging this through gender budget initiatives that look at government budgets through women's eyes and seek to change priorities and restore a sense of collective responsibility for human well-being.

Indeed, Helena Hofbauer draws on the experience of the gender-sensitive budget analysis in Mexico to show that it can be a critical tool for NGOs and women's activists to use in promoting women's economic and social rights. As she argues "budget analysis can help quantify the cost of the provision of specific rights and analyse the resource allocation accordingly" (2002, 101). Another vital area of activity is the political mobilisation of women at the local level to claim specific economic and social rights. Here we have space only for three examples. In El Salvador, La Asociacion de Mujeres por la Dignidad y la Vida has been organising a campaign "Demanding My Rights" since 2000. Within this there is a specific program, "Economic Justice for Women", that campaigns for the promotion and protection of women's social and economic rights. This program defends women's labour rights, and conducts educational and advocacy work on the impact of trade agreements and privatisation on women.

In some countries, political mobilisation is explicitly linked to a human rights framework. Thus, in Nigeria, the Social and Economic Rights Action Centre (SERAC), has prepared a "shadow report" on Nigeria's economic, social and cultural rights practices, and has specifically documented the various economic and social rights violations that occurred as a result of forced evictions in different slum communities around

Lagos. This information has been used to develop several campaigns to promote and protect women's economic and social rights. In India, in 2002 the All India Democratic Women's Association used World Human Rights Day (December 10) to demand the reali-sation of the right to be free from hunger. Thousands of women all across India blocked roads demonstrating at government offices, State Assemblies, and grain warehouses to demand a universal public distribution System for foodgrains.

This chapter has reviewed the ways in which some international women's networks are focussing attention on the ICESRC as an arena for activism, both in terms of improving the Convention as a normative framework, and in using the reporting mechanism to "name and shame" governments. The strength of this approach is the ability to deploy the powerful vocabulary of "economic and social rights" which positions women as agents, not supplicants for charity; and which focuses not only on reducing gender gaps in living standards but also on improving the living standards of both women and men. Its weakness is the weakness of the ICESRC implementation mechanism in a world where economic and social power is more and more concentrated in the hands of big business and dealers in financial markets. In the future, it will be important to build stronger links between the legal activism around the ICESRC, the development of feminist alternative economic and social policies, and grassroots mobilisations for economic and social justice.

9

Women's Situation in India

Domestic violence is common and a serious problem. According to a 1996 survey in Uttar Pradesh, 30 percent of married men acknowledged physically abusing their wives. In a survey of 10,000 women released during the year, more than half of the women said that violence was a normal part of married life. The Health Ministry released a different survey during the year that indicated that, of 90,000 women surveyed, more than half acknowledge being battered. Dowry disputes also are a serious problem. In the typical dowry dispute, a groom's family members harass a new wife whom they believe has not provided a sufficient dowry. This harassment sometimes ends in the woman's death, which family members often try to portray as a suicide or kitchen accident; recent research suggests that a significant percentage of kerosene attacks also are due to domestic violence. Although most "dowry deaths" involve lower and middle-class families, the phenomenon crosses both caste and religious lines.

According to National Crime Records Bureau (NCRB) statistics, 6,917 dowry deaths occurred in the country in 1998, including 2,229 dowry deaths in Uttar Pradesh, 1,039 in Bihar, 598 in Madhya Pradesh, 500 in Andhra Pradesh, 420 in Maharashtra, 200 in Karnataka, 176 in Tamil Nadu, and 21 in Kerala. Under a 1986 amendment to the Penal Code, the court must presume that the husband or the wife's in-laws are responsible for every unnatural death of a woman in the first

7 years of marriage—provided that harassment is proven. In such cases, police procedures require that an officer of deputy superintendent rank or above conduct the investigation and that a team of two or more doctors perform the postmortem procedures. According to human rights monitors, in practice police do not follow these procedures consistently.

The issue of rape has received greater political and social attention than in earlier years. In July the NHRC directed the Andhra Pradesh government to pay $1,100 (50,000 rupees) in compensation to each of four Dalit women who were raped in Godavari district. The NHRC overturned a state ruling that had denied the women monetary compensation because the victims and their attackers were members of low caste and tribal communities. The press consistently reports that such violence against women is increasing, although local women's organizations claim that there simply has been increased reporting. Only 10 percent of rape cases are fully adjudicated by the courts, and police typically fail to arrest rapists, thus fostering a climate of impunity. In May the Central Bureau of Investigation initiated an inquiry into the alleged gang rape of three women by police officials in Pilibhit district, Uttar Pradesh in August 1998.

According to a complaint filed by a witness, three officers of the Madho Tanda police station in Pilibhit district entered the victims' home late on the night of August 16-17 and raped the three women. On May 30, a court in Jalpaiguri, West Bengal sentenced Kashinath Tripathy and Bhuson Barua to life imprisonment for the 1982 rape of a girl in Jalpaiguri. In September in Kulkul village, Orissa, a group of villagers hacked to death a 60-year-old tribal woman, Namsi Ho, allegedly for practicing witchcraft. Police arrested four persons in connection with the killing. On October 16 and November 19, in Ganjam district, Orissa, villagers accused Kumari Behera, of sorcery, and tortured and branded her with hot iron rods. Five persons were arrested in connection with the assaults. According to NCRB statistics, in 1998 there were 15,031 reported rapes, 16,381 abductions of women, 6,917 dowry deaths, 41,318 reported cases of torture of women,31,046 cases of molestation, and 8,123 cases of sexual harassment.

The NCRB recorded 131,338 crimes against women in 1998, compared with 121,265 in 1997. In 1997, 678 cases of gang rape were recorded. Gang rapes often are committed as punishment for alleged adultery or as a means of coercion or revenge in rural property disputes and feuds. On February 1, the Committee on the Elimination of Discrimination Against Women (CEDAW) of the U.N. Commission on Human Rights (UNCHR) expressed concern that "there is a high incidence of gender-based violence against women, which takes even more extreme forms because of customary practices such as dowry, sati (the burning alive of widows on their husbands' funeral pyre) and the Devadasi system (the practice of dedicating or marrying young, prepubescent girls to a Hindu deity or temple as servants of God. Devadasis, who generally are Dalits, may not marry. They are taken from their families and are required to provide sexual services to priests and high caste Hindus.

Reportedly, many eventually are sold to urban brothels". The committee further stated that "discrimi-nation against women who belong to particular castes or ethnic or religious groups also is manifest in extreme forms of physical and sexual violence and harassment." Higher female mortality at all age levels, including female infanticide and sex selective termination of pregnancies, accounts for an increase in the ratio of males to females to 107.9 males per 100 females in 1991, from 104.7 males per 100 females in 1981, and from 102.9 males per 100 females at the turn of the century. In some districts of Tamil Nadu, female infanticide occurs despite government and NGO programs intended to counter the practice. In July the district collector of Dharmapuri, Tamil Nadu, formed a team to investigate the murder of a girl in Pararrapatti village. The team exhumed the buried body and arrested the girl's father and another accomplice.

In August the maimed body of a newborn girl was found under a bridge in Tirunelveli, Tamil Nadu. Police believe that the child's mother abandoned her in the public place hoping that someone would take her in. On February 1, CEDAW expressed concern that "India has not yet established a comprehensive and compulsory system of registration of births and marriages. The Committee notes that inability to prove those important events by documentation prevents effective implementation of laws that protect girls from sexual exploitation and trafficking, child labour and forced or early marriage." Numerous laws exist to protect women's rights, including the Equal Remuneration Act, the Prevention of Immoral Traffic Act, the Sati (Widow Burning) Prevention Act, and the Dowry Prohibition Act. However, the Government often is unable to enforce these laws, especially in rural areas in which traditions are deeply rooted.

According to press reports, the rate of acquittal in dowry death cases is high, and because of court backlogs it takes 6 to 7 years on average to rule on such cases. On February 1, CEDAW noted that "there is an urgent need to introduce comprehensive [legislative] reform to promote equality and the human rights of women." Prostitution is widespread, with an estimated 2.3 million prostitutes in the country, some 575,000 of whom are children. Many indi-genous tribal women are forced into sexual exploitation. In Assam's Chars River islands, some women work as prostitutes in exchange for as little as $0.23 (10 rupees). In 1998 prostitutes began to demand legal rights, licenses, and reemployment training, especially in Mumbai and New Delhi. In 1997 Karnataka's government made sexual harassment a criminal offense.

The country is a significant source, transit point, and destination for many thousands of trafficked women. Literacy rates for women are significantly lower than rates for men; the 2000 U.N. Development Program (UNDP) Report for India found that 38 percent of women were literate, compared with 66 percent of men. The law prohibits discrimination in the workplace, but enforcement is inadequate. In both rural and urban areas, women get lower wages than men for doing the same job. Women experience economic discrimination in access to employment and credit. This acts as an impediment to women owning a business, and the promotion of women to managerial positions within businesses often is slower than that of males. State governments have supported micro-credit programs for women that have begun to have an impact in many rural districts. The personal status laws of the religious communities discriminate against women.

Under the Indian Divorce Act of 1869, a Christian woman may demand divorce only in the case of spousal abuse and in the case of certain categories of adultery; for a Christian man, adultery alone is sufficient. In 1997 the Mumbai High Court recognized abuse alone as sufficient grounds for a Christian woman to obtain a divorce. Under Islamic law, a Muslim husband may divorce his wife spontaneously and unilaterally; there is no such provision for women. Islamic law also allows polygyny (under which a man may have up to four wives) but prohibits polyandry (under which a woman may have muliple husbands). On February 1, CEDAW noted that "steps have not been taken to reform the personal laws of different religious and ethnic groups, in consultation with them, so as to conform with the Convention. The Committee is concerned that the Government's policy of nonintervention perpetuates sexual stereotypes, son preference and discrimination against women."

The Hindu Succession Act provides equal inheritance rights for Hindu women, but married daughters seldom are given a share in parental property. Islamic law recognizes a woman's right of inheritance but specifies that a daughter's share only should be one-half that of a son. Under many tribal land systems, notably in Bihar, tribal women do not have the right to own land. Other laws relating to the ownership of assets and land accord women little control over land use, retention, or sale. However, several exceptions exist, as in Ladakh and Meghalaya, where women may have several husbands and control the family inheritance. Thousands of grassroots organizations work for social justice and the economic advancement of women, in addition to the National Commission for Women. The Government usually supports these efforts, despite strong resistance from traditionally privileged groups.

THE PRACTICE OF DOWRY IN INDIA

Human Rights' is a western concept originating from the specific historical and cultural circumstances of the western world. Increasing sensitivity towards this contention can be considered as one of the significant contributions of the more than half a century long, but so far abstract, debate on 'universality versus cultural relativism.'

The concept of human rights incorporates three basic tenets: individualism, which implies that the individual is the basic unit of society; rights, which implies that the basic organising principle of society is rights; and legalism, which means that the primary method of securing these rights is through recourse to formal law, where rights are claimed and adjudicated upon, mainly in an adversarial manner. Human rights discourse and its underlying tenet of individualism is based on the assumption of a universal human nature, where each individual is assumed to be an autonomous, independent, self-sufficient and rational being. Further, it assumes the separation of the individual and society, the individual being in need of protection from the latter. Thus, the perceived aim of this discourse is to protect this being from any kind of external intervention, be it from the society or the state.

Society or the state in this discourse is not seen as a protection, but as something which can easily abuse the power conferred on it. Since each individual is seen as equally important the main aim here is to enable him or her to lead a life unhindered by others as long as that is compatible with others doing the same. It is through the granting of rights that the pursuit of self-interest and the protection of each individual against the society or the state or against each other Dowry means gifts, money or other assets that are given to the daughter by her parents or family at the time of marriage. According to Webster's dictionary the word dowry means, "money, goods or estate that a woman brings to her husband at marriage" are ensured. The endowment of rights is a way of achieving social harmony.

Rights are seen as tools in the hands of each individual to maintain his dignity and worth. Apparently the assumption here is that the individual in society needs to be respected and treated in a certain way since he or she is the possessor of the right and is empowered to raise a claim. 'Law' is the principal mode for realisation or enforcement of these rights. This 'legal' enforcement of rights is also something specific to the western world, where 'law' is assumed to be something man made, a product of reason. This concept is associated with the specific nature of the origin of civil society, through an assumed agreement between those who left the pre-social state of nature, complemented by an agreement between the rulers and the subjects. The main characteristics associated with 'legalism' in the modern sense is that each case of conflict between two opposing parties is viewed as one where an individual's right or entitlement has been breached and can be corrected through 'legal' resolution, by means of written official law, and where one party will emerge as a winner and the other as a loser.

Hindu Philosophy and Human Rights Hindu philosophy does not adhere to any of the three tenets just shown to be inherent in the formulation of human rights. The basic tenets of Hindu thought for the organisation of society can be discerned as collectivism, that is, the view that the family or group is the fundamental unit of society, duties as the primary basis for securing human existence in society, and reconciliation and repentance as the primary method for dealing with violation of duties. Just as the three tenets associated with western philosophy are the result of a particular cosmo-vision and specific historical and cultural developments, similarly these tenets of Hinduism are the result of a specific Hindu cosmo-vision.

The starting point here is not the individual, but the whole complex connotation of the 'Real'. According to this Worldview the human being or the individual does not stand in a privileged position vis-à-vis other creatures, but is part of a big harmonious whole. An important axiom of Hinduism is that God is omnipresent and immanent in all that exists in the universe. It is not the well-being of an isolated individual but universal harmony that ultimately counts. Under this cosmo-vision an individual is not perceived as an autonomous, independent being, but on the contrary each individual subject is perceived to be embedded in a reality, which exists prior to the individual. The individual is not somebody in need of protection from society or the State. On the other hand the society is considered as essential for the existence of the individual.

The Hindu cosmo-vision is based on the hierarchical conception of the Universe, and thus, unlike western belief, rhetoric about the equality of each individual is not part of it. There is explicit recognition of the fact that each individual is not born equal. Here the belief is that each individual's capacities and limitations are determined to a large extent according to his or her surroundings. In continuation of this belief about the relationship of each individual with the 'Whole' the emphasis here is on duties and not on rights. Dharma, not rights, produces a general and all-pervasive way of life as an organisational principle of existence. It guides the way one ought to act. Dharma, then is, the way in which one ought to hold, bear, carry, or maintain. On a cosmic level, dharma is the way in which one maintains everything, the way in which the cosmos or the balance in the cosmos, is maintained. At the micro level, dharma is the way in which every constituent element of the cosmos contributes its share to maintaining the overall balance.

As long as each element of the cosmos performs its specific svadharma, the overall balance does not suffer. As soon as an element, however, deviates from its own dharma, that is, commits, adharma, the balance is disturbed. The concept of dharma defies attempts at translation into English. It is a concept which embraces the whole life of the human being. Thus, the purpose of rights is served by svadharma. The human being has a 'right' to survive only in so far as it performs the duty of maintaining the world. The method of dispute resolution or the concept of law under the Hindu cosmo- vision is also different from that of the western one. Dharma embraces moral opposites, the conflict and the resolution, both ought and ought not. According to dharma, right not only opposes wrong but right can also oppose right. In conformity with this view the aim of dispute or conflict resolution is not the articulation or distribution of individual rights or freedoms but guidance for all the activities of all individuals. Thus, in conflict resolution, which is based more on the basis of customs or the 'living law', there is no situation of one party winning a claim against another but that of reaching reconciliation between the two conflicting parties to guide their conduct.

THE HINDU COSMO-VISION AND THE CONCEPT OF' HUMAN

Are They Incompatible? The above description establishes that the concept of human rights cannot be traced in the classic Hindu cosmo-vision. This leads us to the exploration of the questions raised at the beginning: what does this situation signify, that is, does this lead to incompatibility between human rights and Hindu cosmo-vision? Does the absence of this concept make this cosmo-vision inferior in some manner or render it anachronistic? Is the endorsement of human rights treaties and their incorporation by the Indian government a mistake, or simply an imposition of western values as part of the colonial legacy? The answers to all these questions are negative. Time and again philosophers have asserted that Hinduism can be seen as neither incompatible with the concept of human rights nor anachronistic for the modern world, since the concerns for human dignity and worth underlying the human rights discourse have also been the central concerns of Hinduism, even though emphasis on rights as the central means for pursuing these concerns has not been part of it.

Though there is no stress on the rights of the individual in Hinduism, philosophers do not find it incompatible with the rights philosophy. Nanda asserts: "in light of the tenets of Hinduism..., it would be a fair assessment that Hinduism would not find fault with the international Bill of Rights". Ramajois explains in this context: the entire concept of rule of law is incorporated in Dharma. The meaning it conveys is that an orderly society would be in existence if everyone acts according to Dharma and thereby protects Dharma, and such an orderly society which would be an incarnation of the Dharma, in turn, protects the rights of individuals. Rules of Dharma were meant to regulate the individual conduct, in such a way as to restrict the rights, liberty, interest and desires of an individual as regards all matters to the extent necessary in the interests of the other individuals, i.e. the society, and at the same time making it obligatory for the society to safeguard and protect the individual in all respects through its political and social institutions.

Freedom of the individual, the central concern of human rights discourse, has also been a prominent one of Hinduism even though there are differences between the concept of freedom as understood in Hindu philosophy and that underlying western philosophy. Under Hinduism, each individual is considered as an end in his or herself and is believed to be endowed with the capacities for self-realisation. Thus everyone, irrespective of race, caste, class, or sex, is perceived to possess equal potential to become 'Brahmin' and is free to choose their own way of attaining the Brahmin status. This freedom is an inherent endowment of each person, something inevitable in the existence of the universe. Here freedom is not something that anybody has to demand or claim, or if willing can waive.

Each individual as well as the ruler is supposed to ensure the situations of self-realisation irrespective of the claim. The right conduct expected from each person is not only to enrich his individuality by free development from within, but also to respect and to aid and be aided by the same free development in others. Thus, every individual is to understand freedom not in separation from society but in connection with society, while performing his or her responsibilities according to their station in life. Accordingly freedom is not understood as a basis for self-interest but for self-discipline or self-sacrifice.

Panikkar has raised an important point in respect of the absence of 'rights' in the modern sense from the non-western philosophies: [T]he very powerful Declaration of Human Rights also shows its weakness from another point of view. Something has been lost when it has to be explicitly declared.... When Human Rights are declared, this is a sign that the very foundation on which they rest has already been weakened. The Declaration only postpones the collapse. In traditional words, when the tabu of the sacred disappears, sacredness fades away. If you have to teach a mother to love her child, something is amiss with motherhood.

Further, contrary to common belief, acceptance of inequality in Hinduism did not lay down privileges for a particular group at the cost of sacrificing the dignity of the other. Intimately linked with the conception of Karma (which can roughly be translated as action and its result) is a belief in each individual's responsibility for his or her behaviour. The basis of the varna (signifying caste or class group) and asrama (indicating station in life) is pyscho-physiological according to the gunatrya (qualities) which are inherent in different proportions in members of the different varnas. It was recognised that change can be effected in gunas (qualities) through effort.

It has been recognised that by effort there may be a change in the caste and therefore varna is not necessarily by birth, but conforms to the principle of evolution. In spite of these basic conceptual differences between Hindu philosophy and human rights discourse, they are not incompatible with each other and this is the reason why Indian endorsement of human rights discourse is neither a mistake nor a result of the imposition of western values. It is indeed a part of the colonial legacy but the incorporation of human rights into Indian legal culture is more a result of historical development than a mere imposition of foreign values. In fact it was adopted voluntarily in the Indian system as a welcome concept, on the initiative of reformers and philosophers well versed in Hindu philosophy, for two reasons.

Firstly, on the political level, the adoption of human rights was a means of struggle against the colonial powers, conducted in their very own language which they had been proclaiming and propagating in the other parts of the world. Secondly, on the social level it was perceived as another useful means to re-emphasise the principles underlying classical Indian thought, which seemed to have lost relevance over the years. While talking about the acceptance of the concept of human rights at the social level it is important to emphasise that in India it has never been adopted or propagated as the sole organising principle of the society. It has always been perceived only as a supplementary means to ensure human dignity, human welfare and human emancipation, in addition to those available under classical Indian thought.

Sri Aurobindo emphasised: In 1925 the Indian leaders had proposed a bill of rights to the colonial Government, which advocated so-called individualistic rights. During the whole freedom movement for India Mahatma Gandhi advocated the necessity of rights to fight against political absolutism. He introduced and propagated the notion of the importance of civil disobedience and consistently stressed the right of self- determination for people. India had also played an active role in the formulation of the Universal Declaration of Human Rights.

Affected she [India] has been, but not yet overcome. Her surface mind rather than her deeper intelligence has been obliged to admit many Western ideas - liberty, equality, democracy and others - and to reconcile them with her Vedantic truth; but she has not been altogether at ease with them in the Western form and she seeks about already in her thought to give to them an Indian which cannot fail to be a spiritualised turn. This adoption was, thus, also based on the changes in circumstances which had already formed the context in which the western style legal system had been introduced and continued to develop its roots in Indian society during nearly two centuries of colonial rule.

These changed situations along with the understanding that the adoption of a foreign belief does not imply the replacement of the existing traditional one was the underlying force for the incorporation of human rights in Indian structure by various social reformers. This incorporation was fuelled by a strong belief in the possibility of the complementarity between western and eastern ways of thought.

UNIVERSALISM VS CULTURAL RELATIVISM

Amidst assertions about the possibility of the complementary coexistence of two ways of thought, one can also contend that, considering the prevalent political and economic situation, the 'universalism versus cultural relativism' controversy is of nothing more than academic interest. It is often argued that the centuries-long foreign rule, coloni-sation and gradual modernisation have carried substantial western influence into almost all non-western countries.

It is often contended by the advocates of the universality of human rights that these rights and the associated mechanisms, like industrialisation, modernisation and capitalism, are the results of cultural evolution, which have been pioneered by the west with the rest of societies following the same course. Even in western society rights emerged during the evolution of society from ancient regimes to modernity. The Universalist thesis is reinforced by the overt adhesion of most countries to the human rights discourse and recently a grand reinforcement came from the declaration of the American Anthropological Association (AAA).

As mentioned earlier, the AAA statement stressing the cultural specificity of the human rights is one of the oft-quoted assertions of cultural specificity. However, these evolutionist contentions, the endorsement by most of the countries of the world of the human rights discourse, and developments like that of the changed position of the AAA do appear to make the 'universalism-cultural relativism' debate redundant. Yet, in spite of all these developments, this debate is certainly of more than academic importance for various reasons. One important fact to be taken into account is that, though there may be a partial truth in the contention that the evolutionary pattern of non-western countries is in line with that of western countries, at the same time one cannot overlook that in the other societies the nature of evolution has been different.

Contrary to the western world evolution in non-western countries has not been spontaneous. In these societies it is shaped by imperialism, colonialism, and consumerism. Thus, the conditions indeed have changed but they have not been reversed. In India the basic beliefs underlying the classical Hindu system such as the importance of the harmonious mutual relationship of the individual and society, emphasis on Svadharma, and belief in the theory of Karma still carry great influence. This recognition of the different nature of the evolutionary process in non-western countries, while it reinforces the concept of human rights, also underlines the necessity of reorientation of the human rights discourse. It underscores the necessity of taking different worldviews and cultural diversity into account. As argued by many authors, who have asserted the cultural specificity of the contemporary discourse, this reorientation is not done with the aim of replacing this discourse with another.

Rather it implies enriching the existing one, making it adaptable and responsive to ways of life different from that of the west. Certainly this task cannot be realised within the abstract bounds of the two extremes of 'universality' and 'cultural relativism'. Universality, in its abstract, essentialist sense, where it implies uniformity of approaches, is certainly out of place for this world. Similarly, cultures as essentialised, homogenous, static, monolithic entities are nothing more than mere imagination. But human dignity and worth are the necessary conditions associated with any human being irrespective of culture or religion. No culture or religion or nation challenges this basic assertion and this is the reason that human rights the AAA have changed its position with the declaration endorsing human rights.

This acceptance is also due to the fact that at implementation level countries usually do not confuse universality of this assertion with the uniformity of approaches. Similarly it is a mistake to understand stress on the impor-tance of culture as complete indifference. This leads us to understand that the concept of human rights and culture are not antagonistic, contrary to the common misunderstanding that the 'universality versus cultural relativism' debate has encouraged. The increasing visibility of the evolving nature of rights and culture has made it easier to overcome this misunderstanding. This evolution is evident from the fact that now it is possible to employ this concept of rights, both for the protection of culture and for protection against culture. In the changed situation, the universal discourse has indeed assumed a global nature but this is a kind of 'globality' which may let differences flourish.

The evolving nature of both rights and culture has made possible the acceptance of the minimal nature of 'universality' in the global discourse of human rights, which can now be responsive to these differences.

Between Acceptance and Resistance A strange paradox surrounds the universal discourse of human rights. It is for women that it sounds most promising but at the same time it is in the area of women's rights that it faces the maximum resistance from different countries. But almost all the contractual parties to the Convention for the Elimination of Discrimination against Women (CEDAW) have entered reservations for the ninety percent of the members of the United Nations - are party to the Convention and an additional 3 have signed the treaty, binding themselves to do nothing in contravention of its terms: application of the treaty in their countries.

Notwithstanding the limitations or contestability of the human rights discourse one cannot overlook the fact that it has served an important purpose of drawing global attention towards the worth of women as human beings. It has enabled women to reveal underlying structures of domination hidden behind the apparently natural reality. It has helped to uncover the hypocritical claims made in the name of cultural protection, it has provided women with a platform to voice their concerns and the possibility to create space for themselves. It is this visible, though for the moment limited potential of rights discourse, which makes the embracing of rights discourse an attractive option for women's movements in all parts of the world.

In such a situation where the discourse has contributed to the well-being and progress of women resistance to it is rather surprising. Yet, since this discourse often comes into conflict with cultural understandings about the role of women in society, with the prevalent gender equations, it is often resisted, as it appears to be attacking age-old understandings. At first instance this resistance seems to be the result of nothing more than mere fundamentalism or sheer intransigence on the part of the patriarchal powers engaged in maintaining the status quo and thus perpetuating patriarchal power structures. Although the power oriented reasons for resistance to this discourse cannot be sidelined, it is also to be noted that not all the resistance to human rights discourse in the name of culture can be solely attributed to them. There are other more profound reasons that account for this resistance.

It is the threat of extinction that solidifies intransigence and generates resistance. Most people see this discourse not simply as supplementary to the existing traditional one, as another means for remedying or correcting the weaknesses in their belief structures, but as the one which seeks to deal with the aberrations or weaknesses by replacing the existing culture with a new, alien one.

On a philosophical level the alien character of the three basic tenets of human rights mentioned above and their unsuitability to the nature and expectations of 'traditional' non-western societies generates antagonism towards them. Human rights discourse's emphasis on the self-interested, alienated individual, on her rights or claims, and on their enforcement through adversarial, formal legal systems threatens to disrupt the fabric of traditional societies where the emphasis is on self-giving or self-sacrifice of the embedded and relational person, on her duties and responsibilities towards society and on the solution of conflicts through mutual adjustment, give and take, reconciliation or repentance.

In western societies, which in the present context are considered to be the locus of women's freedom, where the women's movement has been able to displace more collectivist religious, customary principles in favour of individualistic human rights principles, the societal fabric woven of harmony and mutual understanding is perceived to have been disrupted altogether. As a result western society is presented as one struggling with horrible consequences like high divorce rates, broken families, single parent families, high rates of juvenile crime, teenage pregnancies, domestic violence, high suicide rates, and problems of the aged. Unfortunately it is women's freedom which is often held responsible for these societal problems. Besides, it is not wrong to say that, whatever may be the reasons for these problems, in the end, even in the west, women seem to be suffering more than men from this 'new generation epidemic'.

Resistance to individualistic human rights is used as one of the strategies for containing the spread of this 'new generation epidemic' to non-western countries. Even though we cannot overlook the many new problems that may have crept into modern societies as a result of changed gender equations, this state of affairs raises many complex questions: Is it really women's freedom that has been responsible for higher incidences of 'new generation pro-blems' or do the reasons lie elsewhere? Even if one concedes that women's freedom is responsible for these problems to a certain extent, can solutions be found by 'subordinating' the interests of women to those of the family and/or the society? For cultures where the concept of rights is not viewed favourably especially in respect of women, should the rights discourse be dropped to respect the culture? Certainly none of these questions lend themselves to simple answers.

Before dealing with any of these questions it is necessary to highlight that in most traditional societies there is a tendency to over-emphasise these undesirable changes that may have crept into western societies while neglecting the many positive ones that rights discourse has made possible. Undue emphasis on these aspects probably serves the purpose of idealising traditional structures at the cost of diverting attention from the malaises that need to be addressed if one doesn't want the ultimate replacement of these traditional societal structures. It blinds us to the positive aspects of the rights discourse, which may be useful and in certain situations necessary for preventing the wear and tear of the traditional fabric of the societies. One cannot deny that with the increasing freedom and public role of women, there is a change in family structures.

The roles, attitudes, and expectations of spouses, children and family members have changed considerably. Some of these changes can be considered undesirable but it is certainly a misrepresentation to say that the responsibility for undesirable changes lies solely in women's freedom. In fact it is not the acceptance of freedom but the abandoning of responsibility, by both men as well as women, towards the society and the family that can be held responsible for this state of affairs. Earlier women bore that responsibility even at the cost of their basic survival needs but once they decided to give priority to these needs the hitherto existing stable structures started crumbling. In such a situation one way to save these crumbling structures may be to adjust the freedom and interests of both men and women to the interests of the family and society. It is not by 'subordinating' anybody's interest to the other individual or the group, but by the voluntary balancing of freedom and responsibilities by each individual with understanding of one's social, economic and cultural circumstances that there can be a possibility of the much required harmony within society.

GLOBAL DISCOURSE OF WOMEN' S HUMAN RIGHTS

The above discussion brings home the point that even though resistance to women's human rights cannot be completely ignored it can also not be allowed to overshadow the justified claims of the women's movement against mistreatment in different parts of the world. Notwith- standing widespread religious and cultural differences it cannot be denied that there are certain basic propensities, namely to survive, to self realise and to participate socially, that all human beings share and which provide strength to the global discourse of human rights. Fulfillment of these propensities is as much a requirement for women as it is for men whatever the cultural context may be.

These human propensities give rise to certain basic needs for every woman and man although no person can be abstracted from the social environment, nor can a universally applicable fixed hierarchy of needs be prepared. The hierarchy of needs and accordingly the prioritisation of the basic human propensities are contingent upon the cosmo-visions (i.e., the prevalent understanding within different cultures about the relationship between human being and the universe), and this is where the difference in worldviews affects the operation of the discourse of human rights. It is always dependent upon the subjectivity of the individual, her role, as she perceives it, conditioned by the general beliefs prevailing in the society. Thus, human rights discourse in general and specifically for women can be said to be universal in its objective of creating and maintaining the conditions for the exercise of the freedom to decide on one's own hierarchy of needs.

This position on the global relevance of these needs that make possible the fulfillment of basic human propensities is not an imposition of the values of one culture over the other, for it is the one which no culture denies, as no culture authorises derogation from human life. As discussed with specific reference to Hinduism in the first part, the underlying philosophy here lays stress on creating condi-tions for self-realisation for every individual irrespective of sex, race, class, or status. Certainly one of the methods of fulfillment of these basic propensities is the acceptance of the mutual responsibility of each 'individual' to aid the other(s) in this process. But considering the prevalent social, economic and political circumstances in many countries it has also become necessary to endow every individual with a 'claim' for their realisation while endorsing the necessity for mutual responsibility.

This 'claim' may be of the utmost necessity in situations where any one group of the society is made or forced to bear an inequitable burden of these responsibilities. Moreover, the use of this claim by any aggrieved 'individual' can always provides an opportune occasion for emphasising the mutual responsibility. Again while the concrete reali-sation of these claims will have to be responsive to the relevant social and economic circumstances, still there are certain categories of rights or claims which need to find place, as a means for ensuring the fulfillment of the basic human propensities of each woman, in the legal regimes of all societies and nations irrespective of the cultural context. For the sake of convenience, I divide such rights of women into three groups, i.e. the human rights of women, and their rights in family law and in criminal law. (All three categories can be included in the category of human rights for women. I have made the differentiation in order to list the specific rights relating to different areas that may require differential focus.)

Women need to be ensured certain basic rights in all the three areas, to deal with certain discriminatory and derogatory practices, which are in derogation of the basic needs. These very basic, essential rights against certain practices can be considered as a step towards ensuring the conditions for fulfilling the basic need of survival. As far as human rights of women are concerned, every woman needs to be ensured the right to life. Thus, traditional practices like female foeticide, female infanticide and bride burning, cannot be justified in any situation. Similarly, no discrimination against girl children in respect of health care and food can be acceptable. In the area concerning family law constraints on the requirement of free consent for marriage, discriminatory and derogatory grounds of divorce, denial of a right to maintenance, or to custody or guardianship of children or to inheritance need to be done away with. In the domain of criminal law no kind of violence in the form of witchcraft, female circumcision, dowry deaths, honour killings, domestic violence, or sexual abuse can be excused.

Thus, women need to be given the right to raise their voice where such practices are implemented and endanger their bare survival. Along with ensuring the rights for fulfilling the need for survival, a further objective of human rights discourse is to empower women with freedom to hierarchise their needs of self realisation and social participation themselves. For the purpose of ensuring the two latter categories of basic human propensities, certain rights have to be assured to women unconditionally. These may include access of girls and women to education, availability of opportunities for employment or participation in the public sphere, and protection against discrimination on the basis of sex or biological roles in the society. These basic rights can create the conditions enabling women to prioritise their needs in conformity with their cultural context. This assertion of the need to ensure the 'basic needs' of woman seems to be reinforcing the universality thesis and to make stress on the importance of culture appear futile.

Adapting global discourse to local demands: Women's human rights and traditional practice of dowry in India

Considering the prevalence of cultural diversity in our world it may seem futile to try to discover or formulate abstract or general principles for ensuring a balance between global and local. What this balance signifies and what are the measures required for sustaining it can be determined only within a particular cultural framework. Although, in principle, most traditional religious and customary societies tend to ensure an equitable distribution of the responsibilities for maintaining the basic tenets of such societies, in practice, the weight of maintaining these tenets tilts towards women.

Presently in most societies it is women who carry the main responsibility of protecting, perpetuating and transmitting culture and values from generation to generation. Usually any challenge to traditional practices, even those which manifestly violate the basic right to life, is perceived as an attack on culture and values. In such circumstances the most effective remedy for the women's movement seems to be the blanket challenge to culture and advocacy of the replacement of the traditional discourses with modernistic ones based on the universal human rights principle. The assertion made above about not subjecting women to derogatory traditional practices as a means of fulfilling their basic propensities appears to support the approach of the blanket challenge to culture.

Even though Dowry is most commonly associated with Hinduism it is prevalent amongst other religious communities too under different customary practices. In the following part, by taking the example of the commonly known practice of dowry, I shall try to explain that, while making this global claim against subjecting women to excesses in the name of traditional practices, the approaches to be adopted for realising this claim need to be sensitive to the local circumstances amidst which the target practice prevails. The two preconditions for localising this global claim are: an insight into the whole social, economic, cultural and religious framework within which the concerned practice prevails, and finding the means to deal with such excesses within the cultural framework in conformity with the basic values.

The custom of dowry as prevalent in India presents a typical dilemma for the 'universalism and cultural relativism' debate. Dowry is considered to be an ancient practice associated with the institution of marriage in India, which in very broad terms involves the giving of gifts from the bride's side to the groom's side at the time of marriage. In present circumstances, a large number of marriage transactions in India seem to be hard-core business deals, where the girl herself appears to be the least valued consideration. Although this custom has become a source of serious threat even to the right to life for women in many cases, it also carries significant advantages for women in the Indian socio-economic context. Thus, while dowry needs to be strongly condemned for reinforcing the inferior status of women, paradoxically it receives support not only from society but also from women themselves.

Dowry is a complex customary practice most pronounced in South Asian societies. Dowry can be considered directly or indirectly responsible for other derogatory practices against women, such as female foeticide, girl infanticide, neglect of the girl child, malnutrition of girls and women, a high mortality rate amongst women, and a high illiteracy rate. There is evidence to support the view that many women actually expect, want and more or less demand dowry. In such a situation, where a significant section of the population appear to be involved in financial and material transactions around marriage, and claim cultural and religious justification for these, attempts towards eradication of this custom on the basis of human rights principles can be considered as interference with the right to cultural freedom of Indian society.

But, as discussed in the previous section, respect for cultural freedom cannot entail complete indifference towards manifest violations of women's human rights. Thus, notwithstanding the cultural background, dowry related violence cannot be ignored or condoned. The basic human need, that is, the right to survival, being in danger, women need to be protected. However, once we take this stand the next immediate issue is how to do this, especially considering the support that the custom of dowry enjoys in Indian society. Admittedly, this is not a recent problem, and a long standing legal and social campaign has been conducted in India for many decades now to deal with the 'dowry problem'. The Government promulgated the Dowry Prohibition Act in 1961 to deal with the practice of dowry. Various amendments have been introduced in the Act to widen its net and to make it tough. This Act, as well as the penal statutes - the Indian Penal Code, the Criminal Procedure Code and the Indian Evidence Act - has been amended on more than one occasion to deal with dowry-related violence.

The executive has also been active with its specific focus Section 498-A of the Indian Penal Code deals with all cases of cruelty and harassment to women. This section made cruelty to married women punishable with imprisonment for a term, which may extend to three years and with fine. Through the Amendment Act of 1983, Sec 174 of the Criminal Procedure Code was amended empowering a magistrate to hold an inquiry and making the postmortem essential when a woman dies in suspicious circumstances within seven years of her marriage. A new section 113-A was inserted in the Indian

Evidence Act reversing the presumption of innocence against the accused in the case of suicide by a married woman.

Two new sections 304-B in the Indian Penal Code and 113-B in the Indian Evidence Act were added by the Dowry Prohibition (Amendment) Act 1986. Sec. 304-B in the Indian Penal Code created a new offence of 'dowry death', which is defined thus: Where death of a woman is caused by any burns or bodily injury or occurs otherwise than under normal circumstances within seven years of her marriage and it is shown that soon before her death she was subjected to cruelty or harassment by her husband on dowry and other traditional practices in its various women's empowerment schemes.

There are many non-governmental forums that raise their voices against this customary practice and take up the issue on different opportune moments. There is an immense literature both old and recent that has raised the issue and has put forward suggestions to deal with it. In short there were sufficient steps taken in India to conform to global human rights principles even before India accepted the treaty obligations under the Convention for the Elimination of Discrimination Against Women for the protection of women's rights. However, in spite of all these efforts the practice of dowry is thriving with full vigour in Indian society, implying the failure of various governmental and non- governmental measures. Not only this, dowry, which was originally considered to be a high caste upper middle class Hindu phenomenon, today knows no barriers of caste, class or religion. Here it can be suggested with conviction that the most important reason for the very limited success of these efforts to combat this social evil is a lack of understanding about it.

The efforts made so far are based on simplistic and partial explanations of this practice. The women's movement is mainly characterised by its attack on Hindu tradition by its tracing the prevalence of this practice linearly to the classical Hindu conceptual structure and value system. Amidst much rhetoric there is little clarity about what we are fighting against. There is no agreement about what actually is that 'evil' that needs to be eradicated. The best strategy to move ahead on the path of protection of women's rights may be to try to focus on the negative consequences of these practices within the cultural framework of the society.

Punishment for a person guilty of dowry death is a term of imprisonment which shall not be less than seven years but which may extend to imprisonment for life. India became a party to the Convention in 1993 appropriate to deal with the Hindu practice of dowry. While this discourse is not out of place, it needs to be sufficiently indigenized and supplemented by other means which are responsive to Indian society.

UNDERSTANDING DOWRY AND THE DOWRY PROBLEM

There is no general agreement or certainty about the definition or origin of 'dowry'. In strict terms, 'dowry' is what a bride's parents give to the groom or to his family on demand either in cash or in kind. It can be looked as a settlement that is normally constituted of: (1) what is given to the bride, and often settled beforehand and announced openly or discreetly; (2) what is given to the bridegroom before and at marriage; and (3) what is presented to the in-laws of the girl.

The settlement often includes the enormous expendi-ture incurred on travel and entertainment of the bridegrooms party. This definition can be extended to include also the giving of gifts or cash from the bride's parents to her husband, his family or to herself after marriage, either towards fulfilment of the prenuptial settlement or on the basis of further expectations of the groom and his family. There is a common belief that dowry is an ancient Hindu practice, but there is no authoritative opinion available that tell us that 'dowry', as defined above can be traced to the ancient Hindus. According to Altekar the dowry system was generally unknown in early societies and also with ancient Hindus. He specifically mentions that: "there are no references either in Smritis or in dramas to the dowry, i.e. to the pre-nuptial contract of payment made by bride's father with the bridegroom or his guardian". However, there is general agreement that, while the Hindu belief system and practices cannot be held responsible for the custom of 'dowry' as such, there are some elements of the tradition that feed the roots of the dowry problem.

Altekar says there was indeed a tradition of giving gifts to a son-in-law at the time of marriage but this was restricted to rich and royal families. He asserts that these gifts can hardly be called dowry for they were voluntarily made out of affection. In respect of its elements he further clarifies: The dowry system is connected with the conception of marriage as a dana or gift. A religious gift in kind is usually Altekar gives no clear indication about what he means by 'dowry system' here but it can be assumed that he implies it to mean voluntary transfer of property in any form to the bride, groom and groom's family from the bride's family at the time of marriage. accompanied by a gift in cash or gold. So the gift of the bride was also accompanied by a formal and small gift in cash or ornaments.

He traces initiation of this custom to medieval times and to Rajputana but always wrapped in love and affection, with no element of coercion. Another commonly accepted explanation, which traces elements of dowry to the ancient Hindu belief structure, views it as a kind of pre-mortem inheritance of the daughter, who has to leave her natal family to join another. Many authors have put forward the claim that giving of cash or gifts, mainly moveable property, to the daughter at the time of marriage was a kind of compensation for the absence of inheritance rights in their father's property for daughters. Dowry, thus, stresses the notion of female property and a female right to property, it being viewed as an important ingredient of streedhan. It has been claimed that the custom had its origin in agricultural societies where the family's survival was dependent on its holding land. Since women joined the husband's family after marriage, they were not given a formal share in the land, mainly to avoid the fragmentation of land.

Ram Mohan Das states: We find that Manu has made a

very practical approach to the problem. He recommends one-fourth share and thereby provides for the marriage expenses of the daughter. At the same time by allotting one-fourth share he clearly indicates that the brothers should not unnecessarily waste money over the marriage of their sisters. He explains that sons were given a specific one-fourth share of the ancestral property to meet the marriage expenses of their sisters. This share on the one hand was meant to ensure financial security for her and on the other to put a limit on unnecessary marriage expenses. Given the nature of the evidence that is available for knowing and understanding ancient Hindu practices, it is true that there is no certainty whether dowry can really be connected to streedhan or not.

There are conflicting views about this, and some authors have argued that women were merely vehicles for the transfer of property from one family to another, and had no right over property transferred in the name of dowry. But for our purposes, it is important to note that this explanation also lays stress on the discretion that the bride's family enjoyed in respect of the worth of the dowry and on the element of natural love and affection. As is evident none of the available explanations which try to trace the origin of 'dowry' correspond to the understanding of 'dowry' in the modern sense. These opinions underscore the view that, except for some of its elements, and even in respect of those with many variations, it is wrong to consider 'dowry' as an ancient Hindu practice.

On this basis it is not wrong to assert that 'dowry' - a custom that involves pre-nuptial financial settlement between bride and groom's family; transfer of property as a consideration for marriage; continuing extortion from the bride's family even after marriage; torture or killings of young brides either for breach of marriage settlements or with an intention to benefit further from them - has nothing to do with the ancient Hindu belief system. Menski rightly points out: Killing a woman, and certainly killing a bride at the point of entry to that phase of life where she was supposed to be most productive, would become viewed as the most heinous of the violations of the eternal Order (rita) that the Hindu worldview revolves around.

The 'dowry', a custom that is strongly condemned today, is a modern phenomenon - 'a modern custom'. Consequently both the approaches, that is, one that puts the blame squarely on the tradition for perpetuating oppression of women in name of customary practices, and another that defends the practice on the basis of ancient traditional origin, are misplaced. Yet, the complexity of the whole issue arises from the fact that, though 'dowry' as such cannot be traced to Hindu tradition, certain elements of the Hindu belief system and practices feed it. Given this connection with the ancient Hindu belief structure it is necessary to redefine what exactly can be considered the dowry problem and how to deal with it on the basis of these elements. In spite of great variations in the understanding of dowry, one can say that the predominant understandings especially the one that is sensitive towards cultural diversity, suggest that only 'dowry', that is, those financial and material transactions around marriage that have elements of demand in them, should be considered problematic.

There is no clarity about how to view other kinds of financial and material transactions associated with marriage in India, which cannot be considered per se objectionable but which are directly and indirectly responsible for 'dowry' and the dowry problem. Thus, the issue before us is, how would we categorise the transactions that are not based on explicit demand but on the subtle expectations of the bridegroom's family? In these cases, there are usually no express negotiations undertaken or settlement reached between the bride's and bridegroom's family, yet, on the basis of social norms, bride-takers nurture certain expectations. These expectations may vary according to the groom's physical appearance, his educational status, his social status and his earning capacities. The bride may have to bear harassment in her marital home if the expenditure incurred by her parents in terms of giving cash and other things or in arranging for 'entertainment' of the bridegroom's party does not meet the latter's expectations.

This harassment may, in some cases, also lead the bride to commit suicide. Should this kind of financial and material transaction be categorised as dowry, and should the resulting problems be treated as dowry problems? Further, where can we place the huge expenditure that the bride's parents incur voluntarily, as performance of their duty towards their offspring with an aim to ensure a secure future for her? In such cases there is usually no element of demand or duress involved, but, considering the societal norms, parents may incur heavy expenditure (which may be beyond their capacity) as a way of showing their affection towards their daughter; as fulfilment of their duty towards offspring; as a mark of respect and fulfilment of their duty towards the bridegroom's family; and also as a means to gain social status.

This kind of expenditure may not be contingent upon any specific, desirable characteristics of the bride or the bridegroom or the social and economic status of the bridegroom's family. Should this type of expenditure and financial transactions be considered objectionable? In the available literature dealing with the dowry problem, there is no clarity as to whether these types of transactions and expenditure should be included in the definition of dowry and be typically considered as dowry problems. In case of transactions made with an aim of meeting societal expectations there is still some kind of harassment involved bringing it within the ambit of the dowry problem, especially where the subtle harassment leads to some kind of fatality. Cases where there is no element of demand or duress involved cannot be stretched to the common understanding of the dowry problem, as there does not seem to be anything objectionable if parents want to give something to their offspring out of natural love and affection.

But can we simply ignore such societal norms and the transactions based on them, especially considering the fact that they do have a bearing on the typical preference for the male child in India? In the present context dowry should be seen as including any kind of financial and material transaction in connection with marriage, whether made before, at or after marriage by the bride's parents to the bride, groom and his family. This is in conformity with the widened definition of dowry incorporated in Dowry Prohibition Act, 1961 after amendment in 1984. This states that dowry is any property or valuable security given or agreed to be given either directly or indirectly – (a) by one party to a marriage to the other party to the marriage, or (b) by parents of either party to a marriage or by any other person, to either party to the marriage or to any other person, at or before or at any time after marriage in connection with the marriage of said parties but does not include dower or mahr in the case of person to whom the Muslim personal law (shariat) applies.

Dowry should include expenditure incurred by the bride's family on the entertainment of the bridegroom's party. The dowry problem is constituted not only of those cases where marriages become a bed of violence or death for women or where money has been extorted from the bride's parents. The dowry problem should be understood to include any kind of harassment, torture or killing of women for bringing in insufficient dowry as well as any actual or psychological burden on girls' parents to undertake financial expenditure for their daughter's marriage. This definition of dowry may appear to be confusingly linking two aspects of dowry, one involving the transfer of any form of property from parents to a child and the other involving the extortion of any form of property from the parents of a girl child.

It is necessary to somehow link the two aspects to deal with the dowry problem given the present situation in India, where general expenditure and transfer of wealth in marriage, even though voluntary, has generated rather unhealthy competitive tendencies to gain social status. These so-called voluntary expenditure and transactions play a significant role in shaping general societal expectations around marriage and ultimately feed the dowry problem. Further, these apparently 'innocent voluntary transactions' are far from the original Hindu principle of bestowing wealth upon a daughter as a part of the performance of a societal duty. Far from the original belief concerning the duty of parents towards child and society, such transactions have become a means of aggrandizement for many Indian families and certainly such tendencies cannot be defended on the basis of the Hindu worldview.

To deal with the dowry problem it is necessary to address these various kinds of transactions associated with marriage in India, that is, those having an explicit extortionist element, those made under implicit social and psychological pressure, and also those that can be considered to be actually based on natural love and affection. However, addressing all the three kinds of transactions mentioned above does not mean attacking all of them, and trying to eradicate all kinds of financial transactions around marriage. Addressing them would mean understanding and analysing all the possible elements of dowry to be clear about what needs to be eradicated, what can be subtly challenged for its underlying assumptions, and what is to be supported in this customary practice.

It also means accordingly devising strategies by understanding the limitations of state-based legal measures or rights-based social action for these purposes. Thus, while vehemently attacking 'dowry' - a pre-nuptial settlement as a consideration for a marriage contract - and various forms of 'dowry'-related violence through explicit legal and social measures, it is also necessary to address the specific underlying assumptions about the status of man and woman in society, in all these apparently 'innocent transactions' that contribute to the dowry problem. Indeed assumptions concerning male supremacy or unequal relations between men and women are not specific to the Hindu belief system. Such assumptions are universal and so far no legal and social system has been able to do away with them. It cannot be asserted with certainty whether such assumptions can ever be taken care of but this should not deter us from addressing them.

Undeniably, in an Indian context it is of the utmost importance that such subtle challenges should not result in a sidelining of the more urgent issues like saving the lives of women and protecting them from harassment. What is required is sensitive strategic planning about which parti-cular aspect of the problem is to be highlighted, through what means and in what manner. Inclusion of all kinds of financial and material transactions concerning marriage in our understanding of the dowry problem underscores the complexity of this custom of dowry and brings home the point that addressing it as a 'standardised' women's rights issue on the basis of a linear explanation will not help the cause. It alliances with families of high status. These people are keen to get rid of the black money, so they spend it lavishly during weddings. In this process the level of expectations in marriage market has changed altogether. Men of honest means and moderate income find it extremely difficult to remain honest in order to compete with this class with a free flow of black money.

Various elements of the dowry problem will have to be dealt with through different approaches, and the modernist women's rights approach can be only one of them. Fighting the dowry problem Human rights discourse, with its basic tenets of individualism, rights and legalism and the remedies that may be suggested by it, is not appropriate on its own to deal with rather complex traditional practices, like dowry and many others, which are usually embedded in a different worldview. For this specific case of the dowry problem, this discourse may encourage 'love marriages,' which underscore the importance of individual consent, and campaigns emphasising proprietary and other rights for women and recourse to law to protect and ensure these rights.

These remedies cannot take care of other culture-related elements that contribute, even though indirectly, to the dowry problem, and that they have limited relevance even for the cases where there is manifest violation of women's rights. It was mentioned at the beginning that the practice of dowry receives widespread support as a cultural practice in India, even from women themselves, for whom it is considered to be oppressive. It is associated with a culture which lays great emphasis on the responsibility of every individual towards each other and towards every constituent element in the Cosmos, a culture that sets certain prescribed norms of behaviour and responsibilities for people within different relationships, familial or otherwise. Associated with this worldview is the belief that the marriage of a daughter is an important religious and moral obligation of parents, as a means for ensuring a secure future for her and also as a contribution to the universal Order by providing a way for her procreative powers to be utilised for the continuation of progeny.

It is this sense of religious and moral duty that has come to be exploited in the present circumstances by bride takers. Usually a girl's parents succumb to the pressures and demands of the contemporary materialistic world to fulfil their responsibility. One can say that presently the practice of dowry in India to a large extent is associated with this heightened sense of responsibility towards their offspring within the Indian socio-economic context. Large numbers of girls in India lack economic independence because they lack either education or sufficient employment opportunities. There is no state social security system which might extend financial assistance, even for bare survival, to those in need. Marriage seems to be the only means to ensure financial and social security for girls. Large expenditure is also a kind of investment to ensure a good status for the girl in her new home. Admittedly, it does indeed serve, to a certain extent, the purpose of bringing psychological and financial security.

That is why dowry receives support from all sections of the population, and the anti-dowry law, which seeks to put a financial ceiling on or to prohibit financial and material transactions in connection with marriage, has not met with much success so far. On the other hand, some critics have rightly pointed out that it is not appropriate to defend dowry as a means of transferring property to girls, since in many cases brides have no control over the movable or immovable property which has been transferred as dowry. There is a general perception that arranged marriages are a primary vehicle for the exchange of dowry. Consequently it is believed that their replacement with 'love marriages', where two individuals decide to form their alliance with no or minimal family involvement, may be a remedy to the problem. It is true that under the system of arranged marriages, as prevalent in India, the financial and social status of both parties is a predominant deciding factor, increasing the possibilities of pre-nuptial negotiations. It also follows that parents may dislike their sons contracting 'love marriages' as that takes away a good opportunity for them to enhance their financial or social status.

Nevertheless, even if we accept these considerations as arguments against arranged marriages, it is necessary to realise that in the Indian context advocacy for the replacement of arranged marriages with 'love marriages' does not present a realistic option. In practice, with modernisation Indian society has developed an indigenous variety of 'love-cum-arranged marriages', where 'dowry' in the strict sense may be ruled out but transactions occur that are within our definition of dowry. In Indian culture and in Hindu philosophy, where the family, usually the extended family, instead of the individual is the basic unit of society, marriage is not simply a union between two individuals. It is not only seen as a means of extending kin relationships, but also, and primarily, as a means of procreation for the continuation of the family lineage and humanity.

Further, in India the beliefs that 'marriages are made in heaven' and that marriage is a sacramental union with the objective of many births, have not been displaced by modernisation. Thus Milton Singer has stated: While modernizing influences are undoubtedly changing many aspects of Indian society and culture, they have not destroyed its basic structure and pattern. They have given Indians new alternatives, new choices of life-style, but the structure is so flexible and rich that many Indians have accepted many modern innovations without loss of their Indianness. They have, in other words, been able to combine choices that affirm some aspects of their cultural tradition with innovative choices. Thus individual consent, as understood in the western context, does not seem to play a predominant role in the formation of the marriage alliance.

We may speculate about future developments, but presently, the system of arranged marriages in India being associated with a specific worldview of Indian society, it seems that its abolition is not a practicable remedy for the dowry problem. The granting of inheritance rights to women is also advocated as a real remedy to the problem. While this remains a different and important issue in itself, past experience shows that it is not likely to go far towards dealing with the 'dowry problem'. The Hindu Succession Act, 1956, in sections 6 and 14, has considerably changed the formal rules of inheritance for women by granting daughters rights with sons in their father's property. Yet large numbers of women prefer not to claim their rights. Especially where the father has left just one dwelling house or some other rather small portion of property, most women waive their share for reasons like love and concern for their brother(s), the desire to avoid conflict with their near and dear ones, the desire to avoid becoming involved in legal problems and expense, and the wish to escape social criticism.

Further, for practical as well as conceptual reasons stress on creating awareness of legal rights in respect of dowry, on claiming proprietary rights to dowry, and on facilitating recourse to the formal legal system for seeking gender justice, may be only partially successful in India. Practical insufficiency of resources hinders the operation of the formal legal system. While we may emphasise the necessity of such rights and a legal system to enforce them, we should not forget that recourse to the formal legal system for the protection of rights in India is not a function of awareness. Even people who are well aware of the availability of all these legalistic mechanisms, and who have access to them are hesitant in making use of them. We have much evidence to prove that even very affluent and highly educated girls and their families bring a case for dowry only in extreme circumstances.

This attitude again is related to the specific worldview of Hindu society, according to which people prefer to perform their duty to others irrespective of the others' behaviour and without laying emphasis on the rights that correspond to those duties. These complex situations tell us that the dowry problem has to be dealt with through equally complex measures, by adopting different strategies for the elements associated with different forms of dowry. These may include various social and economic measures, like focussing on the education of girls, better employment opportunities, social ostracism of the people involved in 'dowry' exchanges, and social denunciation of people using marriage as occasions for vulgar displays of wealth. Undeniably there is also an immediate need to tackle the violence related to dowry, and heinous crimes like physical violence, bride burning and killings must be dealt with strictly.

Rights discourse can be particularly helpful in this regard by raising awareness amongst women about the operation of the formal legal system, about their right to seek a remedy through law. We need to advocate incessantly enhanced operation of the criminal justice system in India. The express violations of the law relating to dowry prohibition, and an application of human rights discourse based on legalism calls for penalisation of cases involving harassment. However, in view of socio-economic circumstances in India, it may not be advisable to advocate a uniform method of legal penalisation in all cases involving dowry and dowry harassment.

Even in cases which may involve proven giving and taking of dowry and subsequent conflicts or harassment, legal penalisation, or legal separation of spouses, may not always be the best solution. In the Indian context the particular circumstances of some such cases may require solutions through mutual settlement and counselling. Some writers have undetrandably expressed scepticism about the utility of soft methods like negotiation, counselling or mutual settlement. Manjaree Chowdhary points out that Crime Against Women Cells, established for dealing with atrocities against women have assumed a mediatory role, seeking to effect reconciliation rather than pursuing the matter under prescribed criminal law.

She asserts that a woman who is trying to make a complaint about dowry harassment often finds herself dragged into a process of negotiations which she neither wants nor understands, receiving virtually no information or advice different from what her family or society would have given her. Such scepticism is not ill-founded, yet in my view, considering the socio- economic conditions in which the Indian criminal justice system is embedded and operates, one should not disparage the utility of negotiation and settlement procedures. Any formal or informal body dealing with complaints concerning the practice of dowry needs to be sensitive to the demands of these local circum-stances and may have to condone or ignore an express violation.

Contrary to the expectations of discourse based on legalism, here the legislative prohibition of dowry may have more of a symbolic nature, and its implementation may have to fluctuate between explicit condemnation and appropriate tolerance. It is interesting to note that the Dowry Prohibition Act, which is often denounced as an ineffective, paper tiger, can be considered to be sensitive to the demands of Indian social reality. Menski has pointed out: It is recognised in the countries of South Asia that the state's law serves different purposes to much of western law. Thus, it is equally typical that the state law considers the conse-quences of its own rejection and violation, and even provides for it in explicit terms.

Following this pattern the Dowry Prohibition Act, while prohibiting dowry, recognises that it cannot be outlawed completely. Thus section 6 of the Act lays down that any dowry shall be for the benefit of the wife or heirs, thus anticipating that dowries will continue to be given. Further, the lawmakers being aware of the cultural association of dowry, the anti-dowry law does not prohibit voluntary financial transactions. Section 3(2) of the Act excludes presents of a customary nature from the definition of dowry. Thus it aims to deal only with the abuses of the dowry system, and targets only those transactions with an extortionist element. The rationale seems to be that it is not objectionable to give gifts, in cash or in kind, to mark one of the most important events of life, especially when such gifts are made out of love and affection.

Nevertheless this aspect of the anti-dowry law is widely criticised by anti-dowry campaigners. Both sides are right to a certain extent. While there is no rationale for prohibiting the voluntary transfer of property from parents to child, the critics are also right because such voluntary transactions underwrite objectionable assumptions about the status of man and woman. It has been rightly pointed out: The complex mechanisms of bride-giving and wife-taking in South Asia's mainly patriarchal cultures are premised on the concepts of male supremacy, so that girl's father is automatically treated as inferior to boy's father and the wife-givers have to 'serve', as it were, the wife-takers.

It is necessary to remain clear that in such cases the evil that needs to be fought is not the financial and material transactions around marriage, but the notion of male supremacy that underlies these transactions. It is also necessary to be clear that formal legal measures for the protection and enforcement of the rights of women cannot effectively deal with this aspect. Yet legal discourse is not redundant in challenging such assumptions. It can be helpful, but, as argued by Kapur and Cossman, only in a redefined role, beyond its understanding as an instrument of reform or of oppression. Law needs to be reconceptualised as a site of discursive struggle, where competing visions of the world, and of women's place therein, have been and continue to be fought out. While legal discourse reinforces deeply gendered assumptions, relations and roles, it also has the potential to help create new identities.

Perceiving law as a process or as a discourse may allow us to use law in multifarious ways. Thus, while legal results can be responsive to the immediate demand of the situation, each occasion can provide an opportunity to challenge underlying assumptions and values, can provide a platform for social activists and activist judges to voice their concerns. This reconceptualisation of law as a site of discursive struggle may also allow a more useful and interactive role for law in relation to tradition. This interactive role can go a long way in bridging the much-criticised gap between socio- economic realities and formal legal rules. From tradition one can find instructive measures to deal with customary practices like dowry. Reliance on tradition can also help invoke the element of 'self-restraint', an absolute requirement for dealing with abuses of customary practices, which surely cannot be tackled with law as an external mechanism. Our example of the custom of dowry exemplifies these arguments.

We have seen that 'dowry' arises typically as a problem in the form of an abuse of a customary practice, and that this is a modern phenomenon. Hindu conceptual thought does not authorise or prescribe pre-nuptial negotiations, though there is evidence that it allows for the transfer of movable property. Further, as discussed before, with its underlying concepts of universal harmony and svadharma, it cannot sanction any kind of violence or harassment of women, especially of newly wed brides. Admittedly, a reliance on tradition may be challenged especially on the ground of its underlying notions of male supremacy. But it may be replied that despite this notion, we have no Hindu scriptural evidence that justifies any kind of disrespect or mistreatment towards the lower status of bride givers.

Further, this kind of behaviour may also be excluded on the ground that marriage relations are reciprocal, in the sense that bride givers are also bride takers. Svadharma in the Hindu belief structure might be interpreted as meaning for bride givers that they would perform their duty at best by adorning the bride with gifts according to their ability, and for bride takers that they would accept the bride without any consideration, as the most precious asset on which all ritual and social attention is focussed. Oppression of the individual within or by a family is antithetical to the underlying idea of the necessity of freedom for self-realisation.

The global demand for ensuring and protecting rights against excesses committed in the name of culture and tradition cannot be met without sensitivity towards tradition and local circum-stances. The diversity, complexity and fluidity of every culture exclude uniform solutions. They call for multilateral approaches and multifarious roles for the actors involved. The task necessitates an insight into cultural values to make any proposed changes acceptable. In many cases the justification for fighting against deep-rooted traditional practices, which may have turned oppressive under changed circumstances, can be derived from the same culture on which the practices are alleged to be based.

Reliance on tradition will raise the legitimacy of and understanding for reforms in the eyes of the people. However, reliance on traditions which do not account explicitly for rights does not render the rights discourse irrelevant. It may be used to attract attention towards the basic foundations of traditional systems. It is required to reveal the degeneration of those systems, and to show that the oppression which is grounded today in a particular culture, is in fact groundless. In tradi-tional societies the point of focus is the family and not the individual. However, that does not mean that these societies do not value an individual as an individual for his or her own ends.

Their characteristic view sees everybody's ends associated with those of others. Thus, even when one seeks the meaning of one's own life as an autonomous individual, it is seen that in many circumstances decisions about one's own life need to be sensitive towards their effect on the whole matrix of the family or the society. While most non-western cultures perceive freedom as an essential condition, not for pursuing self-interest, but for exercising self-discipline and self-sacrifice, they at the same time caution against self-negation and provide remedies to deal with the imposition of self-negation on an individual.

While emphasising the necessity of reliance on cultural frameworks it is necessary to observe that almost all religions and cultures have certain underlying stereotypical aspects, which discriminate against women. Thus, rights discourse is universally required to enable challenges to these aspects, which perhaps may have been justified at the time of their origin but need to be removed in the wake of technological advances or changed social and economic circumstances. But then, having accepted the relevance of rights discourse it is important to repeat once again that its universality does not imply uniformity. In fact, one cannot expect uniform approaches even within a single society, and to expect the same at the global level is simply naïve. One needs to remain sensitive towards the possibility of adopting different approaches for different situations, trying to judge rationally the cultural system in its different aspects.

Bibliography

Andrews, B., Brewin, C. R., Rose, S., et al. 2000. "Predicting PTSD Symptoms in Victims of Violent Crime: The Role of Shame, Anger, and Childhood Abuse." *Journal of abnormal psychology* 109: 69-73.

Bachman, R., and Coker, A. L. 1995. "Police Invol-vement in Domestic Violence: The Interactive Effects of Victim Injury, Offender's History of Violence, and Race." *Violence and Victims* 10: 91-106.

Bachman, R., Dillaway, H., and Lachs, M. S. 1998. "Violence against the Elderly: A Comparative Analysis of Robbery and Assault across Age and Gender Groups." *Research on Aging* 20: 183-198.

Baldinger, B. G., and Nelson, D. T. 1995. "Crime Victims and Psychological Injuries." *Trial* 31: 56.

Bazemore, G. 2000. "Crime victims, restorative justice and the juvenile court: exploring victim needs and involvement in the response to youth crime." *Violence and Abuse Abstracts* 6.

Berns, Nancy S., *Framing the Victim: Domestic Violence Media and Social Problems (Social Problems and Social Issues).* Aldine Transaction: 2004.

Birmes, P., Carreras, D., Ducasse, J., et al. 2001. "Peritraumatic Dissociation, Acute Stress, and Early Posttraumatic Stress Disorder in Victims of General Crime." *Canadian journal of psychiatry* 46:649-651.

Bisson, J. I., and Shepherd, J. P. 1995. "Psychological reactions of victims of violent crime." *The British journal of psychiatry* 167: 718.

Bjerregaard, B. 2000. "An Empirical Study of Stalking Victimization." Violence and Victims 15: 389-406.

Black, J. 1995. "Rethinking the naming of sex crime victims." *Newspaper Research Journal* 16: 96.

Blackburn, S. 1999. "Gender Violence and the Indonesian Political Transition." *Asian Studies Review* 23: 433-448.

Boudreaux, E., Kilpatrick, D. G., Resnick, H. S., et al. 1998. "Criminal Victimization, Posttraumatic Stress Disorder, and Comorbid Psychopathology among a Community Sample of Women." *Journal of Traumatic Stress* 11: 665-678.

Bradshaw, W., and Umbreit, M. S. 1998. "Crime Victims Meet Juvenile Offenders: Contributing Factors to Victim Satisfaction with Mediated Dialogue." *Juvenile & family court journal* 49: 17.

Breault, K. D., and Kposowa, A. J. 1997. "The Effects of Marital Status on Adult Female Homicides in the United States." *Journal of Quantitative Criminology* 13: 217-230.

Bubar, Roe, and Pamela Jumper Thurman. 2004. "Violence Against Native Women." *Social justice: a journal of crime, conflict & world order*. 31(4): 70 (17 pages).

Chilton, R., and Jarvis, J. 1999. "Victims and Offenders in Two Crime Statistics Programs: A Comparison of the National Incident-Based Reporting System (NIBRS) and the National Crime Victimization Survey (NCVS)." *Journal of Quantitative Criminology* 15: 193-205.

Cling, B. J., *Sexualized Violence against Women and Children: A Psychology and Law Perspective*. The Guilford Press: 2004.

Cretney, A., and Davis, G. 1997. "Prosecuting Domestic Assault: Victims Failing Courts, or Courts Failing Victims?" *The Howard Journal Of Criminal Justice* 36: 146.

Davis, K. E., and Frieze, I. H. 2000. "Research on Stalking: What Do We Know and Where Do We Go?" *Violence and Victims* 15: 473-487.

Denkers, A. J .M., and Winkel., F. W. 1998. "Crime victims well being and fear in a prospective and longitudinal study." *Sage Urban Studies Abstracts* 26.

Dunn, J. L. 2001. "Innocence Lost: Accomplishing Victimization in Intimate Stalking Cases." *Symbolic Interaction* 24: 285-313.

Dwyer, D. C. 1995. "Response to the Victims of Domestic Violence: Analysis and Implications of the British Experience." *Crime and Delinquency* 41: 527-541.

Epstein, J. N., Saunders, B. E., and Kilpatrick, D. G. 1997. "Predicting PTSD in Women with a History of Childhood Rape." *Journal of Traumatic Stress* 10: 573-588.

Erez, E., Laster, K. 1999. "Neutralizing Victim Reform: Legal Professionals' Perspectives on Victims and Impact Statements." *Crime & Delinquency* 45: 530-553.

Fenwick, H. 1996. "The rights of victims of crime: Protection from harassment and intimidation?" *The Journal of criminal law* 60: 84-93.

Gartner, R., Dawson, M., and Crawford, M. 1998/1999. "Woman Killing: Intimate Femicide in Ontario, 19741994." *Resources for Feminist Research* 26: 151-173.

Gaumer, C. P. 1995. "Protecting the Innocent: Victim-Witness Rights in Illinois." *Illinois bar journal* 83: 568.

Grant, J. M., Folger, W. A., and Hornak, N. J. 1995. "College Students' Perception of Victim Responsibility in an Acquaintance Rape Situation." *College Student Journal* 29: 532-535.

Handsley, E. 1997. "Suits Against the Police for Failure to Protect Victims of Violent Crime: A Feminist Perspective on the Use of Dichotomies." *The Anglo-American law review* 26: 37.

Hart, B. In: Eds. 1996. *Battered Women and the Criminal Justice System*. Thousand Oaks, CA: Sage Publications, pp 98-114.

Henley, N. M., Miller, M., and Beazley, J. A. 1995. "Syntax, Semantics, and Sexual Violence: Agency and the

Passive Voice." *Journal of Language and Social Psychology* 14: 60-84.

Herman, S., and Wasserman, C. 2001. "A Role for Victims in Offender Reentry." *Crime & Delinquency* 47:428-445.

Johnson, K. W. 1997. "Professional Help and Crime Victims." *The Social service review* 71: 89-109.

Kalaher, K. 1997. "The Proposed Victim's Rights Amendment: Taking a Bite Out of Crime or a Dog With No Teeth?" *Seton Hall legislative journal* 22: 317.

Kamphuis, J. H., and Emmelkamp, P. M. G. 1998. "Crime-Related Trauma: Psychological Distress in Victims of Bankrobbery." *Journal of anxiety disorders* 12: 199-208.

Katz, J. 1997. "Staying Alive: Women Who Saved Their Own Lives." *Cosmopolitan* 222: 188.

Kenney, J. S. 2002. "Victims of Crime and Labeling Theory: A Parallel Process?" *Deviant behavior* 23: 235-266.

Kumar, G. S. J. 1997. "Victimization of Women: Coping with Violence." *International Journal of Sociology of the Family* 27: 139-155.

Kury , H. Ferdinand., T. 1998. "The Victim's Experience and Fear of Crime." *Sage Urban Studies Abstracts* 26.

Landau, T. C. 2000. "Women's Experiences with Mandatory Charging for Wife Assault in Ontario, Canada: A Case against the Prosecution." *International Review of Victimology* 7: 141-157.

Linares, L. 2004. "Social Connection to Neighbors, Multiple Victimization, and Current Health Among Women Residing in High Crime Neighborhoods." *Journal of Family Violence*. 19(6): 347-358.

Lipsky, S, R Caetano, C. A. Field, and others. 2005. "Is There a Relationship between Victim and Partner Alcohol Use During an Intimate Partner Violence Event? Findings from an Urban Emergency Department Study of Abused Women."

Journal of studies on alcohol. 66(3): 407 (6 pages).

Loring, M. T., and Beaudoin, P. 2000. "Battered Women as Coerced Victim-Perpetrators." *Journal of Emotional Abuse* 2: 3-14.

Lowenstein, L. F. 2000. "Victims of Violent Crime Leading to Post-Traumatic Stress Disorders." *The Police journal* 73: 256-262.

Lurigio, A. J. 2000. "Are all victims alike? The adverse, generalized and differential impact of crime." *Violence and Abuse Abstracts* 6.

Macleod, M., and Paton, D. 1999. "Victims, violent crime and the criminal justice system: Developing an integrated model of recovery." *Legal and Criminological Psychology* 4: 203-220.

Madriz, E. I. 1997. "Images of Criminals and Victims: A Study on Women's Fear and Social Control." *Gender & Society* 11: 342-356.

Marietta, J. D., and Rowe, G. S. 1999. "Violent Crime, Victims, and Society in Pennsylvania, 1682-1800." *Pennsylvania history* 66.

Marion, N. E. 1995. "The Federal Response to Crime Victims, 1960-1992." *Journal of interpersonal violence* 10: 419-436.

Martens, P. L. 2002. "Immigrants as victims of crime." *Violence & Abuse Abstracts* 8: 3-84.

McPhail, Beverly A. 2002. "Gender-Bias Hate Crimes: A Review." *Trauma, Violence, & Abuse: A Review Journal* 3: 125-143.

Mesch, G. S. 2000. "Women's Fear of Crime: The Role of Fear for the Well-Being of Significant Others." *Violence and Victims* 15: 323-336.

Meyers, M. 1997. *News Coverage of Violence Against Women: Engendering Blame*. Newbury Park, CA: Sage.

Miethe, T. D., Meier, R. F. 1995. "Crime and Its Social Context: Towards an Integrated Theory of Offenders, Victims and Situations." *International journal of the sociology of law* 23: 295.

Miller, L. 1998. "Psychotherapy of Crime Victims: Treating the Aftermath of Interpersonal Violence." *Psychotherapy* 35: 336-345.

Moreland, L. 2001. "How can the Prison Service help the victims of crime?" *Prison service journal* 134: 27- 29.

Nettleton, H., Walklate, S., and Williams, B. 1997. "Three Models of Probation Involvement with Victims of Crime." *The Liverpool law review* 19: 203.

Pain, R. H. 1995. "Elderly Women and Fear of Violent Crime: The Least Likely Victims? A Reconsideration of the Extent and Nature of Risk." *British Journal of Criminology* 35: 584-598.

Peltzer, K. 2000. "Risk for traumatization among violent crime victims in an urban community sample in South Africa." *Curationis* 23: 22-27.

Petersilia, J. R. 2001. "Crime Victims With Develo-pmental Disabilities: A Review Essay." *Criminal Justice and Behavior* 28: 655-694.

Pino, N. W., and Meier, R. F. 1999. "Gender Differences in Rape Reporting." *Sex Roles* 40: 979-990.

Ruback, R. B., Menard, K. S., Outlaw, M. C., et al. 1999. "Normative Advice to Campus Crime Victims: Effects of Gender, Age, and Alcohol." *Violence and victims* 14: 381-396.

Sebba, L. 2001. "On the relationship between criminological research and policy: The case of crime victims." *Criminal Justice* 1: 27-58.

Shalhoub-Kevorkian, N. 1999. "Towards a Cultural Definition of Rape: Dilemmas in Dealing with Rape Victims in Palestinian Society." *Women's Studies International Forum* 22: 157-173.

Wadham, J., and Arkinstall, J. 2000. "Rights of victims of crime explain how victims' rights will be affected by the Human Rights Act." *The New law journal* 6943: 1023-1024.

Weinrath, M., and Gartrell, J. 1996. "Victimization and Fear of Crime." *Violence and Victims* 11: 187-197.

Weisman, C. S. 1995. "Armed by Fear: Self-Defense Handguns and Women's Health." *Women's Health Issues* 5: 3-7.

Yee, J. L., and Greenberg, M. S. 1998. "Reactions to Crime Victims: Effects of Victims' Emotional State and Type of Relationship." *Journal of Social and Clinical Psychology* 17: 209-226.

Yee, J. L., Greenberg, M. S., and Beach, S. R. 1998. "Attitudes toward Various Modes of Coping with Criminal Victimization: The Effects of Gender and Type of Crime." *Journal of Social and Clinical Psychology* 17: 273-294.

INDEX

E

F

G

H

I

L

M

N